'With a resurgence of the nationalist right in the world and a fading away of the populist left, the centre ground has the opportunity and responsibility to reinvent itself for a new era. Will it do so? This book is a timely call to action.'
Lord Peter Mandelson

'This book should be studied in every school across the globe. Its quiet voice of reason needs to be heard loudly now above all!'
Anthony Seldon, author of *Johnson at 10*

'With authoritarianism and extremism on the rise around the world, this book's clear-eyed case for our cherished liberal values is urgently needed. Democracy, liberty, human rights and the rule of law are all under threat, but this book shows how critical they are. Its positive alternative to the destructive politics of fear and division offers something we all badly need today: hope.'
The Right Honourable Sir Ed Davey MP,
Leader, Liberal Democrats

'In this age of unreason and extremism, this collection of essays provides a rallying cry against the siren calls of populism and offers hope of real solutions to the biggest challenges of our time.'
Wes Streeting, Shadow Secretary of State
for Health and Social Care

THE CENTRE MUST HOLD

Why centrism is the answer to extremism and polarisation

EDITED BY YAIR ZIVAN

Elliott&Thompson

First published 2024 by
Elliott and Thompson Limited
2 John Street
London WC1N 2ES
www.eandtbooks.com

ISBN: 978-1-78396-793-3

Translation credits:
'Faith, Philosophy and the Foundations of Centrism' by Dr Micah Goodman
Translation: Thea Brody, SZ Translation

'The Case for Centrism' by Yair Lapid
Translation: Thea Brody, SZ Translation

'The Centrist Method' by Polly Bronstein
Translation: Sahar Zivan, SZ Translation

Picture credit:
Page 258: Kevin Kal Kallaugher, Kaltoons.com, *The Economist*, 2 June 2023.

9 8 7 6 5 4 3 2 1

A catalogue record for this book is available from
the British Library.

Typesetting: Marie Doherty
Printed by CPI Group (UK) Ltd, Croydon, CR0 4YY

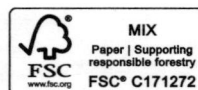

MIX
Paper | Supporting
responsible forestry
FSC
www.fsc.org
FSC® C171272

'For hope of the future surely lies in the revival of the Center – in the triumph of those who believe deeply in civil liberties, in constitutional processes and in the democratic determination of political and economic policies. And, in direct consequence, the main target of both totalitarian extremes must be the Center – the group which hold society together.'

Arthur M. Schlesinger Jr[1]

CONTENTS

INTRODUCTION

Yair Zivan

On the evening of 13 June 2021, a new Israeli government held its first meeting in one of the nondescript committee rooms in parliament. A few hours earlier a coalition made up of eight political parties had been confirmed by Israel's parliament with the slimmest of majorities. Sitting in that room waiting for the photographers to take a few final shots, as the two leaders of the new government shared a joke, it was impossible not to be struck by the diversity of the ministers around the table – from the progressive left to the nationalist right and including Israel's first Arab party in a governing coalition. But the heart of that coalition ran through the political centre. Not only was the largest party in the coalition a true centrist one – Yair Lapid's Yesh Atid – but the ethos of the coalition was quintessentially centrist. I served as senior advisor to Yair Lapid in his role as foreign minister and prime minister, and the next eighteen months gave me a front-row seat to how a centrist-inspired government can work.

Our government did much to be proud of during that time and had an extensive list of successes across a whole variety of fields – but ultimately its political diversity, which was almost unprecedented in global politics, proved to be its downfall. The fringes of the coalition, from the left and the right, tore the fragile partnership apart and the centre was not strong enough to prevent it. While the key players were consistently willing to compromise and cooperate, the political fringes, under pressure from the extremes on their side, ultimately resorted to 'all-or-nothing' politics. That left us all with nothing. At the end of December 2022, I watched from afar as a new government was sworn in to replace us. It was by far the most right-wing and conservative coalition ever elected in Israel – and its divisive actions and policies led to one of the most disastrous years in the country's history.

The experiences of those eighteen months, one of the great political experiments of modern times, and the centrist leadership I saw up close as we met with counterparts from all over the world led to the conception of this book. It is an attempt not only to explain what centrism really is but to lay out the positive vision it has for the world, to see if it can answer the questions being asked of political leaders in the twenty-first century and, critically, to assess if it is strong enough to stand up to the threat coming from the political extremes. I met some of the contributors to this book during my years working in politics, while others simply share a deep commitment to the centrist idea. Each has written about their own area of expertise or passion; each brings a unique perspective.

Centrism is based upon a clear set of ideals and principles: the importance of moderation and pragmatism; the embrace of complexity; the deep commitment to liberal democracy; the belief in equality of opportunity, and that through balancing the tensions that exist in every nation we can make people's lives better. The first section of the book explores these ideas and the roots of centrism, and gets to work dealing head on with the challenges it faces; the second looks at some of the biggest issues confronting society today; the third shows how centrism can provide answers to specific policy areas; the fourth demonstrates how centrism works, with examples from across the world; and the fifth offers a path forward for the future.

I entered government a committed centrist and left with a conviction deeper than ever that centrism can provide the answers to the challenges of our time; it is the antidote to the extremism and sustained attacks on liberal democracy that are sweeping much of the democratic world. But for that to happen we first have work to do.

Gallons of ink have been spilled on the crisis of democracy, the divisions within society, the spread of misinformation and the rise of extremism. Some of that is undoubtedly true, some is exaggerated. The populist right, for example, is clearly rising across much of Europe, visible in many election results, while a populist left discourse dominates on campuses and in academia.

Resentment, anger and despondence all drive populist sentiment. People who feel a sense of loss for a world that once was and fear the world that is coming are drawn to politicians who offer simplistic solutions, especially if no one else is willing to take those valid fears seriously. Populists can neatly reduce any issue to two basic messages: the solution is always straightforward and failure is always someone's fault. There is no problem that can't be solved by a tweet or a five-word slogan. Populists always have an easy, if ultimately unworkable, answer. If the problem is rapid technological change, they'll take us back to the glory days. If it's overpowerful elites, they'll smash the system. If it's inequality, they'll bring down capitalism. If it's globalisation, they'll close the borders. And whatever you're angry or fearful about, they will always find you someone to blame. Populism, at its core, is the attempt to divide society into two easily distinguishable groups. Often it's the 'real' people vs those working against them in some way, whether that's the elites, the deep state, newcomers or outsiders. Or sometimes it's the oppressed and oppressor, in which the latter is always attempting to subjugate the former, based on race, ethnicity, gender or economic status. The individual doesn't count, only their identity classification. Whatever form populism appears in, this divisive approach leaves no room for nuance, context or complexity. There is no room for introspection, for debate, or for self-criticism.

That is why populism goes hand in hand with political extremism, dividing us and preventing us from finding any common ground. Extremists want us to believe that compromise is never necessary, that it is a symbol of weakness and failure. They too always have a simple solution to all the problems of society – total commitment to their ideology. When they fail to deliver on their promises, it isn't due to faults within their ideology but because people failed to embrace it fully enough, usually blamed on some imagined moment of weakness in which compromises were made that supposedly undermined the purity of the ideology.

But what if those people who guarantee easy solutions to complex issues – who seek to exploit genuine economic difficulty and sincere cultural fears – are the problem? What if we're not as divided as they want us to believe? What if, in fact, many of us are eager to inhabit a political centre ground?

Not only do the populists and extremists fail to offer real solutions, they've become one of the foremost problems: an obstacle we must overcome to move our countries in a healthier direction. It's not enough to brand them as irresponsible or racist or anti-democratic, although they may be all those things. Someone has to offer a better alternative. That alternative can't come from another brand of extremism or a different strain of populism, it must come from the centre. It is the centre which offers the antidote to the politics of intransigence and inflexibility; it is the centre which can counter the messages of despair and divisiveness.

In his first victory speech, French President Emmanuel Macron said, 'I will do everything to make sure you never have reason again to vote for extremes.' That should be a rallying cry for centrists because it's aimed at us. It's not a criticism of the extremists and it's certainly not a criticism of the public – it's a challenge to centrists to do more to give the people a clear alternative and connect with their genuine, well-founded fears about the future.

Centrism, as envisaged in the pages of this book, is not the middle point between two ever more extreme tribes on the left and right. Centrism, when properly articulated and implemented, sets the agenda that others must respond to and so becomes a driving focal point of politics. But something has been missing from the centrist message. If the great challenge to democracies today is the emotional pull of populism and the way in which it is amplified by sections of the media and the algorithms of social media, then centrists must find a way to break through with an emotional appeal of their own. There are good reasons for people to be concerned about the impact of AI on the future of their jobs or for their despair at stagnating wages while the cost of living rises. Centrists must show genuine compassion and understanding of the anxiety that large swathes of the public feel and then offer a better path forward.

We will never beat the extremists at their own game, nor should we ever seek to. If illiberal extremists drive the agenda with fear, then liberal centrists must do the opposite. One of the major effects of fear-driven politics is that it destroys trust in public institutions and poisons the public sphere. It creates what political scientist Lee Drutman of the New America Foundation calls the 'cynicism and mistrust doom loop'. He summarised it in his newsletter, *Undercurrent Events*, in September 2023 as follows: 'muddling authority thus undermines authority. This distrust fuels cynicism. Cynicism drives both demand for and consumption of misinformation.' This cycle only serves to strengthen the extremes and weaken moderate liberal centrists. It is why centrists must lead the fight to preserve liberal democracy and the institutions which sustain it. As Germany's minister of justice, Marco Buschmann, writes in his essay, 'Centrism and the rule of law are two sides of the same coin . . . it is the role, belief and duty of centrists to defend those checks and balances which lie at the heart of our system.' And there are successful models for doing so.

In 2020 the Republican and Democratic candidates for governor of Utah recorded a campaign advert together. In that advert they both asked the public to vote for them but did so while standing next to one another as they insisted, 'We can debate issues without degrading each other's character . . . We can disagree without hating each other.' Of course, only one candidate could win that election, but subsequent research shows that those who saw the advert were less likely to support political violence or undemocratic practices (such as refusing to accept the result of an election). If repeated in elections across the world, those sorts of campaign tactics could help to reduce the polarisation and extremism that undermine liberal democracy.

The best defence, though, is for centrists to help people feel that even when things are genuinely difficult, as many believe they are now, they can be better. To show people a path that seems plausible. To offer them hope.

Hope is a powerful emotional driver. It works across borders and across generations. Political consultants and marketing experts have debated for years whether it can compete with fear. It can, and there are plenty of examples where it has. Bill Clinton's 1992 election campaign was infused with messages of hope including a particularly famous and impactful sixty-second advert, 'A Place Called Hope', named after his birthplace. Barack Obama focused his election campaign, as well as an iconic image and the title of a best-selling book, around the word 'hope' with great success. Going further back, in 1960 Frank Sinatra re-recorded his hit song 'High Hopes' as the anthem of JFK's election campaign. Communicating a hopeful, authentic message that has broad international relevance is key to strengthening the appeal of centrism.

The former chief rabbi of Great Britain, Lord Rabbi Jonathan Sacks, one of the great thinkers and writers of our time, wrote that 'optimism and hope are not the same. Optimism is the belief that the world is changing for the better; hope is the belief that, together, we can make the world better. Optimism is a passive virtue, hope an active one.' The 'politics of hope', as Rabbi Sacks termed it, not only inspires an emotional reaction but drives action, forming healthier societies that are more cohesive, tolerant and open, as opposed to politicians with authoritarian and illiberal tendencies who imbue societies with fear and create violence and prejudice. Centrists, therefore, need to play an active role in building those societies, which they will then also benefit from politically – creating a positive re-enforcing loop.

The politics of hope is strongest when it is infused with patriotism, acknowledging the public's sense of pride in the tradition, community and character of their society. People want to feel pride in the place they live and want to know that the unique characteristics that make up their identity are genuinely respected. They want to be part of an uplifting story. When the far left reject classic symbols that form part of the identity of the country, they are rejecting the identity of large sections of the public. When the far right refuse to acknowledge the complexity of a nation's history, with all its faults and failures, they are rejecting the experiences of many of those who make up a modern society, in particular minorities.

It is here that centrists borrow from Edmund Burke, despite his traditional (and often misplaced) association with conservative politics. Burke spoke of society as a contract between the generations of the past, the present and the future. He wrote, 'A disposition to preserve and an ability to improve, taken together, would be my standard of a statesman.' In other words, respect the past but don't try to recreate it, respect identity and culture but don't be afraid to modernise them gradually and carefully, respect the values of your grandparent's society but don't hold your children's future hostage to it.

To many in the UK, the royal family, Shakespeare and Churchill are essential symbols of what it means to be British. None of them is perfect, all have flaws which could easily be used to argue they have no place as part of the modern national consciousness, but they are part of the rich tapestry that makes the UK unique. The same is true of the Founding Fathers of the USA, the revolutionary political past of France, the iconic cultural influence of Italy or the ancient philosophies of Greece.

We can strengthen society by respecting traditions and still be committed to improving it going forward. That is something centrists are uniquely placed to do. George Orwell, in his 'Notes on Nationalism', wrote that patriotism is 'devotion to a particular place and a particular way of life, which one believes to be the best in the world but has no wish to force upon other people'. Centrists can offer a hopeful national story which is patriotic without being jingoistic, which respects the past without dreaming of reliving an idealised version of it and which embraces cultural icons with the same nuance with which we approach our daily lives. Ted Halstead and Michael Lind, in their excellent book *The Radical Center: The Future of American Politics*, aptly called this 'the tradition of renewal'. When a strong national story is combined with a willingness to look forward and engage with a changing world not through fear but with hope, centrists can strike the emotional connection needed with the public.

And then comes the substance: the work of getting things done. Centrists believe in a clear set of principles and a defined approach to policymaking.

It is not enough to talk about 'common-sense solutions' or 'sensible politics'. Those are abstract terms which mean different things to different people – and often mean very little to most. The 'we believe in common sense' style of politics risks playing into the accusation of arrogance that is so often levelled at centrists. It can come across as patronising because it suggests that all other ideas and beliefs are irrational or foolish.

Instead, centrists must find a way of communicating what common sense really means: that we believe in embracing complexity and difficulty in any sector, whether education, national security, economics, international development or technology. There are centrist answers to the specific dilemmas facing individual countries and the world as a whole. These approaches to the major challenges we face are laid out in this book, perhaps for the first time in a global and comprehensive manner.

Centrism seeks out the most productive and effective approach to tackle the competition between globalisation and local communities, civil rights and security, religion and democracy, free markets and social-safety nets. Its approach is dynamic, not static, as it is modified by circumstance and context, adapted when new information becomes available.

It is by no means an easy act to balance these ideas. When globalisation doesn't protect local communities too many get left behind, but isolationist policies that reject the international community leave too many opportunities untapped. Free markets that leave the poor to fend for themselves destroy healthy societies, but welfare states can strangle the free market, destroying enterprise and innovation. Policies that try to impose total equality in society disincentivise hard work and individual success, but ignoring structural inequality ensures whole communities are almost guaranteed to fail. Centrism is the never-ending work of managing competing tensions, of setting national priorities that accept those tensions exist rather than wishing them away.

Centrists believe in such incomplete answers as part of an imperfect world; those seemingly partial solutions help us to continue living together by creating a broad-based shared narrative, a tolerance and understanding of differing points of view, a continuation of government rather than wild swings of the policy pendulum. When centrists govern, it is with the aim of making sure no one is entirely overlooked, even if no one will get everything they want.

While extremists seek total victory and dominance over the entire political system and to remove dissenting voices, centrists understand the dangers of that approach – it is the driving force behind some of the darkest periods in human history. If centrists try to compete with extremists for one-dimensional solutions they are bound to fail along with them, and it's a failure none of us can afford. And so centrists must do the opposite and do it willingly, not as a measure of last resort but as the key to building successful policy that allows us to live harmoniously in one society. That is the higher value.

To those on the fringes of politics, compromise is treachery, a betrayal of the purity of their positions. They would rather fail. To the old social democrats and classic conservatives, compromise is too often a necessary evil to make the system work. They aim to achieve the narrowest workable majority. To centrists, though, it is a core tenet of liberal democracy itself. It is the way to get things done and make them last.

Take, for example, the debate about the best approach to combatting terrorism. The left focus overwhelmingly on addressing root causes of terror (real or imagined) and the right almost exclusively on the use of force. The centre must acknowledge the truth: fighting terrorism is complicated. The solutions aren't immediate and never will be. We will get it wrong sometimes. We may have to change strategy along the way. The fight may never actually be over. We constantly have to balance the tools at our disposal with the values that define us. We need to fight terrorism with force, while at the same time offering a path that rejects violence, that defeats the ideological foundations which lie at the heart of terrorism. As Jonathan Evans, the former head of the British Security Services, writes in his essay: 'A counterterrorist strategy is most likely to succeed if it recognises the complexity of the problems it must address.'

The complexity of policymaking, even across seemingly less controversial fields like education or health care, requires hard decisions when setting priorities. There is often no obvious right answer. The temptation to always say 'both' when presented with a choice is overwhelming but unrealistic in a world of limited resources. Whichever path you choose demands something of the government. It demands that the government trusts the public. People understand that resources are limited, and that the government can't give them everything, but they want to know three things: that those in power care, that they have really thought about what is most important, and that they are acting responsibly. People don't expect perfection, but they do expect better. That's why centrists must insist on good governance and on a form of communication that does not shy away from acknowledging the complexity of making and implementing policy. Let the public know that you're making hard choices and show them that, even when they disagree with you, you're making the decisions with good intentions.

In 1996, after winning his second term, President Clinton declared: 'The lesson of our history is clear: When we put aside partisanship, embrace the best ideas regardless of where they come from and work for principled compromise, we can move America not left or right, but forward.' The idea was to create policies that transcended the traditional party positions, rather than being held back by them. The key was to offer something new, something different, something that yielded results. It was a message that was reflected by Third Way politicians in Europe and adapted successfully by Tony Blair in the UK. They understood, as we need to understand today, that the public is far more interested in outcomes than outdated definitions of ideology. If a policy works, if it makes their lives better, if the trade-off is reasonable, then who really cares how much of it can be claimed by modern advocates of Marx or Hayek?

Ultimately, centrism subscribes to a belief that we can make people's lives better through an acceptance of complexity and moderation rather than a search for simplicity. And as former Australian prime minister Malcolm Turnbull writes in his essay, 'In a frenzied world, the respect, compromise and moderation at the heart of political centrism are the best guarantees that our democracies will endure.'

That's what political centrism has to offer, and it is a dramatic break from the trajectory of our modern political world.

SECTION 1

WHAT IS CENTRISM?

The principles of centrism have been shaped by the reality of the modern world but they also have deep philosophical roots. Centrist ideas can be found throughout history, from ancient Greece to the Enlightenment to the Founding Fathers of the USA, and they provide the foundations on which modern centrism, as articulated in this book, is built. William Galston, Micah Goodman and Aurelian Craiutu draw the foundations of centrism from the civil rights movement, James Madison, ancient Chinese tradition, Western philosophical thought, Jewish texts and the writing of Arthur Schlesinger Jr. They make the case for pragmatism, moderation, humility and holistic thinking, all core elements of the centrist approach. Between their essays, Jennifer Rubin makes the case for the inseparable and mutually dependent connection between centrism and liberal democracy. Defending the foundations of liberal democracy and the values at the heart of it is a task that unites centrists across the world.

One particular strength of centrism is the ability to adapt and to learn from criticism, to improve and to act accordingly, and the changes it has undergone over the years are dealt with in this first section as well. These changes show a consistency of principle combined with an acknowledgement of the changing world. The major criticisms often heard in the media and from political opponents are taken on in good faith and deconstructed without being dismissed.

Having established its beginnings, evolution, challenges and critics, the section concludes with a coherent, articulate, inspiring and positive case for centrism.

1

REFLECTIONS ON CENTRISM

William Galston

When writing on centrism, many authors begin by ritually disclaiming all efforts to equate the concept with some mathematical midpoint between extremes. Although this rejection is warranted in the end, it is worth pausing for a moment to review the reasons why some political scientists have taken this conception seriously.

Centrism finds its natural home in broadly democratic understandings of politics in which the opinions of citizens shape policies and determine which parties will be entrusted with temporary power. In these circumstances the ability to mobilise majorities is decisive, and understanding how best to do this is essential.

Assume for a moment that the attitudes of citizens are arrayed along a single left–right continuum and distributed in a 'normal' bell curve, with the largest number clustered at or near the midpoint. If so, the centre represents the point at which it is easiest to construct a majority while minimising its reach along the continuum – in other words, while maximising agreement within the majority coalition. It is easy to see why practical politicians would prize advisors who can help them achieve this kind of majority.

In the real world, of course, matters are more complicated. Even if there is a single dimension that dominates politics, opinion may not be distributed in a bell curve along it. As many commentators on US politics have noted, there has been a decades-long movement of citizens from the centre towards the periphery on both left and right, pushing the two major parties away from the overlap that defined the operational centre of politics in the middle decades of the twentieth century and towards partisan polarisation.

There is a second and even more significant problem with the simple view I sketched: voters are no longer (if they ever were) arrayed along a single ideological or policy dimension, such as the role of government in the economy. Rather, their views are multidimensional. In the simplest formulation of this more complex reality, voters have varying views on both economic and cultural issues. Some lean left on economic issues and right on cultural issues, as many populists do. Some 'libertarians' do just the reverse, and so forth. Still, unless one of the quadrants in this two-dimensional space contains a majority of the electorate, the problem remains of constructing a majority with sufficient internal coherence to persist over time.

In conceptualising the democratic centre, then, the actual distribution of public sentiment cannot be expunged entirely. Centrism considers the existing correlation of political forces, even though it does not simply situate itself within them. As Tony Blair rightly observes in his essay later in this book, however, centrist politics is about more than 'triangulation'. It represents a reflective response to emerging public problems and relies on the ability of its leaders to persuade the public that new approaches are needed. It begins with politics as it is, but tries to find new possibilities within current realities.

What guides this quest for innovation? The authors in this volume all embrace some version of liberal democracy, which already commits them to some version of political pluralism. Liberal democrats modify pure majoritarianism by insisting on protecting individual rights, however majorities may feel about them.

This commitment to pluralism extends beyond regime-level politics to include policy as well. As James Madison famously observed, in circumstances of liberty, individuals and groups are bound to diverge in both their interests and their beliefs. The alternative to accepting social pluralism is using power, public or private, to suppress it. This

4

means, in turn, that politics must seek to balance competing interests and conceptions of good lives, a process that often requires compromise.

It is possible to regard this form of politics as merely a concession to reality. But centrists often go further, embracing epistemological humility. Not only does human reason not suffice to choose among competing religious doctrines, but also there are many opinions with legitimate but competing conceptions of what gives meaning and purpose to life.

Humility in understanding suggests moderation in practice. After all, one may argue, finding a way to accommodate competing conceptions is not only the best way of honouring their equal claims; it is wise politics as well. Proceeding too far, too fast in any one direction can be seen as unfair to those who may feel marginalised by non-incremental social change.

To state this argument is to see its limits: some circumstances may require immoderate action. In his famous 'Letter from a Birmingham Jail' (1963), Martin Luther King Jr speculated that the greatest obstacle to civil rights might not be Bull Connor's dogs and water cannons or the Klan's robes and burning crosses but rather white 'moderates' who embraced the aims of the civil rights movement while rejecting its means as 'extreme', criticising the movement for demanding too much too soon, for wilfully if non-violently breaking the law, and for disrupting social order. King replied that 'law and order exist for the purpose of establishing justice and [that] when they fail in this purpose they become dangerously structured dams that block the flow of social progress'. A year later, the Republican Party's presidential nominee, a leader cut from very different cloth, declared that 'moderation in pursuit of justice is no virtue', a principle that King would have endorsed while deploring the way Barry Goldwater used it.

All of which is to say that centrism cannot inflexibly embrace a single mode of political practice. While it inclines towards gradualism, it must recognise that some circumstances require bolder and more disruptive strategies. This reflects the limits not only of moderation but also of the epistemological humility that undergirds it. A defensible pluralism requires a distinction between legitimate and illegitimate ways of living. Centrists must be willing to say that certain forms of social life are beyond the moral pale and that it is morally wrong to balance them against the claims of their critics. Rather, centrists must be committed to reforming these ways of life as fast as circumstances permit.

Indeed, centrists typically embrace reform as the antidote to both the classic conservative defence of the status quo and the radical call for revolution. As practical politicians within liberal democracy, they reject the charge that this form of government is fundamentally flawed while acknowledging that its practices often fall short of its principles. In this respect, among others, Martin Luther King was a centrist. Like Abraham Lincoln, he accepted the principles of the American Founding Fathers and deployed them to criticise racial injustice. He situated himself between Black Americans too drained of self-respect to challenge segregation and those who insisted that only a violent revolution could overcome centuries of oppression.

In practice, however, calls for reform often fall flat with groups whose grievances against the status quo are deep and visceral. A reasonable, evidence-based politics finds itself on the defensive against the politics of passion, as it did in the UK during the struggle over Brexit, when arguments about the long-term economic consequences of separating from the EU proved less compelling than did fervent denunciations of Polish plumbers and lost sovereignty.

From time to time, centrists have a chance to present themselves as insurgents, as did Bill Clinton in 1992, Tony Blair in 1997, Emmanuel Macron in 2017 and Yair Lapid in 2022. Tellingly, three of these leaders gave way to conservative parties in which populists enjoyed increasing power. The fourth, France's Macron, lost his parliamentary majority during his successful re-election campaign and has found it difficult ever since to govern his country. The most likely beneficiary of his weakening hold on the French electorate is not the Socialist left of Jean-Luc

Mélenchon but rather the populist right of Marine Le Pen. In a similar vein, the principal beneficiaries of the weakening of Germany's long-dominant centre-right and centre-left parties has been not the far-left parties, but rather the increasingly radical right-wing AfD.

Centrists must figure out how to counter this challenge, which has been fuelled by the decline of the industrial working class and the rise of an educated professional elite whose cultural preferences antagonise less-educated voters. Abstract talk of a better balance between globalisation and domestic production won't get the job done, and neither will a new generation of policies centred on the promise of technological progress.

Many centrists suffer from an inability to take culture seriously and won't reoccupy the commanding heights of politics until they learn how to do so. Centrists must set aside crude materialist presuppositions that treat cultural debates as diversions from the 'real' economic challenges Western democracies now face. Issues such as immigration, ethnic loyalties and resentments, nationalism, traditional values and the role of religion in society cannot be dismissed as diversionary. Doing so will only drive a deeper wedge between centrists and voters without professional degrees or jobs.

This is to say that there is not only a centrist morality and politics but also a centrist sociology. Since Aristotle, political analysts have understood the relationship between moderate politics and a strong middle class. For the three decades after the end of the Second World War, the middle class increased in size, prosperity and self-confidence throughout the West. Since then, many members of the middle class – especially those who attained this status through industrial rather than professional occupations – have experienced downward pressure on their economic wellbeing as well as diminished security in the face of economic and social change.

Making matters worse, these changes have been highly correlated with geographical differences. Since the 1970s, large cities (especially capital cities) have thrived while small towns and 'peripheries' have fallen behind. Populist leaders have scored gains by mobilising non-urban voters against educated urban elites, to the detriment of centrist politics. Rebuilding public support for centrist parties and policies will require their members to get out of their comfort zones, literally and figuratively, and re-engage with the groups of voters they have surrendered to conservative populists.

In the USA, political analysts will continue to debate the extent to which President Joe Biden has governed from the centre. But there is no debate about the fact that in the USA, as elsewhere, the principal challenge to mainstream politics is coming from the populist right, not the socialist left. Former president Donald Trump may well regain his office in the November 2024 presidential election, with incalculable consequences for the alliance of Western democracies.

All of which is to say that this is no time for centrist triumphalism. The challenges to moderate governance, democratic reform and liberal democracies are graver today than in many decades. Centrists should work with a renewed sense of urgency to shore up the parties that defend their creed and to offer policies that renew hope among social groups that have turned away from the centre towards a new right whose commitment to liberal democracy is very much in doubt.

2

CENTRISM AND THE FIGHT FOR LIBERAL DEMOCRACY

Jennifer Rubin

We live in a political era in which far too many words have lost fixed, agreed-upon meaning. Radical authoritarians who would take a meat cleaver to democratic institutions call themselves 'conservatives'. Others unsubtly rename overt racism, sexism and homophobia as 'anti-woke'. If reactionary radicalism can masquerade as conservatism and fascism as common sense, then useful interchange is impossible. In such an atmosphere, then, linguistic precision is critical. Accordingly, before we engage in an analysis of the relationship between centrism, a widely misunderstood term, and liberal democracy, also misunderstood, it behoves us to define both terms.

Popular misconceptions of centrism should not distract us. Indeed, we can easily define centrism as what it is *not* – a waystation between political extremes, a mushy tendency to compromise or a fondness for style over substance. Those mischaracterisations are ably deconstructed by other authors in this collection. Rather, centrism has a positive and specific meaning. We can reduce it to a formula: moderation + heterogeneity.

Moderation, as authors such as Aurelian Craiutu, a fellow contributor to this book, have defined it, is a commitment 'to promote necessary social and political reforms, defend liberty, and keep the ship of the state on an even keel'. It requires humility, restraint and 'a tolerant and civil virtue related to temperance and opposed to violence [that] respects the spontaneity of life and the pluralism of the world and can protect

9

against pride, one-sidedness, intolerance, and fanaticism in our moral and political commitment'. But moderation alone can amount to dilution of virtuous positions, leading to perverse results. If one recognises climate change as a scientific fact, then exercising 'tolerance' for climate deniers is not an option. When confronted with one political party that assaults truth and democracy and another that defends it, some one-sidedness is in order.

To avoid such moral and intellectual predicaments, centrism requires another element: the ability to combine solutions, analyses and policies from a range of political sources, to appreciate that wisdom does not exist solely on one side or another. Conservatives have something to offer in commending the benefits of free-market capitalism while progressives' devotion to equal opportunity and remediation of historic inequalities has value as well (all, of course, in moderation). Centrism recognises that, for example, capitalism and regulation, individual merit and social justice, and diversity and cohesion not only can coexist but must. Centrism appreciates the inherent intellectual conflicts in free societies (freedom and equality, national self-interest and human rights). We cannot, and must not, resolve such conflicts entirely in one side's favour. Centrism, in short, stands for the proposition that ideological tensions are best resolved when we borrow the best from conflicting perspectives.

Liberal democracy refers to a system which protects individual rights and recognises the people as the ultimate source of power. The essential attributes of liberal democracy include the rule of law, limited government, the peaceful transfer of power through popular elections, a free press, an independent judiciary, civilian control of the military and renunciation of violence as a political tool. At the heart of liberal democracy, then, is an unavoidable tension between individual rights and popular sovereignty. Minority rights and majority rule are the x and y axes that set the contours of most debates: how much individual accumulation of wealth derived from free-market capitalism do we curb through taxation? When does freedom of religion give way to popular will or competing values? How do demands for national security coexist with the right of privacy? And how much individual liberty should we sacrifice to tackle a national emergency or contain a pandemic?

Faced with two principles of liberal democracy in constant tension, if not conflict, it should not be surprising that centrism, the ideological perspective designed to combine the best of contrasting perspectives, should be critical to its survival. Conversely, severe polarisation (the opposite of centrism), widely regarded as the enemy of liberal democracy, exerts resistance to compromise, fosters an all-or-nothing mentality, diminishes respect for political opponents, weakens critical institutions and provokes refusal to cede power (because political opponents are cast as an existential threat to society). But if we can see that polarisation stresses the foundation of liberal democracy, it is not self-evident how centrism reinforces it.

And upon close examination one finds plentiful evidence that without devotion to centrism (moderation + heterogeneity) liberal democracy will falter. There are at least three ways in which centrism acts to reinforce and protect liberal democracy: 1) centrism is essential to manage and maximise the benefits of diversity; 2) centrism is critical to maintain respect for an independent judiciary, which is the lifeblood of liberal democracies; and 3) centrism is a fundamental aspect of democratic norms that supplement the rule of law and democratic institutions.

Diversity

In liberal democracies, pluralism – of race, religion, ethnic origin, sexual orientation and political opinion – is both a fact of life and an outward manifestation of individual rights. George Washington, in his ode to religious liberty delivered to the Hebrew Congregation of Newport, Rhode Island, declared:

> All possess alike liberty of conscience and immunities of citizenship. It is now no more that toleration is spoken of, as if it was

11

by the indulgence of one class of people, that another enjoyed the exercise of their inherent natural rights. For happily the Government of the United States, which gives to bigotry no sanction, to persecution no assistance requires only that they who live under its protection should demean themselves as good citizens, in giving it on all occasions their effectual support.

Washington, in singing praise for religious diversity (not simply tolerance by the majority for minority faiths), rebuts the argument that differences must be assimilated entirely for democracy to function. Given the diversity in human experience and viewpoint, uniformity is neither desirable nor possible in liberal democracies.

And yet pluralistic liberal democracies must reach consensus on certain issues, provide the conditions for widespread prosperity and defend their institutions and security. And here is where centrism plays such a vital role. Centrism is the wellspring not only of humility and restraint; it provides the impetus to borrow from conflicting sides. Centrism encourages elected leaders to forge alliances that may shift over time, that cross partisan lines and that provide the stability and sense of unity necessary to function.

It is a truism that in US politics, if you want to achieve progressive aims, elect a centrist. And in President Biden – a man able to achieve momentous domestic progress and forge an unprecedented international alliance in support of Ukraine – one sees a full flowering of centrism. He can neither overwhelm nor ignore opponents. Instead, he combines spending with deficit reduction, an historic investment in green energy with market-based incentives.

Despite disagreement on many issues, President Biden found allies across the aisle on everything from infrastructure to microchip production. His goals were progressive, but in exuding moderation and borrowing the right amount of policy from right and left, he brought ballast to the presidency at its most turbulent time. Biden provided a sterling example of centrism's capabilities: better outcomes come not from overpowering or ignoring one side but by borrowing, luring and co-opting them. It is not coincidental that at a time when liberal democracy was stressed as never before in US politics, a self-styled centrist was best able to navigate to success.

A credible judiciary

Be it in Poland, Turkey or the USA, the perceived politicisation of judiciary at the hands of right-wing ideologues has endangered liberal democracy itself. A judiciary co-opted by reactionary politicians soon loses the qualities that the law of rule, an essential aspect of liberal democracies, provides. Politicised judges who reflexively side with the politicians who appointed them inevitably discard precedent and lack intellectual coherence to reach predetermined outcomes. In doing so, they soon jettison their legitimacy and lose public support. A court that earns the scorn of voters soon faces threats to impede its independence and/or limit its jurisdiction.

If one considers the US Supreme Court, compare the two former Republican-appointed justices widely regarded as centrists (Sandra Day O'Connor and Anthony Kennedy) with the trio appointed by President Trump. In selecting O'Connor and Kennedy, President Ronald Reagan departed from ideological litmus tests – in the former to appoint the first woman to the high court and in the second to gain consensus after two failed nominees. The result: justices respected for their independence, common sense, flexibility and judicial restraint. They helped the high court stay tethered to a modern USA, moving incrementally and adhering to precedent on hot-button issues like affirmative action and abortion. Public support for the high court remained high for decades. By contrast, a court transformed into a right-wing partisan pugilist saw its approval crater. Critics now deride its partisanship, and a ferocious political tumult roils the country, throwing jurisprudence and society (including medical practice, voting maps and the administrative state) into a period of chaos.

As voters come to see the judges as something other than neutral arbitrators, the court loses legitimacy. And when a court fails to restrain its own 'side' from excesses, it endangers the foundational principles of liberal democracy.

Democratic norms

Democratic norms go beyond the letter of constitutional law, cajoling politicians to act in good faith and lending support to institutions. When democratic norms evaporate, authoritarianism – complete with an assault on objective reality, political deployment of violence and suppression of a free press – fills the vacuum. These attacks on democratic norms have spread across western and eastern Europe, budding democracies in the Middle East, and areas of Latin America. And sadly, the USA hasn't been immune.

Without democratic norms, laws can never perfectly insulate us from populists and extremists. Such norms stem not simply from personal virtue, but from a spirit of centrism, an understanding that your side's defeat does not mean the apocalyptic fall of the nation. A peaceful and effective transition of power is a part of the democratic process. If centrism holds firmly to the belief that neither side has all the answers or all the virtues (even if they are not evenly distributed), then democratic norms will be secure. Centrism rejects Manichaeism, allows the natural ebb and flow of political power and respects co-equal branches of government. Simply put, centrists don't start or tolerate coups.

The future

We have no shortage of warnings about the decline of democracy, nor of explanations for threats to its survival. Failure to spread economic prosperity, demographic change, decline of civics education, religious fundamentalism, information bubbles and globalism have all contributed to democracies' slide into mixed government – partially democratic and partially not. Some combination of these factors inevitably leads to support for a strongman who vows to fix intractable problems that 'messy' democracy cannot solve. But perhaps we are looking in the wrong places.

We can address all those challenges to liberal democracy, provided the spirit of centrism pervades. If one sincerely believes there are no permanent victors and no permanent losers, that solutions to problems stem from no single ideological pedigree and that humility, tolerance and pragmatism are essential to governing complex, diverse modern countries, then sizeable, even staggering problems – from climate change to poverty, from injustice to election disputes – can be effectively addressed within the context of liberal democracy. Centrism that can accommodate diversity, preserve a credible and independent judiciary and secure democratic norms is essential and foundational to liberal democracy.

Having seen the fate of liberal democracies when centrism falters, we should appreciate the urgency to cultivate centrism. Liberal democracies' future depends upon it.

3

FAITH, PHILOSOPHY AND THE FOUNDATIONS OF CENTRISM

Micah Goodman

T he political centre has its roots in the ancient past. The primeval intuition that defines the centre was born in ancient traditions that cultivated the idea that balance is at the heart of the ideal way of life. There is no one clear way to attain balance; the history of human culture offers two different approaches: the 'golden mean' model most notably favoured by Aristotle and the model of holistic equilibrium advanced by Heraclitus.

The Aristotelian model of balance is well defined by Maimonides, a twelfth-century Rabbi and scholar considered one of the foremost thinkers in Jewish history. He writes: 'The two extremes of each quality are not the proper and worthy path for one to follow or train himself in.' One must locate these two extremes and place oneself at the midpoint between them: 'The upright path is the middle path of all the qualities known to man. This is the path which is equally distant from the two extremes, not being too close to either side.' The middle, the point between the extremes, is the path one should follow. Maimonides praises the golden mean, calling it 'the path of God', and states that 'one who follows this path brings benefit and blessing to himself'.

Heraclitus proposes a different version of balance. In his view, balance is attained not from the middle but from the whole. Heraclitus does not seek the midpoint between opposites, but the whole that contains both opposites alike: 'Harmony consists of opposing tension, like that of the bow and the lyre.' There is a secret to reality, one for which the bow and the lyre are metaphors. The bow is a tool of war and the lyre is a tool of music, but both are dependent on taut strings. The taut string of the bow shoots arrows and the taut string of the lyre produces notes. What causes the string to become taut and carry out its action? The fact that its two ends are pulled in opposite directions. What would happen if the two ends of the bowstring were not stretched in opposite directions? The string would not be taut and the bow would not shoot arrows. According to Heraclitus, the bow is the organising metaphor for the whole of reality. The opposites within reality are what holds it together. 'God is day and night, winter and summer, war and peace, abundance and hunger, but he takes various shapes, just as fire.'

God, meaning the force that acts upon the world and holds it together, is the meeting of opposites. If winter prevailed year-round and rain fell ceaselessly, there would be no life. If summer dominated all year without a drop of rain, there would be no life. The world exists not because of winter or summer, but because of the contrast between the two. Reality is the string of the lyre, and its ends must be pulled in opposite directions for it to create musical harmony. The ancient Chinese symbol of yin and yang is a familiar expression of this idea. One side is black, the other is white, and where is the truth? The truth is not found in one of the sides, nor is it in the middle point between the two; it is in the whole that contains both sides together.

The *Zohar* is an immense mystic corpus containing many different writings of the Jewish tradition. Among the most mysterious of these is the *Sifra di-Tsni'uta* (the Book of Concealment), the secret within the secret. A concept appears in the *Sifra di-Tsni'uta* by which the godly world, the world of the *sefirot* (divine attributes), is organised as *mitkala*, Aramaic for 'scales'. As we know, the balance of a scale depends on there being an equal weight on each side; and if the human world is a reflection of the world of the *sefirot*, then when the divine world is thrown out of balance, so too is all of human history. Dualists think the world will become harmonious when one side defeats the other; but according to the *Sifra di-Tsni'uta*, harmony appears when the two sides balance one another.

This is an ancient concept common to various mystic traditions, each offering a different metaphor by which to understand the divine balance of reality – the string of a musical instrument, the weights of a scale, and of course yin and yang. What these ancient traditions have in common is that they seek balance not in the middle, but in the whole. The truth is not found in the midpoint between extremes, but in the whole that contains both extremes within it.

The political centre can draw inspiration from these two different models. One is the ethics of the golden mean formulated by Aristotle and Maimonides. This is politics that distances itself from both the right and from the left. The second model is that of yin and yang. This ancient Chinese tradition offers a different path of balance. Inspired by this model, holistic politics is not a middle ground between the right and the left but a politics that contains right and left.

Buridan's donkey

Can holistic philosophy be converted into political action? This is seemingly an impossible transition, because holistic philosophy tends to be very open at the conceptual level but paralysed at the practical level. One thought experiment, referred to as 'Buridan's donkey', which has been formulated in different ways throughout the history of philosophy, does a good job of illustrating the major weakness in holistic thinking. In the Middle Ages, the analogy became common in the branch of philosophy that studies decision-making and the freedom of choice, and echoes of it can be found throughout the intellectual arena ever since, from Western philosophy textbooks to the writings of the Persian philosopher Al-Ghazali. Over the years, the analogy became attributed to the French philosopher Jean Buridan, although it does not appear in his writings. It is a guided imagination exercise.

Imagine a closed room in which the air does not move. On one side of the room is a pile of grain, and on the other side is another pile. The two piles are perfectly equal in size. In the exact centre of the room stands a donkey. What will happen to the donkey? If one instinct pulls it towards one pile of grain, and a second instinct of identical force pulls it towards the second pile – it will starve to death. It will remain immobile between the two piles. It will become a pile of bones, not due to shortage but to paralysis.

Someone who manages to break free of the binary pattern of thinking and view the world through a holistic lens sees the good in every phenomenon and the spark of truth in every notion. Such an individual can believe in a certain stance and in its opposite with equal conviction and may become completely paralysed as a result. One who sees the light in the political right and the truth in the political left is liable to freeze in place. The holistic approach forges passiveness.

People who believe that the opposing stance is a disaster are more devoted to their own stance and are willing to fight for it. This is the major advantage of binary thinking. It may narrow our mind, but it increases our effectiveness.

Is this tragic trade-off necessary? Are we doomed to choose between two problematic options? An open intellectual and spiritual life that neutralises the desire to act, or a life of active energy that stems from a narrow and binary spiritual world? Is there, to borrow a modern political term that appears elsewhere in this book, a third way?

The answer of Ecclesiastes
Ecclesiastes proposes this third path.

> Be not righteous over much; neither make thyself over wise: why shouldest thou destroy thyself? Be not over much wicked, neither be thou foolish: why shouldest thou die before thy time? (Ecclesiastes 7:16–17).

This verse speaks out against excess – and, surprisingly, comes out against all forms of it. Not only should one avoid excessive foolishness, one should also avoid excessive wisdom. Not only should one avoid excessive wickedness, one should also avoid excessive righteousness. How do we neutralise the tendency towards excess? Well, Ecclesiastes does not suggest taking the golden mean between two extremes but proposes a completely different approach.

> It is good that thou shouldest take hold of this; yea, also from this withdraw not thine hand: for he that feareth God shall come forth of them all. (Ibid.:18)

Ecclesiastes seeks not the middle ground between righteousness and evil, but the path that contains both righteousness and evil. To be God-fearing, says Ecclesiastes, is to express one's full range, which contains both good and bad; and a God-fearing individual 'shall come forth of them all'.

How do we follow the holistic guidance of Ecclesiastes? How do we live a life in which we take hold of the one (righteousness) and from the other (evil) withdraw not our hands? How do we maintain the balance created when we try to fulfil our obligation to all? The answer can be found in Ecclesiastes 3:1–8:

> To every thing there is a season, and a time to every purpose
> under the heaven;
> A time to be born, and a time to die; a time to plant, and a
> time to pluck up that which is planted;
> A time to kill, and a time to heal; a time to break down, and a
> time to build up;
> A time to weep, and a time to laugh; a time to mourn, and a
> time to dance;
> A time to cast away stones, and a time to gather stones together;
> a time to embrace, and a time to refrain from embracing;

A time to get, and a time to lose; a time to keep, and a time to
cast away;
A time to rend, and a time to sew; a time to keep silence, and
a time to speak;
A time to love, and a time to hate; a time of war, and a time
of peace.

This well-known chapter is one of opposites. Weeping opposite laugh-
ter, silence opposite speaking, love opposite hate. But these are not
binary opposites, because they do not cancel each other out. A world of
love is not a world without hate; a world that has war is not a world
without peace. There is a place under the heavens for an idea and
the opposite idea, for a phenomenon and the opposite phenomenon.
How is this possible? Well, it is possible because each one has its
moment. Ecclesiastes concludes the section with these simple, clear
words: 'He hath made every thing beautiful in his time.' There is truth
and there is good in every phenomenon, as long as it appears with
the right timing.

How do we follow the guidance of 'It is good that thou shouldest
take hold of this; yea, also from this withdraw not thine hand'? We take
hold of everything. Of war and peace, love and hatred, good and bad.
We take hold of everything, but not at the same time. Every human
matter has a moment that is suitable for it.

A zealot is one who thinks that a certain value is always the correct
one. Zealots are blinded by ideology, and therefore blind to time and
context. They are focused on their own world view and fail to notice
what is happening in the real world. A zealot of peace is someone who
believes that peace is always the solution; a militarist believes that exercising force is always the solution. Ecclesiastes says: 'a time of war, and a
time of peace'. There are people who tend to believe that all problems
can be solved by talking, and there are those who tend to hole up in
silence. Ecclesiastes says: 'a time to keep silence, and a time to speak'.

There is no solution that always works; there is no notion that is always correct. What makes a notion correct is not only its content, but its timing. There is justice in war, and there is justice in peace; there is strength in love and there is a place for hatred. The determining factor is not only the content of the matter, but the question of whether this is the right moment for it.

Ecclesiastes invites readers to change the way they evaluate ideas. Instead of asking which idea is true, ask which is more suitable for the current, fleeting moment in history, the current context. The question is not how much truth there is in capitalism, but whether this is the moment for capitalism or does the current climate require a larger degree of state intervention?

Ecclesiastes 3 can be read as a very sophisticated type of holistic approach, one that is immune to Buridan's donkey syndrome. Though all ideas are of value, not all ideas are suitable for every time.

From here it follows that binary thinking is less, not more, practical because binary thinkers are blind to the unique characteristics of the present moment. They believe there are stances that are never correct, and stances that are always correct. They are convinced that the value of ideas comes from their foundational ideology alone, and binary thinkers are therefore less attentive to reality. Ecclesiastes 3 introduces a different approach to reality, one that allows us to fall in love with different ideas on one hand, and pay special and practical attention to the changing dynamics of the world on the other.

People who are locked into binary thinking have a hard time being pragmatic. They reject entire worlds of abundance that they identify as impure. Those on the political right are unwilling to seriously consider proposals, plans and ideas that come from the left, and why? Because they come from the left. Those on the left who are allergic to anything that has a whiff of the right have a hard time evaluating whether a certain right-wing idea could work and improve the world. Binary thinking amplifies the feeling that some worlds are fundamentally unacceptable, and the practical sphere of action becomes narrower and less effective as a consequence.

In contrast, those who believe that there is some truth in every claim and ideology can very easily adopt a pragmatic approach. They need not ask which stance is true and just, because they have already answered that question. They know that there is truth in all the stances. Being exempt from the question of justice, they are therefore free to ask the question of benefit. In fact, it is precisely because they believe there is a spark of light in every stance that they are free to ask the simple question of which stance is most effective.

As a result, the holistic approach paves the way to a highly flexible and practical way of thinking. Holistic thinkers are not locked into one path; all worlds are open to them emotionally, so they are free to select proposals, ideas and plans from different worlds and use them to take the most effective action. They can approach the right and find useful ideas within its diverse world; they can approach the left, pick out the most effective programmes, put them together and drive action that will effect real-world change. This is a flexibility that binary people do not have. They do not approach the opposing viewpoint because they fear it will defile them. The binary thinker focuses on negating, while the holistic thinker focuses on building. Binary ideology is therefore confined to one path, while the holistic spirit can create alloys using elements from opposing sources.

The common perception that binary thinking generates effective action, while holistic thinking creates paralysis, is not true. It is often the spiritual, mystical attitude, which sees light in everything and at times seems disconnected from our modern approach to politics, that can create the most practical, flexible and effective way forward. This is the fundamental difference between centrism and other approaches to politics in the modern world. It is at the heart of why centrism offers the antidote to polarisation and extremism.

4

THE 'VITAL CENTRE' AS A FACE OF MODERATION

Aurelian Craiutu

'The spirit of the new radicalism is the spirit of the center – the
spirit of human decency, opposing the extremes of tyranny.'

Arthur M. Schlesinger Jr, *The Vital Center*

As someone who has written a lot (perhaps immoderately) about
moderation, I have often had the opportunity to reflect on the
relationship between this old virtue and centrism. The two concepts
seem connected in more ways than one. A short chapter of my book
Why Not Moderation? Letters to Young Radicals explores centrism as a
face of moderation and makes the case for a new vital centre today.[1]
Upon rereading it for this essay, I have realised that I still can't figure
out exactly how the two concepts are related, even as I am sure the
connection between them is real, strong and critically important. The
discussion on centrism in my book follows that on compromise and pre-
cedes the chapter on eclecticism and pluralism. This is no accident, for
centrism, moderation and compromise, along with concepts like civility
and prudence, belong to a common semantic field which also includes
their antonyms such as extremism, radicalism, fanaticism and zealotry.

What do opinion polls tell us about centrism? They use different
methodologies, and their results are certainly not infallible. Yet, most of
them seem to agree that a little over a third of US voters today identify

themselves neither as Democrats (liberals) nor as Republicans (conservatives).[2] Those sorts of numbers are repeated, to varying degrees, across the democratic world. What is, then, the best way to describe these voters? Are they independents? This may be so, but is it enough to figure out what they really stand for? Are they centrists? But centrism, too, has been a notoriously difficult term to pin down, maybe until now. Moreover, as this book shows, there is more than one way of being a centrist. Are these swing voters perhaps better described as moderates? That term, too, has often been associated with weakness and being lukewarm or indecisive.

It would be hard to deny that most independents are pragmatic, not extreme; they will happily endorse compromises if they promise to create tangible positive results for their lives. These voters are often frustrated with the establishment and are focused more on solving issues than on engaging in old ideological disputes or new crusades. They are open to appeals from candidates from different sides. It may very well be the case that the independents are the ignored or silent middle that emerging parties seek to empower. In many places, they are the swing voters whose ballots can determine the outcome of narrow elections, as happened in 2016 and 2020 in the USA. In two-party systems, the independents seem to belong to a 'party' *sui generis*, without banners and ranks, whose members are tired of the strident slogans used by the main parties to gain momentum and votes. In multi-party systems, they are often represented by political forces and groups rising from outside the traditional centres of power.

The views of these independent voters are hard to pin down on the classical ideological scale, although they seem to have a clear set of preferences and principles. Many are certainly moderates, although not all independents (or centrists) are automatically moderates. As I have demonstrated elsewhere, moderation is not the exclusive advantage of the centre; it is closely associated with the mean, whose location is not fixed on the political map but depends on circumstances, perception and judgement.³ One understanding of the centre always locates it halfway between the extremes; it can always be found with the aid of a more or less precise formula. The golden mean of the ancients is different since there is no scientific formula for finding it. It could theoretically be halfway between the extremes, but is not always. The mean is defined in relation to the individual who makes a certain decision in a particular context. That is why, as David Hume once remarked, finding the mean is a difficult task since there is no unambiguous way in which to do so. This is mostly because good and evil, in many cases, 'run so gradually into each other, as even to render our sentiments doubtful and uncertain'.⁴ That is why moderation, aiming for the mean, is a broader concept than centrism and can be found on all sides of the political spectrum – on the left, in the centre and on the right.

It is no secret that centrists have been the victim of constant scepticism, derision and ideological intransigence in a world in which reaffirming one's sectarian identity and reinforcing group identity are more important than seeking reasonable compromises with one's opponents for the promotion of the common good. The titles and subtitles of recent articles and books leave little room for doubt. According to one of them, centrists lack realism for they are 'pining for a golden age that never was'.⁵ Another one goes further, adding a note of sarcasm and irony: 'Centrists look at a burning planet, a racist in the White House – and plead for moderation.'⁶ Yet another article categorically declares that centrists, not extremists, 'are the most hostile to democracy'.⁷ The overall message conveyed by these critics and sceptics (mostly, although not exclusively, from the radical left) is that the centre is already dead or represents a 'death trap' in our age of hyper-polarisation and tribalism. Who would want to embrace it then?

The question seems rhetorical, especially within the pages of this book. It is not uncommon to label centrists as weak, hollow and undecided. Some view them as mushy, wishy-washy or unmanly. Cowardice, immorality and duplicity are also added by their critics to the list of real or imaginary centrist sins. They argue that the centre is little more than a dead end and have no hesitation in declaring centrism obsolete or extinct.[8] The most generous critics go as far as to admit that centrists' hearts might be in the right place, but their minds are often muddled, full of slogans and platitudes about compromise and common sense. Centrists, so the argument goes, are sentimental rather than pragmatic, letting their optimism get the better of their scepticism. They have no chance of success in contemporary sectarian politics.

It was not always so. Only forty years ago, centrists (in both parties) amounted to about 60 per cent of the US Senate. Since then, they have been the victims of big donors, ruthless primaries and gerrymandering. In the aftermath of the attack on the Capitol on 6 January 2021, as the author of a recent article in *The Economist* remarked, 'only cynical political calculation could pinpoint the sensible centre of American life as equidistant from both parties'.[9] It is difficult to find a centre equidistant from both extremes as long as 'a party in thrall to Donald Trump is dangerous in ways a party resigned to Joe Biden is not'.[10] One party – the GOP – appears to be far more dysfunctional than the other and has emerged as 'an insurgent outlier . . . unpersuaded by conventional understanding of facts, evidence, and science'.[11] Searching for a centre equidistant between the two parties seems unwise in this case.

Now, it is important to acknowledge that centrism can have, and often takes, many forms and colours; the impossibility of one form does not exclude the appearance of others. The centre has at times been an ambiguous term, prone to be used (and misused) for various ideological agendas (few of which would meet this book's definition of centrism). A few historical examples come to mind. In the immediate aftermath of the French Revolution, an 'extreme centre' appeared in France that, according to its critics, was nothing but the place where opportunist politicians met and came up with strategies to win and maintain power. In the nineteenth century, liberalism developed as a doctrine of the centre or *juste milieu*, but its priorities, fears and hopes constantly shifted, giving the middle different shapes and priorities over time. As centrists, liberals began fearing despotism and religious fanaticism, then sought a middle ground between revolution and reaction, before confronting the rise of socialism and the power of the proletariat.[12] The 'vital center' that Arthur Schlesinger Jr advocated at the outset of the Cold War started from the assumption that 'communism is not the wave of the future, and is, if anything, a passing stage to which some may temporarily turn in the quest for modernity'.[13] Its modest agenda stood in sharp contrast to the maximalist politics embraced by both the extreme left and right.

What about today? The centre that some dream of is certainly not to be identified with the conventional politics of the centre of the existing political spectrum, 'shifting as the spectrum shifts',[14] without a solid compass. Neither is it a simple reaction to the excesses of neoliberalism or woke culture. In this respect, I follow in the footsteps of those who argue for a muscular, realistic and vital centre that embraces eclecticism and pragmatism. Is this a utopian goal in our present circumstances? I don't think so. As I argued in *Why Not Moderation?*, this new vital centre cannot (and should not) be dependent on (or merely follow) the initiatives of the extremes. It must define the terms of the debate and force the extremes to respond to it. Such a centre is more than a mere balance of power approach that seeks a simple equilibrium in the competition between various political forces and groups in society. The new vital centre, one that embraces moderation, relies on a few major assumptions.

First, as I have argued elsewhere, 'it rejects any form of single-mindedness that tends to degenerate into the fanaticism and zealotry of single causes (abortion, free speech, identity politics, woke culture, etc.)'.[15] As a form of political eclecticism, it honours the complexity and hybridity of life that can be contemplated through many windows and from diverse viewpoints. Above all, it rejects any 'fantasy of wholeness',[16] according to which we can identify a single overriding interest, principle or value that should be at the centre of social life and public policy. The advocates of the new vital centre believe that in modern society it is impossible to find a single cockpit or central command station that has the key to everything. Capitalism's critics, such as Karl Polanyi and his followers, or the present critics of neoliberalism, from Wendy Brown to Quinn Slobodian, sometimes refer to the free market as exactly such a single cockpit. They affirm that modern society has become a large market society governed exclusively by the logic of the free market regulated by demand and supply. Yet, as another economist, Wilhelm Röpke, reminds us, many areas of life will always remain *beyond* the spheres of supply and demand, largely unaffected by them.[17] Friendship, grace, chivalry and beauty, for example, are not governed by the principles of the free market and never will be. These areas of life are no less important both in our daily lives and in our approach to government.

Second, embracing ideological crossovers, the advocates of the vital centre acknowledge that our lives cover a multiplicity of realms that, in turn, follow different axial principles, as Daniel Bell argued five decades ago.[18] The techno-economic realm has functional rationality as its axial principle, whereas the political realm follows legitimacy, in conjunction with free competition and the rule of law. The cultural realm has expressive symbolism at its core, with personal authenticity and self-realisation attached to it. The autonomy of each of the three realms must be respected, for they follow different types of logic and have diverse rhythms of change. Between them, there are often tensions and contradictions that must not be glossed over. A criterion that is appropriate to one of the three realms is likely to be inappropriate to evaluate the other two. Profit, for example, is a useful measure for the economy, but not for politics or culture. Centrism understands and embraces this complexity. Applying the right approach to the right problem at the right time is at the core of the vital centre as I understand it.[19]

A few concrete examples might be helpful here. A centrist position may not work well if we frame issues as either/or choices (usually

29

involving moral or religious issues), but it may be effective when it comes to concrete matters that allow for more-or-less choices like taxes, infrastructure, immigration, debt ceiling, deficit reduction, health care, gun control, reducing the cost of prescription drugs, or clean air and water. Such topics are of vital importance to voters and are amenable to centrist pragmatic solutions. Yet, they are not often discussed by the media because they do not involve stark black-and-white contrasts that appeal to wide audiences and capture their imaginations.

Another good case in point is education. It would be an error to apply criteria of strict economic efficiency to evaluating and funding primary and higher education. When true to their mission, universities are not for-profit organisations constantly seeking to innovate, nor should they live entirely in the past, rejecting adaptation to the present. They have always been fragile institutions that allow for the study of obscure and odd subjects of apparently little immediate utility. As Abraham Flexner, the founding director of the Institute for Advanced Study in Princeton, once wrote, 'the pursuit of these useless satisfactions proves unexpectedly the source from which undreamed-of utility is derived'.[20] A centrist approach to education would honour 'the usefulness of useless knowledge' and seek at the same time to promote necessary reforms to tackle the increasing bureaucratisation of our institutions of higher learning, spread opportunities for learning widely and promote uninhibited freedom of inquiry and discussion. It would endorse neither the radical claims made by the authors of the *1619 Project* nor the conservative tone of the *1776 Project*, two ideological ways of interpreting America's past.[21] Instead it would seek to broaden the conversation on the reality of slavery and racism in the history of the USA and celebrate at the same time the real achievements of the Founding Fathers who created America's imperfect but enduring Constitution.

Third, the vital centre seeks to be realistic and accepts that there are different types of centrist positions based on the *nature* and *scale* of the problems involved. According to this view, the political good is multidimensional rather than one-dimensional. Policy issues are not black and white, but grey; they always involve inevitable trade-offs and painful costs. In many cases, there is no absolute way of determining the best course of action; we are confronted with a plurality of goods, values, views and opinions. Instead of having to choose between right and wrong, we are often obliged to choose between what is partially right and what is partially wrong.[22]

Centrists of this mould are realists who follow the ever-changing contours of political life; they are not monomaniacs fixated on one single idea or theme. As moderates, they can defend limited government and embrace reasonable welfare policies; they are much less ideological and much more pragmatic about the size of government than the old left and right. They can be conservative in morality and religion, and radical in other spheres (culture or private life). Centrists of this kind believe that there is no single measuring rod that allows them to find the perfect solutions to every complex problem. They do not believe in blueprint thinking or miraculous panaceas. Instead, they embrace complexity and hybridity that reflect reality better than ambitious one-size-fits-all theories.

The level at which these problems are addressed often makes a huge difference. A centrist pragmatic position on a concrete issue like education or police reform might be effective at the local level, while centrist solutions to infrastructure, health care or new energy sources may be more effective at the state or federal level. This is another way of saying that scale and size matter. Some issues may be best solved at the local level through cooperative solutions and voluntary associations; others involve the intervention of the government and courts at the state or federal level.

That is why centrists agree that we need to go *beyond* classic dichotomies such as market vs state, left vs right and embrace eclectic solutions that may seem like ideological hybrids. They recognise that modern society can no longer be interpreted as an integrated holistic web.

31

As Elinor and Vincent Ostrom and their collaborators associated with the Bloomington School of political economy and public choice showed, we need to go beyond market and states to explore the *polycentric* governance of complex social, economic and political systems.[23] Polycentricity is central to any centrist agenda, equally sceptical of solutions that recommend either *the* state or *the* market. Centrists believe that a balance between competing principles is needed to make democracy work, and the old comprehensive ideologies by definition fail to offer such a balance.

To conclude, the vital centre (as a face of moderation) can be effective, but only if animated by a fighting creed, realism and courage. There is a world of difference between the parody of the centre that believes in the possibility of eliminating conflict from politics through rational deliberation and overlapping consensus, and a muscular centre that espouses pragmatic policies without making rotten compromises. As moderates, centrists are aware that they must acknowledge the plurality of political values, principles and goods – liberty, equality, justice, privacy, community etc. – and the inevitable constraints of social and political life. In an era characterised by the propensity to make bold claims promising comprehensive and rapid large-scale change ('Drain the swamp', 'Abolish ICE', 'Defund the police', 'Medicare for all', 'Cancel all student debt'), centrists can and must reaffirm the virtues and power of incrementalism. They must remind everyone that (most of the time) gradualism is *not* a moral failure, as radicals claim, and incremental reform may often be 'the best way to address social problems in a climate where it is difficult to agree on basic facts, let alone expensive large-scale interventions'.[24]

Their critics (many of whom are answered in greater detail elsewhere in this volume) will take them to task for their alleged inconsistency. Yet centrists do not envisage any way of being perfectly consistent or eliminating life's contradictions and tensions; instead, they seek to leverage them into a source of strength. Their core values are moderation, honesty, humility and respect for nuance.[25] That is why they are prepared to proceed gradually by blending opposites and rejecting superficial alternatives or simplistic binary choices. When the political system they seek to reform doesn't match their theories and blueprints, they do not try to dismantle the system, as radicals tend to do. Their type of incrementalism also has the additional advantage of being democratic insofar as it does not focus on one single way. It starts from the premise that there are many possible ways of reforming society, and experiments must be conducted to figure out which ones work best.[26] Such a centre is well worth fighting for today in our age of hyper-polarisation and ideological intransigence.

5

THE EVOLUTION
OF DEMOCRATIC CENTRISM

Lanae Erickson and Matt Bennett

As Bill Clinton began his second term in office, one of us was serving on the White House staff; the other was finishing her first year of high school. Despite – or perhaps because of – our different ages and vantage points on 1990s centrism, we now spend significant parts of our work life developing and articulating why and how the meaning of 'centrist' has evolved over the past three decades. While the name of the organisation we lead, Third Way, might conjure that earlier era, our politics are distinct from both the Clinton/Blair definition of centre and the conservatism of the old Blue Dog Democrats in Congress.

Between globalisation, shifting social mores, changing electoral coalitions and the authoritarian shift in right-wing politics, today's version of centrism looks a lot different from the one that drove the Clinton presidency or the Blair premiership. We have embraced its strengths – a commitment to pragmatic policy progress and political strategies that can win majorities – and grappled both with modern realities and with its past shortcomings. That reckoning has led to the current iteration of what it means to be a 'moderate Democrat' in the USA which has clear relevance for centrists all over the world. It is now more inclusive, more nuanced and better suited to be the political antidote to today's radical right and far left.

It's important to note how unsurprising it is that centrism has evolved since the 1990s. To be sure, Bill Clinton, along with his allies in the global Third Way movement, were the founders of modern centrism.

They broke some decades-long losing streaks – in which Democrats had won the White House only once since 1964, British Labour had struggled, and centrism as an idea found it difficult to make an impact across the European continent. They laid out a vision for what it meant to be a 'New Democrat' or 'New Labour' in the early 1990s.[1] That philosophy drove Clinton's presidential campaigns and served as the intellectual foundation for his tenure. Clinton's imprint on Democratic centrism was deep and durable. But it would be absurd to presume that philosophy was trapped in amber when he left office and when the rest of the Third Way members followed. Clinton himself would be the first to insist that while the principles and values should endure, the agenda and electoral strategies themselves must change. While he used overt callbacks to John F. Kennedy in his 1992 campaign – including a video of a teenage Clinton shaking President Kennedy's hand – no one thought the governing ethos of the early 1960s should apply thirty years later to a unipolar world on the brink of a technology revolution.

The decades that now separate us from the Clinton presidency have been equally consequential for the USA and the world. The approaches, both substantively and politically, had to change. And they have.

Let's start by giving Clinton's signature achievement – his economic policy – its due. Among other things, it created 23 million jobs, turned deficits into surpluses, increased real wages and afforded new protections and benefits to workers and their families. That success was echoed across Europe. The capitalist core of Clintonian or Blairite economics still drives the philosophy of the centre: work with the private sector to foster growth, but also regulate and tax to ensure the growth is equitable. This belief in the centrality of markets – that are wisely regulated and bolstered by smart public investments – continues to serve as a major breakpoint between the centre and the socialist far left.

But with the benefit of hindsight, it is now clear that centrist politicians of that era were too optimistic about globalisation. It's true that no one could hold back that tide, and there is no path to prosperity without exports and global engagement. Plus, hundreds of millions – perhaps billions – of global citizens were lifted out of poverty by the deals struck in the 1990s.

Still, we should have anticipated that the North American Free Trade Agreement (NAFTA), which Clinton inherited (and tried to modify), would hurt much of the country. NAFTA contributed to a hollowing out of the US industrial heartland. It may have been inevitable, but NAFTA made it faster and worse.

The other major trade deal of that era, Permanent Normal Trade Relations (PNTR) with China, was a foreign policy failure. Much of the free world believed that if Chinese growth was tethered to world economics – if they ate McDonald's and sold us T-shirts – China would become more like the West and join the family of nations. That, to put it mildly, was a miscalculation. Despite deeply entangled economies, China is now one of the USA's top two foreign adversaries, and its tensions with the rest of the West continue to grow.

Today, our movement believes that the isolationist policies championed by the right are dangerous and counterproductive. But international trade deals must promote domestic manufacturing, advance a transition to clean energy, and ensure that countries with lax labour standards or persistent human rights abuses aren't writing the rules for the global economy.

These shortfalls on trade also had enormous political implications. NAFTA's economic impact played a real role in Hillary Clinton's loss to Donald Trump of three essential Midwestern states in 2016, thereby delivering the White House to him. In the UK, some of that same anger towards the EU led to the shock of Brexit. Far-right figures like France's Marine Le Pen either ran strongly in national elections against centrist opponents or, in Italy and elsewhere, actually won based in part on discontent with globalisation, including around immigration.

Drilling down on the US example offers a window into the way the centre has shifted to meet this new reality. In the USA, Democrats have

36

compensated for the loss of non-college-educated voters by bringing in more college-educated, often suburban voters. That means different areas and voters are now delivering moderate Democrats to Congress. In the 1990s, the elected officials pushing the party to the centre were largely Southern or rural white men. Take Lanae's long-time representative, Collin Peterson, from the beautiful North Woods of Minnesota. Peterson was pro-union and supported a range of left-leaning economic policies as the chair of the House Agriculture Committee. He was also pro-life and carried an A+ NRA rating as a 'strong defender of the Second Amendment'. He not only backed the 1996 Defense of Marriage Act but teamed with three Southern Democrats on a Federal Marriage Amendment, which would have barred every state from recognising unions between same-sex couples. His pairing of progressive ideas on labour with conservative views on social policy reflected the views of his constituents. And that was a fact of life, both for the kid growing up in his district and the Clinton aide needing their substantive and political support.

But political realignment spelled the end of Peterson's brand of moderation; he lost his seat in 2020, and now most of the Blue Dogs are gone. Those 1990s-era centrists have largely been replaced by people like Representative Angie Craig, an openly gay, pro-choice, pro-business moderate Democrat who represents a district of the near and distant suburbs of Minneapolis. She advocates just as fiercely for Minnesota's farmers, but she also supports the Equality Act and codifying Roe v. Wade. And though she's a gun owner who knows how to shoot, Craig has garnered a failing 'F' rating from the NRA. But, like Peterson before her, Craig prevails because she represents a centrism that fits the era and reflects the values of the voters who put her in office. In short, the evolution of the Democratic coalition means that most moderate Democrats in elected office today hail from places that are more suburban, more college-educated and more open to inclusive social policies than the centrists of the 1990s.

The US centre-right is harder to track, in part because it was buffeted by the hurricane of Donald Trump and his MAGA movement. What it meant to be 'conservative' was turned upside down – suddenly it was the left defending the FBI and the military and Democrats who were arguing against Trump's trade protectionism. And old ideological lines in Republican politics were erased by a more urgent focus on questions going to the heart of the USA's democratic system: could our government, elections and courts be trusted? In the USA, the centre-right lost almost all purchase on elective office, with the ranks decimated in primaries that they lost to Trump loyalists.

A few moderate Republicans may be beginning to re-emerge, but it is not clear that their party can maintain a coalition that includes both Trumpian true believers and small-government policy wonks. This shift in the nature and faces of the centre extends to the broader movement of organisations that drive and support it. Over the past decade, for example, Third Way has partnered with LGBT groups to pass hate crimes legislation and repeal 'Don't Ask, Don't Tell', played a leading role in advancing the marriage equality movement (including shaping the first-ever winning ballot initiative campaigns in 2012), worked closely with Sandy Hook parents to push Congress to pass sensible gun safety laws and supported crucial reforms to our country's law enforcement in the George Floyd Justice in Policing Act. One look at our website belies any comparison to 1990s-era social policy. While gaps remain on some issues, today's moderate Democrats are basically aligned with progressives on the goals around most culture war questions. Where there's a rub, and there are some on ideas like 'Defunding the Police', it comes largely on questions of tactics, messaging and strategy.

One major benefit of this transformation is that it has created an opening for centrists to be represented by a broader array of messengers. Gone are the days of exclusively white, male, rural (or in the case of the USA, Southern) moderates. Today our movement is represented widely, if not primarily, by women, people from diverse backgrounds, including first- and second-generation immigrants, LGBT people and others who may not have felt as welcomed by the 1990s version of our politics. Those who have become the face of Democratic centrism in the USA include Michigan governor Gretchen Whitmer, Transportation Secretary Pete Buttigieg, Representatives Abigail Spanberger and Lisa Blunt Rochester; these are not your father's Democratic moderates. They – *we* – represent a varied set of voices, all of which are proud to call themselves pragmatic progressives. Non-white voters are core drivers of our push for sustainable solutions that prioritise what works over ideology, as these voters have no interest in making perfect the enemy of good. In fact, in the USA voters of colour are the ones who delivered arguably the most centrist president in our lifetimes: Joe Biden.

In addition to these massive changes to the moderate brand, agenda and approach, another transformation has had a major impact. The takeover of the political right by forces who seek power at any cost, are willing to ignore the rule of law and foment hate and division is nearly complete. That has profoundly changed how the centre thinks about sensible law-making. In a two-party system, each political party reacts to the evolution (or in this case, devolution) of the other. In multi-party systems it creates space for new centrist parties to rise and take vast swathes of the public with them. Today's populists, sometimes labelled National Conservative and sometimes supporters of 'illiberal democracy', punish those who dissent from their attempts to undermine democracy, and abandon ideology for allegiance to demagogues. That means that while centrists still believe in working across the aisle as a necessity of governing, we cannot pretend that we're dealing with partners of a few decades past.

We have had to go all in against the attack on liberal democracy, often allying with the left and anyone willing from the moderate right, to defend democracy and the fundamentals of our way of life. While we have significant policy and political disagreements with those on the far left and classic conservatives, it is simply not comparable to our divergence with the far right. Indeed, the most imminent danger the left poses is creating a caricature of centrists that the populist right can use to win in close elections.

This right-wing threat has necessitated a change in how we approach others in the broader centrist movement as well. Centrists must not fall into the trap that extremists often set by prioritising purity over power. In the 2020s, the rise of the authoritarian right means that we simply cannot afford to lose elections to those who would undermine democracy. Principled debates are important in charting a course for government, but they cannot be done without an eye towards their political implications. Losing touch with voters no longer means a few years of disagreement with the ruling party over policy; it means handing the reins of government to profoundly dangerous forces of illiberalism.

We note, with amusement and some dismay, that 1990s fashion is back in style. But a resurgence of Doc Martens and flannel does not hearken a return to the Clinton-era centrism of that time. Yes, we are still the winning wing of our camp and the pragmatic visionaries who drive real progress. But we have learned from our mistakes, addressed many of them, and now face an existential threat to everything we believe in. That means the centre must pull together behind our leaders and help them articulate a clear and modern vision for the future – and build the electoral coalition that will support it. Because, at this moment in history, nothing less than liberal democracy is at stake.

6

CENTRISM AND ITS CRITICS

Philip Collins

A middle way

From the politics of the middle ground defined in the USA by President Eisenhower, through Harold Macmillan's Middle Way in the UK to the Third Way shared by President Bill Clinton and Prime Minister Tony Blair, the path between political extremes is a well-travelled one. These examples would not be as instantly recognisable as they are had they not been successful. It is therefore maybe not surprising that such a notable political venture should attract criticism and counterblast. Indeed, we can usually learn a lot about the virtues and the vices of a political faith from the assault made on it by acute critics. Yet in this respect political centrism seems something of an exception. It appears to attract a critique that is, by turns, ill-judged and ill-tempered.

There are three critiques to which centrism is regularly subjected. I shall call them the position critique, the victory fetish critique and the disguise critique. Sadly, these critiques do not cohere into a single line of inquiry. Indeed, most of the critical scrutiny yields little by way of insight, little that the committed centrist might wish to incorporate into his or her own body of thought. There is surely constructive criticism of centrism out there, but it doesn't come from the current group of critics. Perhaps there is one exception to this, which is that the critical writing on centrism should lead to a renewed alliance between the radicals and the moderates in any movement, an alliance which has been a fruitful source of progressive change.

The position critique

First, the argument from position. This is the claim that the political centrist takes a position, as a matter of course, halfway between the dominant political parties of the pure left and right. They are the honest political positions and the centrist is merely the balance between them. The centrist thus finds a hybrid point, not out of any genuine conviction but more out of a failure to realise that the true path of righteousness exists to the left or to the right (depending on the vantage point of the critic). Centrism, on this account, is nothing more than the coordinates on a map or the seats in the middle of the National Assembly between the high clergy and wealthy on the right and the lower clergy and poorer folk on the left.

This definition is descriptive and simple to understand but fails to provide any reason why the centrist would choose to do this. Why would anyone go into politics at all if all they wanted to do was to take every cue from those around them? This critique also has the serious weakness that it makes centrism entirely empty and thus hardly worth bothering about, leaving centrism itself unchallenged. On this account, centrism is not a philosophy; it is a mere position. There can therefore be no fraternity between centrists in different nations or over time, as the precise political spectrum onto which they will map their politics will never be similar enough. Centrists are thus the playthings of other parties. Wherever the main parties of the right and left happen to be located on a linear political spectrum, the centrist sits happily in the middle, sure in geometric certainty, with no beliefs to speak of. Centrists share a method at times, but nothing else. The effect of the critique from coordinates is that centrism simply vanishes.

The victory fetish critique

The deficiency of this critique is obvious, which is why it usually becomes the predicate of a second counterblast to centrism. The dedicated centrist, according to the view which I shall call the victory fetish, has no strong notion of what politics is designed to achieve, but he or she is obsessed by the prospect of electoral victory. The choice to be a centrist is a matter of calculation over principle, in the belief that there are more votes to be harvested in the middle of the spectrum.

It is worth noting at first just how much this critique is conceding to the centrist. The claim that victory will be won in the centre of the political spectrum is, for any given general election, either true or false. If it is false, then the centrist will simply fail. If centrism did not turn out to be a viable strategy for winning elections, then we should not need to bother with it anyway. An irrelevant and discredited creed that always led to defeat would hardly merit much of a critique at all.

But if it is true, then is it not irresponsible of the putative radical to waste his or her political passion on a losing cause? It does seem, in point of fact, that centrism has been a rather successful strategy for winning elections. There are plenty of electorates which seem to like the politics of the centre, even if some vocal political activists tend not to. In a democracy this is a significant fact the critics of centrism might wish to reflect on. The election victories of Bill Clinton and Barack Obama, Tony Blair in the UK and Emmanuel Macron in France gave those governments at least the possibility that they might make some progressive improvements to their respective countries. Electoral victory was the necessary price of admission, and victory in politics is not something to be shied away from. If the capacity to win elections is the best that the critics can offer, then centrism is going to come away unscathed.

Note too how the victory fetish critique is subtly incompatible with the position critique. Centrism defined by coordinates would shift to the left if the party of the left became more radical, because the midpoint on the spectrum would also shift to the left. It would make this move by definition because centrists are supposed to keep the two main parties of left and right equidistant. Yet a centrist with a victory fetish would only make this move if the electorate had also shifted to the left, which is by no means the same thing as a political party making that move. The position centrist would shift to the left, the victory fetish centrist would not. It is worth noting too that the only person who keeps his or her head in a time of polarisation is the position centrist. If the right and the left flee to the extremes, the position centrist stays in exactly the same spot. Clearly, there is no serious critique here, either in a belief-free position or a motiveless passion for victory. Centrists, as this book shows, have a clear set of beliefs and a healthy desire for political victory.

The disguise critique

This is what leads to a third critique of centrism, which I shall call the disguise theory. At some level the critic of centrism knows that victory for no purpose at all is a strange motivation. And even if the centrist does win elections for reasons that are the pure pursuit of power, the experience of office brings with it the imperative to make political choices. The electorally successful centrist will be defined by revealed preferences in government. The disguise critique suggests that, although the centrist has disguised his or her true intentions as a clever ruse to get elected, those interests become apparent in office. This critique takes four forms which place the centrist in quite different places on the political spectrum and make different allegations about the degree of conscious agency involved in centrist politics. The centrist, according to the critics, has no position of his or her own and must therefore be a disguised liberal, a conservative, a coward or a socialist.

The first and most radical instance of the disguise critique is that the centrist is a bedfellow of all that is worst. The centrist provides a cover for, variously, free-market neoliberalism, dismantling the welfare state, eroding the rights of workers, ignoring old industrial towns and imperialism and colonialism abroad. In this critique, the centrist is an ally of neoliberalism. The rhetoric of the centre is applied to uphold the politics of the right. Neoliberals are at least honest about their creed and prepared to advertise it openly. The centrist is cunning enough to wear a disguise and is therefore, being both a neoliberal and a fraud, worthy of even more opprobrium. There is a version of the radical disguise critique in which the centrist is the unwitting ally of the neoliberal villains but the result is the same, and the disdain perhaps even greater. The unwitting centrist, having been used, is no longer quite so deviously malign but he or she is stupid instead.

The second instance of the disguise critique, which is not compatible with the first, is that the centrist is in fact not a neoliberal but a conservative. The centrist is alleged to believe in the neutrality of all institutions and remains wilfully blind to structures of racism and misogyny because he or she occupies a privileged position within the status quo which must not be disturbed. The centrist is thus borrowing the language of progress to ensure that nothing happens. The conservative centrist is not a counter-revolutionary like the neoliberal centrist, but he or she is an enemy of right-thinking people all the same. The best retort to this rather strange accusation is to look at the record of the governments led by leaders who were happy to call themselves centrists. All around the world – the USA, Canada, the UK, Australia, France, Germany – centrist governments have been conspicuously active. Roy Jenkins' reforms in the UK or Lyndon B. Johnson's civil rights legislation in the USA, to take just two examples, hardly left their nations unchanged and both were administrations that were, at the time, charged with being excessively concerned with electoral victory.

Indeed, as soon as a critic is confronted with the reality of a centrist government in office, there will be a quick switch to the third instance of the disguise critique which is that the centrist is a leftist who simply lacks courage. This centrist is not a neoliberal nor a conservative, but someone who is just insufficiently left-wing. There is a germ of truth in this. Political movements need a radical edge. There are many egregious practices – segregation, the banning of interracial and same-sex marriages – that once prompted radical demands for change. It is commonplace that the radical demand of one era becomes the standard issue of the next. But this is the case for an alliance between the moderate person and the radical. The moderate shares the objectives but fits them to the political moment. The moderate is also responsible for ensuring that the demands brought into the mainstream are reasonable and that radical policies from left and right which would do more harm than good remain on the fringes where they belong.

The fourth instance of the disguise critique comes from the political right and levels the accusation that, behind the mask, centrists are really socialists. They have understood that electoral victory will be elusive and so are pretending to be something they are not. Edmund Dell's baleful history of the British Labour Party, *A Strange Eventful History*, is a book-length study of how democratic socialism has always failed because the first term has proved to be incompatible with the second. The right-wing disguise critique suggests that the centrist has worked this out and is therefore posing as a moderate but is all set to enact the socialist policies for which nobody would ever vote. There is, at the root of political centrism, a kinship with philosophical pragmatism. As John Dewey said in his *Political Writings*, 'philosophy is of account only if, like everyday knowing and like science, it affords guidance to action and thereby makes a difference in the event'. This is an insight the centrist applies to politics and it is one that is usually denied to the critics. The position critique of centrism effectively erases it as an idea altogether. The victory fetish critique of centrism concedes the success of centrism but fails to explain it. The various disguise critiques of centrism attribute beliefs to the centrist that the critic either likes or loathes. It is as if the critics cannot believe there is a viable political philosophy other than their own. As Bishop Berkeley once said about philosophers, they are prone to throw dust in their eyes and then complain that they cannot see.

These critiques can be countered in empirical action. Their best retort is the set of achievements carried out in the name of political centrism. But the creed needs to be defined and argued for, and it is that greater clarity that this book exists to supply. Then people who are happy to be regarded as centrists will feel they are living up to Dewey's test for political action: 'action which is not informed with vision, imagination and reflection is more likely to increase confusion and conflict than to straighten things out'.

46

7

THE CASE FOR CENTRISM

Yair Lapid

The president of Israel sat in the filthy changing room of a football stadium and waited. It was close to midnight. Someone approached him and handed him a cell phone. 'Mr President,' I told him, 'I'm calling to say that I have succeeded in forming a government.'

The date was May 2021, and of course this was not how it had been supposed to play out. The plan had been for me to finish forming the government at least an hour earlier, and President Rivlin had been meant to award the Israel State Cup in line with tradition at the end of the final, and then receive my official announcement in keeping with protocol. But the negotiations for forming the government became increasingly complicated, voices were raised in the large conference room, the leader of the Labour Party threatened to blow up the talks, and just as we were getting word that all was lost, the door to the conference room opened and my parliamentary advisor burst in, white as a sheet. 'The match ended in a draw!' she shouted. 'It's gone to extra time! The president is stuck at the stadium! We can't get him out of there!'

In the end, of course, everything turned out well. The president's aides pulled him out of the stadium despite his objections (former president Rivlin is an avid football fan), and the negotiations over the formation of the government concluded, as is the way with these things, minutes before the allotted legal deadline and not before everyone at the table swore at least twice that they were going to get up right now, go home and never come back. Politics always walks a narrow tightrope between drama and comedy, but we all knew that the government formed that night was completely different. It wasn't a right-wing government, it wasn't a left-wing government, it was a pragmatic government.

Ever since the Jacobins sat their revolutionary backsides down on the left side of the French parliament, the democracies of the world have maintained the same steady pendulum swing: sometimes the right rises to power, other times the left. The names may change, but the pendulum continues to swing. Sometimes they are the right-wingers, the conservatives, the fascists, the capitalists, the local patriots, those with 'constrained visions', in Thomas Sowell's definition; and after a few years they are again the left-wingers, the socialists, the Bolsheviks, the progressives, the universalists, the humanists. Even when the world changes and the problems change with it – even when the left replaces social democracy with trans rights and the right replaces patriotism with anti-immigrant sentiment – politics remains binary. We cannot always explain exactly what we are *for*, but it is completely clear to us who we're against. Everyone is standing on one side of an imaginary border and shouting at those on the other side to go to hell.

The government we established shattered this principle. It consisted of no fewer than eight(!) parties from across the political spectrum. There were unequivocally right-wing parties (at the head of one such party stood my friend Naftali Bennett, who served as prime minister as part of our rotation agreement), there were unequivocally left-wing parties, two centrist parties, and even – for the first time in the history of the country – an Arab party of supporters of the religious 'Islamic Movement in Israel'. All these parties made sure to tell their political 'base' that they had not abandoned their traditional position on the political spectrum, and that they had joined the government only to fiercely protect the vital interests of the left/right/Jews/Arabs. In the interests of keeping the peace, I didn't point out the obvious: That we just weren't there any more. From the moment the government was formed, everyone belonged to the political centre.

It was a 'horseshoe' government, as in French writer Jean-Pierre Faye's excellent metaphor. This is predicated on the logic that the radical left and the radical right, the two ends of the horseshoe, are much closer to each other than to the centre of the horseshoe. They feign a profound hatred between them, but in practice they often find themselves aligned, in particular inhabiting a similar emotional world: both want to destroy the old world in favour of a radical agenda, both share a profound hatred and infinite suspicion towards the 'establishment', both are addicted to conspiracy theories and live within a media 'bubble' in which there is no room for other opinions or even facts that could sow doubt among true believers.

The strengthening of the extremist elements stems from their sharp and catchy slogans (those who don't mind lying 'for the cause' always have an advantage), in a world that is becoming increasingly complicated and whose public finds it increasingly difficult to understand its purpose. But we – the centrists – must also shoulder part of the blame for the rise of extremism, because the political centre fails time and again to present a conceptual alternative to the edges of the horseshoe.

Time after time, the centre repeats the same mistake: it presents itself as a faded version of the left or the right, instead of insisting that it operates under completely different rules of engagement and in a completely different political field. To bring voters to the polling booths, centrists avoid conflict with the extremists, so as not to lose their support. The result, of course, is that the voters don't show up and the centre's ability to govern is impaired. This is true in bipartisan systems, and offers an explanation for the faltering of both major parties at different times. It is even more true in multi-party systems, where a party with two or three seats can enable the formation of a government or bring it down.

Unfortunately, that is what happened to us. Our government survived only a year and a half, and collapsed when it became clear that eight parties were perhaps too many. Unsurprisingly, those who replaced us were a nationalist-messianic coalition based on the parties of the radical right. The extremist government that Netanyahu formed tried to immediately complete the pendulum swing, to change our system of government, emasculate the Supreme Court and turn Israel into an undemocratic country. In response, one of the largest and most inspiring protest movements of the last century was born. Hundreds of thousands of people took to the streets every week to protect values such as a functioning democracy, liberal nationalism, fighting corruption and the separation of powers.

The government, for its part, raised the bar and dangerously accelerated the anti-democratic process. The terrible result was that our enemies understood that Israel was weakened internally and saw an opportunity to attack. On 7 October 2023, Hamas terrorists invaded our country. Israel suffered the worst massacre the Jewish people had been through since the Holocaust. War broke out. At the time of writing, the struggle hasn't finished. The final results will be written in the history books but the basic principle was proven in the clearest and most painful way imaginable: the more Israel is a democracy and the more moderate the country, the stronger we are. If the country moves away from liberal centrist values in favour of populism it becomes weaker militarily, diplomatically and economically.

I believe this struggle, between radicalism and democracy, will be the one that defines global politics in the coming years. The separation into left and right is artificial and outdated, and the real struggle is between the moderates and the extremists.

Not the moderates from the right and the moderates from the left, but simply the moderates. Not the extremists from the right and the extremists from the left, but a destructive partnership between populists and radicals. The only thing that can stop them are decent centrists who know how to build a civil community based on integrity and dialogue.

We are not looking for the ideal way of life; rather, we seek to create the conditions that will allow different ways of life to coexist.

The major challenge of the centre is to explain that moderation is not a compromise between world views – it is a world view in its own right. More than this, it is the only world view that can address the challenges of this era.

We refuse to give up, because we are not driven by the question of what we want to take from others, but rather what we can give to others.

The centre is not a restricted version of right or left, but an optimistic political system based on the idea that people who disagree can work together in pursuit of a common goal. The centre is not a location on the political spectrum, but what sociologist Edward Shils called 'a phenomenon of the realm of action'. The centre's goal is to create a constant balance between the contradictions of modern life: a road built in the north is one not built in the south. Optimising industry increases unemployment. One who believes he must wage a just war for his people needs to consider that many of his people are likely to be killed.

Running a country is not a zero-sum game, and it is not an exercise in social engineering. Politics does not take place in a vacuum; it takes place in the real world. It builds – or destroys – the lives of real people. In the era of globalisation and the information revolution, the major ideologies are simply no longer fit for purpose. Words like 'socialism', 'capitalism', 'right' and 'left' are inadequate for a world full of contradictions. They were defeated by the technological revolution, by a world with no clear borders, aggressive social media and the new classes created by globalisation. The old perceptions, deaf to the changing times, cannot give us effective infrastructure for running a country. Denmark and Afghanistan are both 'countries', but they are two completely different bodies in moral, administrative, economic and political terms. Is there any one thesis that can be used to run them both?

The populists and the radicals will certainly not solve the dilemma for us. They may be good at marching and yelling, but time after time it becomes clear that they are utterly unable to govern societies. No catchy slogan, no matter how loudly it is shouted, will solve a complex issue like securing domestic production in the global market. No wall – physical or conceptual – will succeed in protecting from the inherent tension between the modern welfare state and the waves of immigration eating away aid budgets. We cannot keep averting our gaze from the oppression of women or the LGBTQ community just because it is done in the name of religious conviction. In the world in which we live there are no simple answers to complex questions, there is only the intelligent and level-headed management of changing situations. It's not the thesis, it's not the antithesis, it's the synthesis, stupid.

Our great challenge is communicating this to the public. The centre always does this uncomfortably and with an insecurity that shines through. Entire generations of political strategists and publicists have told us all that 'elections are all about emotion', that 'there's no such thing as a campaign that isn't negative' and that 'you must be able to explain it in five simple words'. I would offer this one piece of advice for centrists in response: fire your publicist and hire someone else. Find someone (ideally young) who understands that if they are working for a centrist party, their role is not to be a pale imitation of the populists, but rather to find a way to communicate the idea that the world is complex and would best be run by responsible and realistic people. Here are six simple words for your new publicist: the centre is positive, not negative.

During my tenure as prime minister, we held complicated and crisis-filled negotiations with the union of high school teachers. They threatened not to start the new academic year if we didn't raise their salaries. On the other side, our powerful minister of finance, Avigdor Lieberman, banged on the table with his large fist and announced that he wouldn't add a single shekel to their salary. Everyone played their traditional role in this theatre production, but 1 September, the start of the academic year in Israel, was getting closer. It looked like the schools would not start on time. I led a marathon of discussions with all the relevant figures to solve the problem. In one of these discussions, I asked: 'If you had $100 and a student who lives in the impoverished periphery, where would you invest those $100 – English classes, or a hot meal at school?'

Those present stared at me, slightly surprised, but I persisted: 'This child is going to live in a globalised world where the difference between success and failure is speaking languages. If he doesn't master English, he'll never break the cycle of poverty he lives in. On the other hand, all the research shows that children who don't eat a hot meal in the afternoon struggle at school and don't live up to their potential. So we have to decide – where do you want to invest that money?' It took a bit of time, but in the end those at the meeting understood what I was trying to tell them: there are no definitive answers. The world consists of conflicting interests and limited resources, and our role is to navigate among them and reach practical solutions, not absolute justice. The school year, by the way, started on time.

Dilemmas of this kind obviously have political ramifications. The education and future of their children is something people vote on in elections. The centre's political-communication theory must be rooted in a daring premise that the publicist you have just fired didn't understand: the mother of that child in the periphery isn't stupid. She understands that her child must speak English, she understands that this has a cost, and she will be willing to discuss it if she just recognises that we truly care about the fate of her child. Our job is to explain to her that anyone promising easy solutions is insulting her intelligence. We won't win this confrontation (or the elections) if we add insult to injury.

We must tell her that the centre is the only reasonable solution in the twenty-first century, because it at least bothers to stay updated and connected to the changes happening in the world. The centre offers a cautious connection between truths that until recently contradicted one another: we can believe in free markets and still take homeless people into our hospitals. We know how to nurture family and community life, but welcome different models of sexuality into it. We seriously address concerns about the climate crisis but remember that the solutions must be cheap and technologically relevant, or else people who are poor will not cooperate with us. We want peace on Earth, but know that peace is guaranteed and upheld by military force. We propose a humane society that is bound in what Émile Durkheim dubbed 'the collective conscience'. We propose leadership that speaks to the good and the noble in humans, out of a deep conviction that it exists. The way to improve the world is to work, create and build wonderful things in it, not to hate people who think differently from us.

That is the case centrists must take to the public. And it is a winning one.

SECTION 2

CENTRISM AND THE BIG QUESTIONS

Any political approach or belief system must be able to provide answers to the biggest questions facing the world. Some of those questions, like the limits of free speech and the role of the state, are as ancient as democracy itself, even if the context surrounding them has changed thanks to new forms of media and modern systems of government. Others are more recent, such as the challenges of globalisation and rapid technological advances. The answers to these questions lie in broad approaches and appreciating the subtlety and nuance in any given situation, but there is a set of principles we can use as our basis, as the essays in this section show.

Tony Blair offers a centrist model for modern government, which he terms the strategic state. It rejects the old dichotomy between left and right and offers a different way to think about what government can do for us in today's world and how it can adapt to a rapidly changing reality. It is a quintessentially centrist approach and a model that governments across the world should seriously consider adopting.

John Avlon's essay on the media lays out a framework for a centrist approach to journalism, exploring how changes in the media landscape have created challenges for centrists politically but also more broadly undermined some of the foundations of liberal democracy. Avlon suggests it doesn't have to be that way, and media executives would do well to heed his call.

The essays by Baroness Ruth Anderson and Børge Brende critically undermine the oft-used argument that centrism is searching for a magical middle point between the positions of ever more polarised fringes.

Anderson makes the case that centrists should lead the fight for free speech rather than leave it to the extremists, arguing that limitations on free speech should be rare and that the last people who should be trusted to police such limitations are those on the political extremes. And finally, Brende, the president of one of the world's most well-known global organisations, makes a compelling case for global cooperation but insists that it can only work when it delivers results that make a difference to people's lives. If globalisation doesn't address the real concerns and grievances of people who feel overlooked by international trade and cooperation, it is doomed to fail and we will all be poorer for it.

The big questions facing the world are the ones where centrists can and must take the lead; this section of the book shows that's possible.

8

CENTRISM AND
THE STRATEGIC STATE

Tony Blair

I believe in progressive centrism: a strong centre ground, not simply as a technical management tool, but one that is utilised to drive forward progressive values and deliver a just society, where the power of government, properly directed, improves the lives particularly of those at the bottom of the ladder. It stands in the liberal/left tradition in its priorities and principles, but recognises that their application depends on understanding the modern world, and is fully prepared to cooperate across political boundaries, including with those from the conservative tradition of politics if it builds a consensus for progress.

Centrism is emphatically not a splitting of the difference between the right and the left; rather, it is a recognition that radical change is necessary and should be based not on ideological preconception but on fact-based conception of what delivers the progressive goal.

The challenge of progressive politics is the same as it has always been: that the sensible people are often not radical; and the radical people not sensible. In an era demanding rapid change, the risk is that the centrist looks like the person whose sole claim to office is their reasonableness. Being reasonable in this day and age is a much-underestimated quality, and far preferable to extremism driven by claimed 'truths' which turn out to be misconceived prejudices.

Nonetheless, to succeed over time, centrism has to be the place of solution, not merely of sense. Centrists have to think imaginatively about how the world is changing and how to create opportunity out of change. It's the place not only of idealism – as opposed to ideology – but of the hard intellectual graft necessary to respond to complex situations with answers which endure because they're well constructed around the world as it is and not as we want it to be.

In my view, the mission of progressive politics for this generation is clear: it is to understand, master and harness the twenty-first-century Technological Revolution. This revolution is every bit as far-reaching as the nineteenth-century Industrial Revolution. It is the 'real-world' event changing everything. How it is harnessed – its risks and opportunities – will shape the future more than marginal debates around tax and spending or divisive 'identity' politics.

This is our task. Of course, there will be conservatives who also 'get it'. But this is a positive not a negative, enabling a consensus to be built. We must also overcome the forces that will, inevitably, seek to derail it or claim that its risks overwhelm its opportunities.

The work needed is immense, requiring a wholesale reimagining of the state and its relationship with the citizen, reforms of public services and an entirely new skill set in public service and in the partnership between private and public sectors.

Centrist leaders must embrace the enabling possibilities of technology, making science and innovation the core of their offer to citizens and their theory of government, rather than relegating this responsibility to industrial policy specialists and e-government bureaucrats. In this way, we can move beyond a twentieth-century fight at the margins of tax and spending or welfare policy and start harnessing the power of technology to reframe the biggest problems facing our societies:

- How do we reform health care so that we're no longer focused solely on spending billions treating ill-health and are instead using the power of new technologies, like genomics and AI, to shift the focus to prevention rather than cure?

- Demographic change and people living longer, healthier lives means changes to the state pension age; but as more people seek to stay active longer, how do we define 'retirement'?
- When teachers no longer hold a monopoly on knowledge and employers are seeking new skill sets around creative thinking and EQ as well as IQ, how should our education system be organised?
- When there are completely new forms of employment and self-employment, how do we establish rules for social justice without destroying the flexibility that employees (and not just employers) want today?

We could go across the whole of the policy agenda and ask similarly fundamental questions.

Inertia in providing answers carries a high cost. It means that a progressive agenda which offers a credible, hopeful view on the future is missing and leaves a space for populists to dominate the debate. Centrists must face up to the unintended consequences of rapid technological progress. Online commerce has driven economic prosperity, but has left high streets in many communities changed forever. Social media is a source of joy, community and political expression for millions of people, yet mis- and disinformation pose a new challenge to trust and democracy.

Technology offers the prospect of dramatically greater opportunity for the many: making the world's information available to all; opening up education through both world-class institutions and peer learning; free and cost-effective tools to support entrepreneurs, creators and retailers; platforms that can frictionlessly match workers with jobs. The recent leap in AI capability opens up new frontiers of productivity and creativity, offering powerful tools that can synthesise information, produce text, images, music and film.

Progressive politicians must show that they understand the trends and forces shaping people's daily experience; and that they are ambitious and optimistic about making full use of technology's potential to improve them. A lack of faith in leaders and institutions to deliver progress on the issues that matter is undermining trust in democracy itself.

To keep pace with this unprecedented change requires a new model of government that shreds simplistic oppositions between the public and the private sector. Arise the Strategic State.

The Strategic State – rather than the Big State or the Small State – marks a new attempt to connect modern politics with the reality of citizens' lives and the ever-evolving transformation happening around them. The private sector and individuals are embracing technology. It is ubiquitous, and gives individuals an ability and a freedom to explore and consume in ways previous generations would find unimaginable. The list of the top-ten global companies looks markedly different from even ten years ago, with all but two being technology companies and driving progress in AI, biotech and climate tech at breakneck speed.

The Strategic State harnesses the benefits of the tech revolution and mitigates its risks. It uses data and technology to drive down the cost of public services, while always trying to improve outcomes. The current path of ever-higher taxes and increasing government costs – particularly when citizens get less in return – is unsustainable.

It is not only focused on correctives or merely reacting to tech but is also proactive about shaping its development. The potential benefits of technology are vast and so the approach should ultimately be optimistic. Leaders must accurately identify the strategic priorities and crowd-in capital, talent and resources to address them. Centrism is uniquely able to deliver this combination of supporting competitive markets to allow innovation to flourish while maintaining an active, agile state that makes investments, shapes the development of technology in the public interest, and judges what supporting digital infrastructure and platforms are required and what needs can be met by the private sector.

The Strategic State embraces the possibilities of tech – to transform services, to overhaul the relationship between citizen and state, to reform institutions and to rethink the most pressing challenges facing society.

In health, from the sequencing of the human genome and rewriting of genetic code to the design of novel proteins using AI and the creation of artificial organs, the biotech revolution has been one of the most profound developments of recent decades. Rapid progress is now also coming about through the confluence of biology and computing, including machine learning and AI. As a16z's Vijay Pande, a biotech expert, has argued, 'This new era of industrialised bio – enabled by AI as well as an ongoing, foundational shift in biology from empirical science to more engineered approaches – will be the next industrial revolution in human history.'

A tech-informed health policy would mean shifting from a reactive to a preventative model, focusing resources on keeping the population healthy rather than just curing illnesses. It means democratising access to care and bolstering research by providing secure, accessible and interoperable electronic health records that put health-care data directly in the hands of patients. And it means creating a single digital front door to allow people to directly access services, where appropriate, across both the public and private sector.

Tech will be central in responding to climate change – both restricting global warming and adapting to the changes already making themselves felt. From the mobility and energy sectors to agriculture and heavy industry, the range of tech solutions available to address climate change is growing. The development and implementation of novel technologies is critical, as decarbonisation targets are extremely ambitious and will be unattainable without them. Tech is the only way climate transition can happen while preserving rising living standards – particularly in developing economies. We need to deploy existing tech at scale, while we innovate and develop new solutions in parallel, to achieve the emission reductions the world needs.

9

CENTRISM AND FREE SPEECH

Ruth Anderson

'The truth is not simply what you think it is;
it is also the circumstances in which it is said,
and to whom, why, and how it is said.'

Václav Havel

There are few people from the last century who more embody the power of freedom of expression as a fundamental human right that can deliver democratic change from the centre, not from the extremes, than Václav Havel.

A dissident, a political prisoner, a playwright, a poet and the first president of a democratic and independent Czechoslovakia, Havel's life story exemplifies the power that can be harnessed from the written word and the real-life impact which embracing freedom of expression as a tool for protest and dissidence can have on a society.

Havel intrinsically understood the potential of the written word to both inspire others and to help build a political network united to deliver change. Uniquely, he also realised the efficacy of words as an opportunity to build solidarity for his cause both at home and abroad, and how *samizdat*, the reproduction of censored materials behind the Iron Curtain, could be used beyond the Soviet Union to challenge state-sponsored propaganda and disinformation.

In other words, Havel understood the power of challenging a state-approved narrative both domestically but also on the world stage, because the status quo can only be affected if pressure is applied at every available point.

One of the most poignant and enduring examples of this effort of global solidarity, where the written word is the agent for change, are the duelling playlets by Havel and Samuel Beckett, which were published on the pages of the anti-censorship magazine *Index on Censorship* in 1984. The playlets *Catastrophe* by Beckett and *Mistake* by Havel reminded the world of Havel's plight and the realities of living behind the Iron Curtain if you were a dissident. As playwrights, they collectively leveraged their respective talents to demand change and they refused to be silenced – for Havel, whatever the consequences.

Havel and Beckett opted to use their voices, their work and their platforms to challenge a totalitarian regime and they understood the power that was afforded to them by the right to freedom of expression.

So my challenge to the current generation of activists is: why have the progressive left and the moderate middle forgotten the lessons which Havel and his allies taught us? Why have they forgotten the power that can be harnessed by embracing their right to freedom of expression? And, most importantly, why is their answer to our current turbulent politics to seek to silence their opponents rather than win the argument and out-organise them at the ballot box?

Over the last decade various populist political movements across Europe and the USA have attempted to hijack free speech as a political tool. Too often we've seen political leaders, mainly from the right but now also from the far left, seeking to weaponise the concept of free speech against their political opponents for electoral gain in order to justify their politics of hate and division.

The mantra 'I've got a right to say what I want to say (without consequence)' has been all too common in the debating arsenal of populist leaders as a new form of political dialogue in Western democracies. These politicians have embraced free speech as a political tool, but their commitment to free speech and free expression extends only to their own words and they routinely seek to shut down those who dissent from their populist positions. They wield free speech – they do not champion it. They demand the right to complete free speech irrespective of how offensive while calling to ban books which present an alternative view to their own.

Yet those groups who have most benefited from freedom of expression as a universal and fundamental human right have seemingly forgotten its importance. While the populist right have embraced the concept of free speech as a mechanism with which to enable their own political rhetoric, their opponents have seemingly floundered in either challenging the narrative or building their political alternative. And, most importantly, they have failed to stop their political opponents from claiming the mantle of the protectors of the democratic value of free speech. What's worse is that they have also forgotten that every positive and progressive change to democratic societies has emerged because individuals worked collaboratively and harnessed the powers afforded to them by the right to freedom of expression. Instead, seemingly either in fear of the politics and tactics of their opponents or because they are seeking to insulate themselves from engaging in difficult issues, they have sought to censor and to silence rather than argue and fight back. They have forgotten their own history. They have forgotten the power that freedom of expression, of speech, of protest and of research can harness. They have forgotten how we win.

That lack of collective memory is now undermining the core fabric of our democratic society. From the fight for universal suffrage to the civil rights movement in the USA to the Stonewall riots, our predecessors in the battle for equality fought tooth and nail to secure the democratic rights we now take for granted. It is time for the moderate centre to remember the battles they fought and for all of us to cherish and harness the fundamental human rights which we were afforded in 1948 by the Universal Declaration of Human Rights. Centrists should add the victories achieved by free speech to our political story, embrace them and learn their lessons as we face the challenges of today.

If you allow your political opponents to be the only voices heard, then they win by default. And if your response to arguments you disagree with is to try and silence them, then you have lost before you've even started; in fact you've probably made your political reality even worse. Suppression of speech forces it to the extremes and then it is the fringes that benefit. It is the absolute worst tactic that centrists can employ. It legitimises conspiracy theories and allows disinformation campaigns to thrive. It aids the creation of subcultures which seek to undermine our social norms and, most importantly, it can lead to echo chambers which never allow debate and discussion. How can we counter what we cannot hear? It leaves us surprised when significant sections of the population believe in ideas we had not even considered worthy of response. It also reinforces the premise that their alternative opinions must have some value; if the 'establishment' seeks to silence an argument rather than engage and demonstrate why the premise is wrong, then you can understand why some people would see the appeal of engaging in banned arguments rather than mainstream positions. If centrists believe in the ability of the public to understand the complexity of challenges and the solutions on offer, then we must also believe in the public's ability to absorb and interrogate information.

But this is nothing new, and everyone exposed to the world of political extremism knows better than to seek to ban the arguments or the ideology – it just makes it more exciting and aids recruitment. That doesn't mean that freedom of speech is without limitation: it must exist within societal and legal norms and it cannot and should not protect against incitement to violence or hate speech.

The most powerful tool against extremism is not only to push it to the fringe but also to make it dull – to take away any glamour or excitement associated with the people and groups promoting it. We can look at how the British Union of Fascists was defeated in the UK in the run-up to the Second World War: their membership fell from a reported 50,000 at its peak to less than 20,000 by the time war was declared. This collapse in support was not achieved by banning them (although that followed after the war began in earnest and they effectively sided with the Axis powers over the Allies) or by banning their magazines or their meetings. It's why the moderate middle need to think carefully about how and why they seek to censor, if at all – because it's typically counterproductive.

Defeating the fascists in the UK was achieved through exposing the ludicrous and hate-filled nature of their politics, by challenging and highlighting their violence; and it was done by shining a light on their true beliefs. It was done by defeating their ideology street by street. It was done by removing the glamour associated with a fringe political party. In 1936 the British government made an audacious move: it chose not to ban a political party but instead banned all political uniforms. There would be no black- or brownshirts in the UK. In one move, the British Union of Fascists lost their collective identity – they lost their glamour. And then they lost their members. This didn't defeat their ideology – in the years and decades ahead there was a new fight for each generation – but it did undermine their political unity and comradeship.

The fight against totalitarianism is why I am such a staunch defender of freedom of expression. The rights afforded to those of us lucky enough to live in a democracy are precious and need to be cherished and protected, especially by those in the political centre. They protect us from political extremes, and when a society embraces every tenet of freedom of expression it can lead to significant developments. One area where this is particularly important is academic freedom.

Academics by definition should challenge the status quo and push the boundaries. Their work facilitates change and progress. They are empowered to think outside the box, to stress-test dominant and settled opinion and offer us alternative world views. Over generations, their work has given us the Enlightenment, nuclear fission and analytical thought – it even gave us the internet. Protected academic freedom is vital in order for a democratic society to thrive and develop. It builds our collective knowledge base and finds solutions to new and old problems.

Which is why it is so damaging for those with a political agenda to attack and undermine academics for doing their job when they don't like their areas of inquiry. Academics should never be hounded off campus because students don't like their research outcomes or analysis. Teachers should not receive death threats for highlighting issues which are outside current mainstream thought or for teaching subjects which are at odds with religious doctrine.

In fact they should be rewarded for challenging the status quo, as that is literally their role if academia is going to survive and our society thrive. It is the responsibility of those of us with a public platform not to shy away from defending those who are investigating challenging subjects because their work empowers us. It provides an academic basis for debate and facilitates a collective discussion about where mainstream opinion should sit. Without the academic framework for debate and discussion all we have is dogma, and that rarely delivers real, positive change. All this is easy to say when we agree with the ideas being put forward or feel like they come from our side, but the challenge for centrists is to protect just as passionately those with whom we disagree.

Universities are cathedrals of learning and enlightenment. They should be considered a core tenet of our democratic life. Those people who spend their days debating and thinking to build our collective knowledge should be applauded. But it is guaranteed access to their works which should be the key concern for us in the current world of culture wars.

Libraries are the shopfront of freedom of expression. The written word is at the heart of every facet of our current debate, and the right to read is as fundamental to the right to freedom of expression as is the right to create. This should be the easiest argument in defence of freedom of expression for moderates. The banning of books is for tyrants. Just look at Afghanistan, Hong Kong and Russia, where books and access to specific titles which challenge the state-agreed narrative are banned without a second thought.

It would be easy to think that this is an issue only for repressive regimes, but it is currently on the front line in the culture wars which we seem to be living through in each of our democracies. The restriction of access to books is one of the first steps taken by those looking to roll back liberal democracy. It should serve as a warning light for us all and become a battle front for centrists.

Let us for a second look at what is happening within a democracy which claims to cherish freedom of speech more than any other country and even protects it, in law, with the First Amendment. In the USA a total of 1,648 books were banned in the last academic year in school districts across the country. They included publications which explored sexuality and the impact of slavery and our recent history. They sought to ban Margaret Atwood and Judy Blume and Toni Morrison and Khaled Hosseini. And in Tennessee, *Maus*, a graphic novel by Art Spiegelman outlining the rise of Nazism and the impact of the Holocaust, was banned 'due to concerns about profanity and an image of female nudity in its depiction of Polish Jews who survived the Holocaust'.

This is objectively ridiculous, and these actions undermine us all. If there was ever a campaign which should be waged by centrists to defend freedom of expression, it is one to stop the banning of books. And as former president Obama is now on the case, let's hope that there will be a new front in the war we can all engage with – because we fail to protect the written word at our peril.

As difficult as the current state of freedom of expression is in our democracies, I am an optimist – so let me bring you back to the power of freedom of expression and how it has been used to bring about change, and as the ultimate tool of solidarity for those people who just want to deliver reform from the centre. Let us remember Havel, whose life was defined by words and who changed the very direction of his country through the collective power he harnessed in utilising his right to freedom of expression. If Havel could deliver democracy from a prison cell by embracing the written word, then each and every one of us lucky enough to live in a democratic country should stop being afraid of free speech. We should cherish it to protect our hard-won rights and embrace it for the political fights ahead.

10

CENTRISM AND GLOBAL COOPERATION

Børge Brende

An unfortunate condition of the current era is that at the very moment when greater global cooperation is needed to address shared priorities such as scaling climate action, strengthening economies and addressing questions around breakthrough technologies, the appetite for such collaborative action appears to be in decline. The recession of support for cooperation has been replaced by waves of increasing competition and confrontation, so much so that the International Monetary Fund has warned of a risk of fragmentation 'that would leave everyone poorer and less secure'.[1]

Though the drivers of this growing fracture are multifaceted, one element has been a steep decline in trust in the global mechanisms that make cooperation possible. This broad loss of faith is born of a sense that the 'system' not only isn't working but is making matters worse. The UN has cautioned that this 'trust deficit' could have dire outcomes, hampering social and economic progress and undermining progress towards achieving the Sustainable Development Goals and other global objectives.[2]

The truth is that the resulting desire in many countries to turn inwards should not come as a surprise. Because, despite the fact that the cooperative global system – in particular, the interconnected economic landscape – has been essential to delivering benefits such as cutting extreme poverty, it hasn't always worked as it should.

Countless words have already been written on the merits of and discontents with globalisation and global collaboration, yet it is worth spotlighting one stark example of what has gone right . . . and wrong. The record speed at which COVID-19 vaccines were developed during the pandemic was a miraculous achievement, made possible by coordination among governments, businesses and research institutions. And it was made possible by the global trade system – the BioNTech/Pfizer vaccine is composed of 280 components from nineteen different countries.

Yet the urgency and cooperation that were present in the development of the vaccines did not carry through to distribution. In the first year of the availability of the COVID-19 vaccines, high-income countries achieved vaccination rates of 75 per cent to 80 per cent, whereas low-income countries saw rates below 10 per cent. This discrepancy was due in large measure to the fact that the global health space had become an area of zero-sum competition as states sought to acquire vaccines faster than others – something that only served to prolong the pandemic to the detriment of everyone.

We are now in the middle of a negative loop in which missteps of past cooperative efforts are fuelling distrust, which in turn is preventing support for future collaboration.

Pursuing centrist geopolitics

Strengthening global cooperation and underlying trust in a cooperative global approach won't be quick or easy. But it will be necessary. Because solving the compounding economic, environmental and security challenges ahead of us – what has been referred to as a 'polycrisis' – can only be done if parties work in concert with one another, even if they do not see eye to eye on every issue.

What, then, can leaders do to increase the effectiveness of and faith in global cooperation?

Here, there is guidance from the world of domestic politics – namely, the centrist approach in many countries that focuses more on forming partnerships of purpose, even with members of opposing parties, that deliver practical solutions and less on aligning according to ideology.

71

Though this approach may sound intuitive, geopolitical motivation is not always driven by a commitment to results but rather to pursuing partnerships based on shared values, ideologies or outlooks. To be sure, there is immense benefit in partnerships of the like-minded – notably, these relationships are often rooted in trust rather than transaction and can therefore increase respective and collective security. But shared values cannot be the sole determinant of what drives collaboration. A desire to respond to shared challenges and to advance shared benefit must be there as well.

Like much else in the centrist approach, the case for centrist global collaboration is strong because it has been shown to be effective.

We know this from the private sector, where there is a long history of what has often been referred to as 'coopetition' – competitors collaborating for the sake of fending off shared risk, accessing new markets or addressing broader priorities like climate change. On the last-mentioned, companies including competitors like Airbus and Boeing and also Microsoft and Apple are part of the First Movers Coalition – an initiative launched by the World Economic Forum and US State Department at the 2021 UN Climate Conference (COP26) to decarbonise heavy industry and long-distance transport through purchase commitments for green technologies.

And we know centrist collaboration can work in geopolitics. Perhaps most notably, during the Cold War the USA and the Soviet Union coordinated on broader environmental preservation and global health, among other areas. The 1987 Montreal Protocol, which has been shown to have successfully reduced damage to the ozone layer of the atmosphere, was one result of this collaboration. Another was the campaign that began in the 1960s to inoculate people around the world against smallpox. Because of US and Soviet coordination, the World Health Organization declared the disease eradicated in 1980.

But we don't have to go all the way back to the middle of the last century. The case for centrist global collaboration has been well articulated by the former Israeli prime minister Yair Lapid, who has termed it 'connectivity statecraft'.[3] The Negev Forum, which has drawn lines of cooperation across the Middle East, connecting Israel with the United Arab Emirates, Bahrain and other countries in the region in pursuit of common economic, energy and security agendas, is just one example.

Still, making centrist approaches a reality can be a challenge, particularly among rivals. Speaking of the delicate coordination between the USA and China on climate action, the US special presidential envoy for climate, John Kerry, said in 2023, 'This has to be cooperative, notwithstanding other differences that do exist.'[4]

At first, cooperation between the two countries seemed promising, despite growing frictions in other areas. At the 2021 UN Climate Conference in Glasgow, the USA and China – the world's two largest emitters of carbon emissions – announced, to much fanfare, a joint commitment to coordinate on climate action. But a short while later, discussions between the two were suspended. Though the talks resumed in mid-2023, they have been fragile – a stark reminder of the challenges inherent in this type of cooperation.

Indeed, reaching across the geopolitical divide comes with risk – political, reputational or otherwise. Parties can be subject to intense criticism by opponents back home and even by global allies for collaborating with ideological or geostrategic opponents (indeed, John Kerry faced criticism from political opponents for his efforts in pursuing climate talks with China).

Mitigating these risks can be achieved by heeding another lesson from domestic politics, namely the adage that 'all politics is local' – meaning that voters often pay closest attention to what affects them and their communities, rewarding those leaders who do as well. When it comes to global collaboration, leaders should ensure that their efforts deliver meaningful results that account for the interests of stakeholders – and keep this aim as the North Star. In this regard, increasingly, trade agreements are incorporating measures to advance gender equity and climate action priorities to ensure these accords deliver equitable benefits to people and communities. The more that collaboration yields meaningful and equitable benefit, the more likely support for the collaboration that generated this benefit will increase.

Towards sustainable trust

Globalisation has plateaued in recent years due to weakened political support for a cooperative system (what the International Monetary Fund has called 'slowbalisation'[5]), but our economies and societies are still inextricably linked. Trade, travel and data flows (as well as global pandemics) all bind us together and there actually appears to be little desire to disrupt these connections. According to DHL, 'International flows have proved remarkably resilient despite recent shocks, with trade and many other types of flows already well above pre-pandemic levels.'[6]

These interconnections mean that developments in one corner of the world affect the other, as the COVID-19 pandemic, the global financial crisis and effects of climate change make clear. In other words, what happens globally reverberates locally.

Addressing issues like rising debt levels and declining economic outlooks, as well as climate change and its impact on vulnerable communities, can deliver local benefits if done properly. It is up to leaders to chart effective, collaborative paths towards addressing these shared challenges and to make that case to their voting public. The more that collaboration is shown to be responsive to the needs of stakeholders, and the more this type of collaboration delivers results, the more likely support for these efforts will grow within and between societies. This heightened trust in cooperation will further incentivise leaders to work together and make progress on shared objectives in a way that provides inclusive benefits for their communities.

11

CENTRISM AND PUBLIC POLICY

Chrystia Freeland

In the aftermath of the Second World War, an army of veterans returned home and went on to lay the foundation of the most prosperous period in human history. Theirs was the era of *Les Trente Glorieuses*: three decades of unprecedented prosperity when our economies grew by 3 per cent, year after year after year. We call them the Greatest Generation, because that is what they were. After liberating a continent, they tucked their medals in a box and set out to make the most of the freedom they had fought for – and for which so many of their friends had paid such an awful price.

Because of them, that post-war era was, for Canada, for North America and for the collective West more broadly, the apex of middle-class capitalism – of an economy that was growing, as President Biden would say, from the middle out. Growth was strong, income inequality was low, taxes were high, and the foundations of our modern social welfare state were laid.

The prosperity and opportunity of that era were certainly not shared equally – particularly if you were a woman, or Indigenous, or not white, or gay. But a collective lingering awareness of how well our system worked at that time still dominates Western politics today.

Les Trente Glorieuses did not last. The middle-class-led, widely shared capitalist engine of economic prosperity started to sputter. Growth slowed, unemployment rose and inequality widened. The solution – to a problem chiefly defined as one of economic stagnation and offered first by the Reagan-Thatcher right – was to shrink the post-war state. For a while, that seemed to work – until the financial crisis of 2008,

75

and the political response to it, revealed that our societies were drifting into plutocracy, with the rise of the global super-rich and the fall of everyone else.

Western democracies are still grappling with the reality that the middle class was hollowed out and left behind, that our economic engine is slowing down, and that it has stopped delivering for working people.

The starkest response to this challenge has been on the populist right. The populists' great strength is the fearlessness of their diagnosis. They are not afraid to say, in apocalyptic terms, that the post-war economic and social consensus is no longer working for working people. They speak of 'American carnage' and of Canada being broken.

What follows from their diagnosis, of course, is more muddled: a combination of regulation slashing, neocon tax cuts and cruel austerity, mixed together with aggressive protectionism, if not outright isolationism. Their muddle should be no surprise. If your objective is to demolish rather than to build, you don't need a blueprint – all you need is a wrecking ball.

But in an age of political extremes, what should be the answer at the centre? Let me share our government's approach on the centre-left in Canada.

Our plan has had two fundamental objectives. First, and most urgently: to grow the economy. Investments in public transit, in electric vehicle battery factories and in a major new pipeline are not just one-off public expenditures. They are investments – decades-long investments – in the economic growth which creates middle-class jobs and makes middle-class communities more prosperous.

Stronger growth has always been the underpinning of an economy that works for the middle class. But growth alone is not enough. That is why, second and critically, we have sought to ensure that growth delivers for the middle class by driving down inequality, raising incomes and ensuring, by design, not by trickle-down, that everyone can truly share in the prosperity which their tax dollars help to drive.

Supported by a growing economy, we have made massive enhancements to Canada's social-safety net, including new and enhanced benefits for parents, low-income workers and seniors. Because when people have the support they need to flourish, they can make a greater contribution to the economy.

As one example: our new Canada-wide system of early learning and childcare is saving middle-class families thousands of dollars each month. And it is also helping women join the workforce in record numbers. As I write this, the labour force participation rate for Canadian women in their prime working years has reached a record high of 85.7 per cent. That compares to just 77.5 per cent across the border in the USA.

I believe this focus – on building an economy that works for everyone – should be the animating principle for centrist democracies as we navigate a clean economic transition which is the most significant economic transformation since the Industrial Revolution itself.

In our essential efforts to tackle climate change and retool our economies during the clean transition, it will be easy for governments seeking to meet this existential challenge to forget that the first and last and most fundamental measure of the success of our policies will be whether they work for working people.

That is why in Canada we are putting Canadians and Canadian workers at the centre of our efforts to combat climate change and build our clean economy.

We put a price on carbon pollution in 2019 – a price that was a ballot issue in two national elections and has been upheld by our Supreme Court. The money we raise goes straight back into the pockets of Canadians in the form of the Canada Carbon Rebate of up to $1,500 a year for a family of four.

Our historic clean economy investment tax credits are more generous when Canadian workers are paid a prevailing union wage, and our unprecedented Clean Electricity Investment Tax Credit will help to double Canada's clean electricity production – while also including requirements to keep electricity prices affordable for Canadian families.

As democracies respond to this second industrial revolution, our efforts to build our clean economies will be meaningless – and quickly rejected – if they do not deliver for the people who build them. We can forget about Paris targets and emissions reductions if we fail on this most important metric.

In the years to come, as our economies continue to recover from the shock of a global pandemic and its painful after-effects, populists will continue to see opportunity in nihilism – a chance to lean into the gloom. An everything-is-broken pitch can be seductive when people are tired, prices are still high and mortgage renewals are looming. As we navigate a period of profound upheaval, a message which stokes fear of change may likewise find a receptive audience.

For those of us in the centre, the fearless clarity of an extreme populist message will be impossible to counter with only a stoic explanation of why that message is wrong or dangerous. Recent experiences, on both sides of the Atlantic, have demonstrated the frailty of that approach.

Instead, the North Star of politics at the centre – as we address the immediate priorities before us and the fundamental challenges of our time – should be a relentless focus on middle-class prosperity. By building economies that truly work for everyone, we will demonstrate to those we seek to represent that we can offer them the brighter future they so rightly seek.

As a cabinet minister who regularly criss-crosses my country, a door-knocking member of parliament who has been elected four times and a journalist who reported around the world, I have found that people value the same things. A job that pays them well, doing work which is respected. The ability to live a dignified and prosperous life, and the confidence that their children's lives will be better than their own.

The centre succeeds when we can deliver on these essential promises. We falter when we do not.

12

CENTRISM AND THE RULE OF LAW

Marco Buschmann

What is centrism?

One of the earliest arguments for political centrism can be found in the work of Aristotle. Virtue, according to the ancient philosopher, is the mean between two extremes. If we apply this concept to politics, the centre emerges as the point that is simultaneously furthest from the two poles – left and right – of the political spectrum.

It could of course be argued that from this perspective, the centre is little more than a political football between the two extremes and is therefore defined by them. The objection is a valid one in that the centre should not be outlined merely as an arbitrary reflex in response to the positions adopted by those extremes. A centrist political stance must be able to conceptually define what sets it apart from both left and right of its own accord, and express the differences positively.

The form these differences take quickly becomes apparent if we regard the extreme positions held on both left and right: both camps define people as belonging to a group – whether race, class or nation. Both view the world as a battlefield on which these groups are pitted against one another. By contrast to this paradigm, political centrism can be framed in positive terms: rather than groups, it believes in the intrinsic value of each individual. Rather than fighting, it believes in voluntary cooperation.

From these lodestars of political centrism – the intrinsic value of the individual and cooperation as opposed to fighting – emerges a clear understanding of the major political themes: in order to defend individuals against tyranny, democracy allows them to participate in state power. To ensure that they are also defended against a tyranny of the majority, political centrism affords individuals a sphere of legal protection that is effective even in the face of a democratic majority. This creates scope for individual freedom and voluntary cooperation – in markets, in culture and in civil society. Furthermore, it creates the necessary conditions to allow the minority to become a new majority through democratic competition.

Central to this process are what we call fundamental or human rights. The fusion of democracy and fundamental rights is today known as liberal democracy. This is the guiding principle of political centrism, anchored in the rule of law. Centrism and the rule of law are two sides of the same coin.

Why centrism needs the rule of law

If we separate fundamental rights from democracy and view the latter not as the participation of individuals in political power but as the absolute power of an absolute majority, the result is what the journalist Fareed Zakaria, with critical detachment, called 'illiberal democracy'. It is an idea that is steadily gaining traction among the political fringes. On the political right, Viktor Orbán has explicitly stated his ambition to establish an 'illiberal democracy' – a form of rule that gives the majority free rein and under which the individual ultimately counts for very little. He has eagerly set about making this a reality in Hungary, while others are following suit. This is also why illiberal democracies invariably rail against the rule of law: the law sets limits that protect the individual, even against the majority. For a majority that wishes to rule unfettered, however, the law is an obstacle.

Many modern conservatives accept that democracy and fundamental rights are inextricably linked. Left-wing politicians too like to talk of fundamental rights on an abstract level. However, some believe that a robust parliament is all that is needed to safeguard fundamental rights in a democracy. This argument seems plausible enough – but history has discredited it.

The proponents of democracy in the early modern era were convinced that a majority of voters would always act in such a way as to ensure the preservation of a democratic culture. They believed that any democracy would, of its own accord, inevitably align with the famous 'golden rule' formulated by Rabbi Hillel in response to the question of how the Torah could be condensed into a single precept: 'That which is hateful to you, do not do unto your fellow.' Variations on this maxim can be found in the world's major religions, and many political philosophies, throughout history.

Many early democrats laboured under the illusion that voters would never elect a government treating its citizens in a way that they would not tolerate themselves. There would be no laws to silence people – for what voter would ever tolerate being silenced? There would be no laws interfering in matters of faith and conscience – for what voter would ever tolerate such meddling by the state in their private beliefs? There would be no laws allowing people's property to simply be taken from them – for what voter would ever tolerate the state taking away their very livelihood? And how could there ever be laws allowing people to be discriminated against, humiliated, or even systematically murdered? Who could ever want such things to happen to them?

The reasoning seems sound. But unfortunately, it has not been borne out by history. We have seen it again and again: in antiquity, a majority voted to execute Socrates because they found his teachings blasphemous. And in modern times, the greatest catastrophe in the history of democracy took place in Germany: the rise to power of the National Socialists and the German parliament's abdication of its legislative role with the Enabling Act of 24 March 1933.

The dangers posed by simple majority rule were explored by the French historian Alexis de Tocqueville. In the early 1830s, Tocqueville travelled throughout the USA to study the practical role of the country's democratic Constitution and its effect on society. He documented his observations and analysis in the book *Democracy in America*, which became a classic of political literature.

The title of one of the book's chapters, 'Tyranny of the Majority', became a catchphrase that remains in use to this day. At first glance, the phrase seems paradoxical: if democracy is the opposite of tyranny, and majority rule is a key instrument by which democracy avoids tyranny, how can the majority be tyrannical? Tocqueville explains the paradox as follows: 'So when I see the right and the ability to do everything granted to whatever power, whether called people or king, democracy or aristocracy, whether exercised in a monarchy or a republic, I say: the seed of tyranny is there [. . .].'

Tocqueville believed that the exercise of power, whatever form it took, must be subject to constraints. He argued that these constraints were anchored in the principle of justice – a law that applied to all of humanity. No ruler was exempt from it. Moreover, no one nation – as a part of humanity – and certainly no majority within a nation – an even smaller part of humanity – had the authority to breach this universal law.

Tocqueville also offered a recommendation on how the principle of justice could be upheld under majority rule. He invoked the 'spirit of the jurist as a counterweight'. By no means was he of the opinion that jurists were better or even more democratic than anyone else. Nevertheless, he wrote: 'they serve as arbiters among citizens, and the habit of leading the blind passions of the litigants towards the goal gives them a certain contempt for the judgment of the crowd'. In other words: jurists are, in a sense, trained to detach themselves somewhat from majority opinions and to focus on what is required by the law.

Current conflicts regarding the rule of law

It follows that in the relationship between a democratic majority on the one hand, and a constitutional court system with the power to repeal laws adopted by this majority on the other, tensions can arise. In fact, it is a relationship that embraces friction. This is not a fundamental flaw or a bug in the constitutional system. On the contrary, it generates the energy required to maintain a democratically legitimate political system that does justice to the fundamental rights of individuals in particular. That friction, that tension, is seen again and again in centrist thinking as a positive driving force that promotes good policy and sustainable results.

This friction also provides vital impetus for the field of constitutional jurisprudence and for constitutional policy. Certain political standpoints tend to coincide with certain stances regarding the interpretation of the constitution.

In the USA, a heated debate is currently under way on how the written Constitution should be interpreted with regard to the right to abortion. Originalists argue that the text reflects the intentions of the framers of the Constitution in the eighteenth century, and nothing more. According to this view, freedoms not found in the constitutional amendments, such as a general right to privacy, do not exist. Originalists believe that to treat the text as a source of guidance on issues in a radically changed world is to abuse it, and to ignore the fact that the text could also have been changed. Currently in Germany, a similar – albeit less heated – discussion revolves around the issue of constitutional change through interpretation. One side believes that judges have relatively little leeway for interpretation, while the other accepts that interpretation of normative texts must give full consideration to social, economic and technological changes. These types of arguments are repeated across much of the democratic world in one guise or another.

It is no coincidence that conservatives in particular tend towards an originalist stance, as this position has the effect of eroding the influence of the constitutional court system over time. This is because it is generally very difficult to make amendments to written constitutions – often intentionally so, to prevent the guarantees they provide from being revoked by the political majority whose power they are designed to limit. The question of when the content of an uncodified constitution changes, meanwhile, is a complex one. Were judges to be bound by originalist constraints in the interpretation of legal texts, they would either have to cling to a world that no longer exists, or increasingly be forced to conclude that the constitution no longer provides meaningful answers. As a result, the balance of power would increasingly shift towards the parliamentary majority. This in turn would put the rights of the individual at ever greater risk of being sidelined by majority opinion.

Disagreements on substance are closely tied to the people involved in them. This is why the judiciary must be independent. If judges hand down rulings that do not have the approval of the majority, it must not be possible simply to replace them. There have nevertheless been repeated attempts, especially in recent years, to undermine the independence of courts. This can be done subtly, by changing procedural rules and rules affecting judges' terms of office, by limiting their powers, or by appointing additional judges chosen by the current majority. In many cases, a constitutional amendment is not even required. This raises the question of whether the constitutional or supreme courts, as 'guardians of fundamental rights', should be made more resilient and given more effective legal protection – because when a majority seeks to curtail the independence of the courts, it is a strong indication that the country is on its way to governing by the 'tyranny of the majority'.

Conversely, judges must be careful not to exceed their remit – that of interpreting the body of law – or they risk inviting a legal conflict themselves. Germany's Federal Constitutional Court, for example, has emphasised that the legislature enjoys broad margins of discretion for the concrete application of the Constitution, as well as prerogatives of assessment that are beyond judicial control. Other constitutional courts have developed an approach to political decisions designed to avoid encroaching on areas that are the preserve of parliament.

In conclusion: any attempt to effectively protect individuals – including against the majority – by means of fundamental rights cannot rely solely on a parliamentary majority's regard for these rights. There must be clear constitutional rules enabling an independent judiciary to defend the fundamental rights of the individual against any threat – including a majority in parliament. This is the essence of the relationship between centrism and the rule of law in a liberal democracy. It is the role, belief and duty of centrists to defend those checks and balances which lie at the heart of our system.

13

CENTRIST JOURNALISM AND DEFENDING DEMOCRACY: NON-PARTISAN BUT NOT NEUTRAL

John Avlon

The US Constitution doesn't mention political parties – but it does mention journalists.

This was not an oversight. The country's founders understood that freedom of the press spurs informed civic debate and accountability for people in power – both of which are essential to self-government.

From the earliest days of the world's most successful democratic republic, there were partisan newspapers that advanced specific political agendas with slashing editorials and slanted reporting. But there was also a competing tradition of non-partisan newspapers that warned about the dangers of extreme partisanship, aiming for objectivity through honest reporting and editorials that aimed to persuade rather than just play to the base. They were not perfect – newspapers are, after all, essentially human enterprises – but they helped establish basic journalistic standards and ultimately increased trust between fellow citizens.

This dynamic was not unique to the USA, but the costs of partisan media to democracy should now be clear. In our fragmented landscape, partisan media profits from polarisation, monetising a narrow but intense niche audience by keeping them addicted to anger, anxiety and resentment. As political warfare rises, trust in media falls. The Pew Research Center documented the trend back in 2004 and concluded that 'virtually every news organization or program has seen its credibility marks decline'. Even C-SPAN – which offers unedited coverage of public events in the USA without commentary – suffered a steep decline in believability. In a hyper-partisan media environment, people become so suspicious that they literally don't trust what they see with their own eyes.

Two decades later, this dynamic is compounded by the proliferation of disinformation and apocalyptic politics, amplified by social media algorithms that reward the most confrontational and conspiracy theorist voices. AI threatens to further erode the idea of truth itself.

This is, to put it mildly, a problem. Because if citizens cannot reason together from a common set of facts, then the larger project of self-government is in danger.

A centrist press – by which I mean independent and fair-minded, driven by consistent principles beyond partisan interests and pursuing facts without fear or favour – is essential for finding common ground. It is essential for defending liberal democracy.

But because the ideal of a centrist approach to news can be controversial, dismissed as naive, corporate, or unattainable, it is necessary to define our terms – both what it is not and what it is.

It is not a form of 'both-siderism' that creates moral equivalence on issues of verifiable fact. You do not put a climate change denier on set alongside a climate scientist – bolstered with peer-reviewed data – have them both make their case, and then turn to the audience with a shrug, and say 'You decide'.

As New York Senator Daniel Patrick Moynihan famously said, 'Everyone is entitled to their own opinion, but not their own facts.' Confronting misinformation is a core responsibility of journalism today. Fact-checking is not evidence of partisan bias, but a reflection of our commitment to tell the truth.

There is likewise no obligation to platform people who repeatedly spread misinformation in the effort to 'hear all sides'. This is what author Isaac Asimov called 'the false notion that democracy means that "my ignorance is just as good as your knowledge"'.

It's a myth that a centrist approach to news means it must be boring. This often takes the form of commodity news – that bland flow of information that avoids taking a stand for fear of offending. But in an era when information is everywhere, differentiation is the soul of a news brand. In general, people who choose to consume news are smart and trying to get better informed. We should respect their intelligence, cover the stories that define our times with wit and personality, and have faith that quality journalism attracts a quality audience. Remember: the heart of a journalist's job is to make important stories interesting.

At a time when party establishments are increasingly run by extremes, centrist journalism does not reflect the establishment. It does not depend solely on the official version of the facts – that's simply being a stenographer for people in power. Instead, the guiding principle is 'trust but verify'.

Dig into the underlying data. Judge intentions separately from results. Be fair-minded: scepticism is a virtue; cynicism is a vice. Don't forget that good news can still be news. And never forget that holding power to account is a core responsibility of journalism. Finally, there's a mistaken idea that journalism from the vital centre can be understood as simply a third way between right-wing and left-wing news organisations. That framing offers a useful contrast in politics – especially given that moderate and independent voters make up an under-represented plurality. But in journalism, the ideas which correspond to the centre are beyond partisan politics: they express fundamental journalistic virtues.

In the wake of the First World War, a group of US journalists led by Walter Lippmann resolved to restrain the partisan and sensationalist tendencies of the press which they believed fed fanaticism and nationalism. The result was a code of ethics, known as the Canons of Journalism, that guided responsible editors and reporters for much of the twentieth century. It stated that 'partisanship in editorial comment which knowingly departs from the truth does violence to the best spirit of American journalism'. It lauded the core virtues of independence and responsibility, the public good pursued in good faith, guided by 'sincerity, truthfulness and accuracy'. It mandated 'clear distinction between news reports and expressions of opinion'. It valued fair play, mandated the issuing of corrections for published inaccuracies and prohibited 'promotion of any private interest contrary to the general welfare' as being contrary to the cause of 'honest journalism'.

Beneath the quaint articulations, these remain bedrock principles. A centrist approach to journalism aims for a vibrant, substantive, fact-based debate that puts the public interest above all special interests. It clearly delineates between reporting, analysis and opinion. A centrist news organisation does not cave into pressure from the mob of the moment. It pursues investigations, regardless of what political party or interest group may be implicated, based on a fair reading of the facts. Lest we forget, facts necessarily do not follow any one partisan line all the time.

Especially online, there are more partisan news outlets than those that explicitly aim for the broad and vital centre. Among the broad and vital centrist press, *The Economist*, *The Atlantic* and The Bulwark are personal favourites. Overseas, the UK's *Financial Times*, Germany's *Die Zeit*, Italy's *Corriere Della Sera* and Japan's *Mainichi Shimbun* have all cultivated centrist reputations.

During the five years when I was editor-in-chief of The Daily Beast, I insisted that our political coverage be 'non-partisan but not neutral'. It meant that we would follow the facts and apply consistent principles without toeing any particular party line. We leaned into original reporting while columnists in the opinion section ran the gamut from liberal to libertarian, criticising the far right and the far left as deserved, without straining for false equivalence. Our readers were reminded that there is no right not to be offended. Our principles, painted on a pillar in the office, stated: 'we love to confront bullies, bigots and hypocrites'. On another pillar was this quote from the Texas columnist Molly Ivins: 'Keep fighting for freedom and justice, beloveds – but don't forget to have fun doing it.' Being a happy warrior is a good mindset for journalism, politics and life. In contrast, ideologues tend to be inflexible and, more often than not, humourless.

Being free of partisan constraints is liberating – a centrist publication can also embrace a 'high-low' editorial sensibility that reflects the full range of artistic, scientific, business and leisure interests that makes human beings more than just political animals.

A centrist approach to journalism does not try to impose ideology on the essentially human dimensions of society. No group has a monopoly on virtue or vice. Objectivity is an elusive goal, but it is an ideal that reporters should not give up on. As CNN's Christiane Amanpour says: 'Objective means cover all sides. It does not mean come to the same judgement about all sides.'

Fairness is another value that can seem saccharine to some. It aims for journalism that considers context, impact and perspective without making excuses for immoral actions or compromising fidelity to facts.

History offers a useful perspective on our problems. As the journalist Renata Adler wrote: 'a radical middle . . . acts out of a consciousness of how much has been gained, how far there is to go and what there is to lose'. It recognises that part of journalism's responsibility in a civil society is to remind people of the history behind the headlines so that they can put current events in context.

A successful news organisation is a badge of identity for its readers and viewers. This means articulating clear editorial principles and presenting news with a human face, with compelling and credible characters engaged in a fact-based debate between the left, right and centre. Ultimately, there should be a focus on finding common ground and solving problems.

Accountability journalism is essential, but it is not enough to restore faith that has been broken by the constant onslaught of partisan media. The good news is that studies show that solutions journalism can help restore trust in media. People are exhausted by ornate fixation on problems – they want to hear ideas on how to fix those problems, from a variety of policy perspectives across platforms. The goal is to make viewers and readers smarter, not dumber – more active and engaged citizens of a self-governing society.

Resist the mistaken belief that you can cover a demagogue like any other candidate. This is naive. It ignores the lessons of history and only succeeds in normalising their lies.

In polarised times, the very act of being independent will provoke overheated complaints by professional partisans that a news organisation is unfair when it disagrees with them. For better or worse, I'm not aware of a single US president who didn't complain about their coverage – that goes for Democrats as well as Republicans – and that pattern is repeated across the democratic world. There is an inherent tension between politicians and the press. And yet, I've always believed that the good-faith goals of journalism and politics are essentially complementary – engaged in a public service devoted to the common good, deeply invested in civil debate, concerned with civic issues and, ultimately, solutions to common problems. Good journalism can, and should, make our politics better.

That's not to say that news organisations should not check their own biases. If you're in a leadership position, work to ensure that your newsroom isn't pulling punches when it comes to legitimate stories involving a political party with which it might personally feel an affinity. After all, a liberal crook is just as bad as a conservative crook. On the flip side, tone comes from the top, so work to make sure that a top editor's or owner's political preferences do not cause reporters to put artificial spin on the ball to please the boss. An additional challenge stems from the decline of local journalism, which has created 'news deserts' and exacerbates age-old urban vs rural divides as reporters increasingly reflect urban sensibilities. A failure to understand the perspective of rural working-class families only further fuels divisions and a sense of mutual incomprehension. Likewise, treating the latest left-wing social beliefs as above reasoned debate fuels alienation and accusations of elitism, especially when they seem to contradict liberal values.

At the end of the day, a centrist approach to news means a commitment to the values that undergird liberal democracy. These include a respect for individual rights and human rights, faith in spirited but reasoned debate, a healthy distrust of mob mentality and a belief that freedom allows the human spirit to flourish.

In contrast, authoritarian and illiberal regimes require a pliant partisan press. They depend on the degradation of truth through disinformation – where often the goal is not to convince but to confuse the citizenry, to push people into a pervasive cynicism that causes them to abandon the idea of objective facts or truth. As an anchor and producer of Ukraine's 'Stop Fake' counter-disinformation news channel told me, 'Russian disinformation is not about positioning left versus right but about using the left and the right against the centre.' This is where misinformation and hyper-partisan agendas often overlap, aided by the professional polarisers pushing this narcotic.

When it comes to broad-based news organisations, journalism from the vital centre is more a matter of a disposition and direction than offering an explicit alternative ideology. But there's another dimension of journalism in which there is an opportunity to create an alternative beyond partisan orthodoxies. Amid a crowded field of right- and left-wing think tanks there is a need for a centrist journal of ideas, something akin to the *National Review*'s role in the birth of the modern US conservative movement, to show that there is a coherent political philosophy with intellectual heft, highlighting signature personalities, a distinct history and actionable policies. The fact that there is significant common ground in the approaches of centrist leaders from different countries – as captured in this book – provides evidence for this idea.

The dangers of partisan news should now be self-evident. We saw it most pungently in the USA when much of conservative media was afraid to publicly contradict former president Donald Trump's lies about the

2020 election results. Their silence, for fear of offending their base and losing market share, ended up enabling an attempt to overturn an election by lies and force. It was the fullest expression of what the Canons of Journalism warned about almost a century before: 'Partisanship in editorial comment which knowingly departs from the truth does violence to the best spirit of American journalism.'

This is a challenging time for journalism on almost every front – a time of dwindling revenue and declining trust. That's exactly why the work of an independent, principled and fair-minded press is more important than ever before.

We need bold journalism from the vital centre to provide a clear alternative to hyper-partisan media which tries to profit from polarisation. A commitment to establishing facts through honest reporting and persuasion through reasoned debate can lead us to common facts and common ground. As the legendary broadcaster Ed Murrow said: 'To be persuasive, we must be believable. To be believable, we must be credible. To be credible, we must be truthful.' When it comes to civic debate and the battle of ideas, the centre must hold to ensure the success of liberal democracy.

SECTION 3

LEADING AS CENTRISTS

This section looks at the most innovative, creative, effective policy ideas in public life today from political centrists. The policies included in this section aren't comprehensive, they don't include every aspect of government policy – transport, policing and infrastructure for example don't appear – but rather a select few.

When it comes to policy, in today's polarised environment even the fundamental motivations that should be at the heart of an issue end up being contentious. Perhaps the most straightforward of those should be education policy, the motivation behind which should always be to give every child the best possible start in life. If we can agree on that, then we can debate the right approach and suggest a framework that balances competing values to achieve a shared goal, as Arne Duncan does in his essay. But, as he explains, even agreeing on the overall goal isn't so straightforward.

One of the added layers of complexity in policymaking is that we don't live in a vacuum. Addressing global energy needs and climate change can't be done locally or even nationally. As Rachel Pritzker argues, the response must be global and must consider needs beyond our own community or country. The threat from climate change is real irrespective of where you live, but how best to combat it depends heavily on other national priorities. If we don't find an approach that works globally, then our chance of making a meaningful difference is almost non-existent.

Adapting to technological change is not straightforward either. There are those who argue that we can't regulate technology at all and we should leave it all to the market. On the other side are those who insist on regulation without a clear sense of what we would regulate, why and, crucially, how. Jamie Susskind's essay offers a blueprint for approaching technological advances and building an effective digital policy. It is an area where politics is lagging behind reality and where centrists are taking the lead.

The issues in this section are complicated and provide no easy answers. This is clear in the essays by Jonathan Evans on counterterrorism and by Michèle Flournoy and Richard Fontaine on national security. They require the balance between competing values that centrism proposes; compromise to build solutions that last; and a relentless focus on outcomes. No solution is perfect, no policy comes without costs, there are always unforeseen impacts (some positive, some negative), and, critically, a policy is worthless if it can't be delivered. But these are issues that must be tackled, and currently most of them are inadequately addressed by too many governments and political parties.

Centrists need to remain focused on outcomes, on making a real and tangible difference to people's lives and to society, as Representative Haley Stevens articulately states, giving an insight into what a centrist government could look like.

14

A CENTRIST APPROACH TO NATIONAL SECURITY

Michèle Flournoy and Richard Fontaine

Politics, despite the saying, has never really stopped at the water's edge. Foreign policy has always been contested, with liberals and conservatives, realists and idealists all competing to shape national security. The pursuit of national interests and values occurs in a decidedly political context, and so it is only natural that the unity or polarisation that characterises the rest of the body politic would impact the approach to foreign policy.

Recent years have seen an overall decline in bipartisanship, precisely when increased global uncertainty demands more of it. Across the world, there are foreign policy issues on which parties remain unified, and more still where they could forge agreement in the future. Yet the increasing polarisation of politics and the hardening of positions on issues foreign and domestic have also produced growing dysfunction. Political leaders too often swing from one foreign policy pole to the other rather than govern from a more durable centre. We can do better. Given the remarkable number, scale and stakes of the challenges we face today, we must do better.

The centrist consensus

For all the disagreements over the years within much of the democratic world, there has existed among most of the national leaderships a general consensus on foreign policy ends. In the USA, they have generally agreed upon a unique responsibility in upholding the rules-based international order that we and our allies designed and built after the Second World War, and from which Americans derive disproportionate benefits. Hence Washington's traditionally expansive – and often expensive – leadership role in many regions and across multiple issues. In much of Europe, closer ties among countries on the continent has received widespread support.

Three central principles have enjoyed widespread acceptance in Western democracies. First, to keep the peace we have sought strong alliances, underwritten by a powerful US military and the stationing of US troops abroad. Second, to increase prosperity we have pursued an open and more integrated global economic system and progressively freer trade. And third, to defend freedom at home and abroad we have aimed to expand human rights and democratic systems around the world.

Where there were debates, they have typically focused mostly on means rather than ends: how big a military is required, and how much defence spending is affordable? How should we pursue free trade, and with whom? What's the best way to support democracy and human rights, and what should we do about friendly autocracies? When should the USA and its allies conduct humanitarian interventions, and which tools should they use?

Today, each of the traditional goals – and not just the means – is under debate. For instance, increasing numbers question the benefit of international alliances, which require both greater spending and some restrictions on unilateral freedom of action. For all the evidence that free trade increases economic growth and expands employment, the USA has put a halt to ambitious trade agreements like the Trans-Pacific Partnership and instead embraced tariffs and restrictions. Today, some on the right question whether traditional efforts to promote human rights are effective or even desirable, while others on the left point to the West's own transgressions – such as the 6 January 2021 attack on the US Capitol – to argue that we lack the standing to urge democracy in other countries.

Most profoundly, bipartisan, elite-level support for strengthening the international order has been undermined by the legitimate concerns shared by a large portion of the electorate. The public is increasingly aware of the huge expense and dissatisfying results of the long wars in Afghanistan and Iraq, and in the USA there is criticism of the fact that the USA continues to shoulder the lion's share of NATO's defence spending burden despite increases in allied military budgets. Washington is, for example, far and away the greatest single-country source of assistance to Ukraine – and for a war that is not taking place in North America. Many people believe that traditional trade agreements have eliminated jobs in key sectors like manufacturing, agriculture and mining, and that any net benefits of trade have not accrued equitably across the population. To a significant section of the voters, the key elements of the traditional approach to bolstering international order – maintaining military might, intervening to punish rule-breakers, exercising paramount diplomatic leadership, strengthening alliances, disbursing foreign aid and pushing for new trade and other economic agreements – don't seem to be worth the cost.

Yet the USA would abandon its centrist consensus – and the global leadership role it instilled – at its own peril. Similarly, Western countries should think long and hard about the implications of abandoning their own global centrist approaches. To do so would invite a world we've seen before. The emergence of the post-1945 international order was a direct response to the first half of the twentieth century, which saw the two most costly wars in history, the worst economic depression ever and the rise of autocrats who thought they could conquer the world, or at least large parts of it. The overriding desire of the post-war leaders was never again to repeat that horror. And so the order they fashioned embraces the principles of sovereignty, territorial integrity, an open international economic system and fundamental human and democratic rights. Though not without missteps and blunders, the eight decades since the international order's establishment have been far better than the thirty years before it.

From a US perspective, America's role in establishing and preserving global order has paid enormous dividends, not least for Americans themselves. The USA and its allies are freer, more secure and richer because of the leadership the USA has exercised. The country's disproportionate burdens have generated disproportionate benefits. And in many cases, there is simply no alternative to US leadership strengthened with support of like-minded allies. We adopt a more isolationist stance at the world's peril and our own. An enduring global US leadership role stems directly from the traditional international centrist consensus and, when informed by lessons learned from past errors, remains the best way to protect and advance the USA's interests and values, as well as those of its allies.

The benefits of bipartisanship

The heartening news is that, contrary to conventional wisdom, bipartisanship in foreign policy is not dead. Two researchers at American University, Jordan Tama and James Bryan, for instance, examined trends across recent decades. Despite identifying concerns about declining bipartisanship, they nevertheless concluded that 'on important foreign policy issues, we find that some degree of bipartisanship is still more common than severe polarization'. Indeed, a common approach is evidenced in the annual passage of defence authorisation language, near-universal support for Finland and Sweden's NATO accession, large majorities across most of the Western world in favour of aid to Ukraine and sanctions on Russia, large appropriations for HIV/AIDS relief in Africa, insistence on continued counterterrorism efforts globally and cross-administration and internationally supported initiatives to forge and expand the Abraham Accords.

'Whenever Democrats and Republicans cooperate on an issue today,' the researchers wrote, 'the media tend to describe this as a rare exception to the rule of strong polarization. Our research shows that such cooperation is not actually rare, but rather occurs regularly, particularly on international issues.' Another group of researchers found that 'strong polarization' in Congress, in which more than 90 per cent of the members of each party vote on opposite sides, is rare on national security matters – it occurred in less than one in ten important foreign policy votes. 'We find', they added, 'that a majority of Democratic legislators and a majority of Republican legislators have actually lined up on the same side on most important foreign policy votes since the end of the Cold War.' With a few notable exceptions, this has been the case across much of the democratic world.

A bipartisan foreign policy approach generates important benefits. Forging cross-party agreement tends to produce more centrist, pragmatic policy that avoids extreme outcomes. It is more sustainable across changing governments, which in turn adds to credibility and capacity for leadership – allies and adversaries alike view policy as durable, rather than subject to lurching between extremes after each election. Bipartisan foreign policy also attracts broader support from the public, which in a democracy is necessary to sustain any approach to global affairs, and it reduces political divisions that foreign adversaries can exploit. It also reduces the risks of politicising the apolitical institutions so critical to the effective execution of national security policy, from the military to the Foreign Service.

None of this is to suggest that bipartisanship always produces good outcomes. The 1964 Gulf of Tonkin Resolution, which authorised war in Vietnam, was a great bipartisan achievement, as was the 2002 Congressional authorisation of the war in Iraq, but both led to terrible and costly mistakes. Today, a rough bipartisan consensus stands against trade agreements, despite their tremendous economic and geopolitical value. Political parties can be wrong, even together. As Madeleine Albright, Stephen Hadley and Nancy Lindborg have written, 'Not every bipartisan policy has been successful, yet virtually every successful foreign policy initiative has been bipartisan.'

It's the overlay of bipartisanship with pragmatism – or centrism – that tends to produce the wisest and most sustainable approach to national security challenges. A pragmatic foreign policy roots interests and values in the kind of world we wish to see, while not ignoring the realities of the world as it is. The USA generally seeks to maintain a global order governed by rules rather than by brute power, one in which countries large and small enjoy sovereignty, disputes are resolved peacefully, markets are open to trade, human rights are considered universal and democracy can flourish. Although the track record in upholding such principles is hardly perfect, they have been championed as ideals that should govern international behaviour. Since the 1940s, Washington has opposed hostile spheres of influence emerging in Eurasia precisely because they threaten that rules-based order. A pragmatic foreign policy would identify the specific steps necessary to realise that vision, estimate costs and risks and match means to ends. It would aim to preserve the core pillars of the international order, even as specific rules and institutions inevitably adapt to changing circumstances to remain relevant and effective. It would seek to ensure that our international activities generate benefits for all, and for the maximum number of allies and partners as well.

The promise

The path forward is not to yearn for some halcyon days of yore when foreign policy mandarins guided the ship of state without reference to its political context. It is, rather, to coalesce political leaders around a common vision, in trusted working relationships, animated by pragmatic policies that secure national interests and values in an increasingly contested and chaotic world. In one example in the USA, the House Select Committee on China represents an effort to bring serious, centrist political leaders together around the key challenge of our time. Individual efforts that link policymakers across the Bush, Obama, Trump and Biden administrations, and the executive branch and Congress, constitute yet another set of opportunities. The China challenge itself may provide fuel for the centrist impulse. The threat that Beijing poses to international order, and to the world we wish to see, is significant. That, in turn, has made previously impossible policy moves materialise.

It has not, however, made the hardest things attainable. While some progress has been achieved, we are not today doing everything in our power to invest in the drivers of our own competitiveness. For example, our political leaders have been unable to forge strategic immigration policies that would ensure that the most talented high-skilled workers come and stay to contribute to our economies. The effort to make room in the defence budget for new technologies and capabilities that are essential to deterring and, if necessary, prevailing in an Indo-Pacific contingency remains woefully slow and incomplete. A bipartisan foreign policy would seek progress across these and other fronts.

Here, however, is where pragmatism becomes vital. The rising China challenge, as an example, can motivate constructive bipartisan action, but it could also reprise some of the Cold War's ugliest and most shameful moments: McCarthyism, proxy wars, Red scares and the rest. The appropriate response to China's rise is to combine strength and resolve with prudence and wisdom.

That might serve as a mantra for taking on other national security challenges as well, from Russian aggression to Iranian influence in the Middle East to terrorism and climate change. A political leadership united in bipartisanship, infused with centrism and pragmatism, is best suited for the world now upon us.

15

A CENTRIST APPROACH TO EDUCATION: REFORM MUST MOVE FORWARD FROM THE CENTRE

Arne Duncan

For almost as long as we have had public education, we have had highly politicised debates about how to improve schools. I first encountered these debates in a personal way as a child in my mother's tutoring programme. She had approached a local public school in Chicago and volunteered to tutor kids after school – for free. Her offer was ignored, so she found space in a church and every afternoon she collected kids of all ages and taught them reading and maths and helped them with homework. As a reward, they got to play in the gym each afternoon. I went there almost every day of my life until college.

A few years after college, I started a public school with my sister. Chicago Mayor Rich Daley asked me to join his administration and eventually he appointed me as CEO of the same school system that rejected my mother, the Chicago Public Schools (CPS). For seven years, my team pushed hard to improve the third-largest school system in the country, transforming under-performing schools, opening new schools, boosting overall student performance and raising graduation rates.

In 2008 Barack Obama, who had visited CPS schools with me while serving as an Illinois legislator and as a US senator, became president of the USA and he asked me to serve in his cabinet as secretary of education. He gave me one important piece of advice: do the right thing for kids and let him worry about the politics. I took him at his word, and we drove an aggressive agenda aimed at raising standards, holding the system accountable and giving parents more public school choice. All of our policies reflected the president's deep belief that equality of opportunity was foundational to the USA and that schools were the path to opportunity.

None of our reforms at the local or federal level would have been possible without support across the political spectrum. While Republican lawmakers gave the Democratic mayor of Chicago the power to appoint the CEO of the Chicago Public Schools, Democrats traditionally provided more financial support to schools. Both were necessary to create the conditions for reform, and during my seven years overseeing CPS I relied on support from the right and the left to drive change. It was a centrist approach that allowed those with hardened positions at both ends of the political spectrum to shift away from old ideologies to pragmatic solutions that put the needs of children first.

For example, conservative business leaders were eager to bring public school choice into Chicago, while the Chicago Teachers Union pushed hard for higher teacher salaries. We did both, opening over a hundred new schools while maintaining labour peace, and the results speak for themselves. A study from Stanford University analysing Chicago test scores in the years just after I left CPS showed that it was among the fastest-improving school districts in the country. We believed that the combination of public school choice paired with increased investment in teachers drove the remarkable results.

Shifting to the federal level, I became secretary of education twenty-five years after the 1983 publication of *A Nation at Risk* – the Reagan administration's harsh assessment of the state of American education. In the years that followed Reagan's report, governors on both sides of the aisle gathered outside Washington to discuss ways to improve education, eventually giving rise to three core policies: standards, accountability and choice.

A great example of centrist education policy was the embrace of the charter school movement. It was inspired by the legendary New York

Teachers Union leader Albert Shanker, who believed charters could be laboratories for innovation that might prompt traditional school systems to break free of bureaucratic restraints. This essentially conservative idea – unleashing innovation by reducing regulation – was initially embraced by teacher unions.

Simultaneously, the education community, in the USA and internationally, had been debating the issue of accountability for years. With support on both sides of the aisle, America adopted the No Child Left Behind Act, which, among other things, mandated yearly standardised testing and transparency. The law also spelled out consequences for chronic underperformance, up to and including closing down low-performing schools and sending students elsewhere.

In the USA this was the first time that states and districts had to publish achievement gaps among low-income and higher-income students, people of different races, students with disabilities and students who were learning to speak English. The system hated it but, driven by a broad centrist consensus, politicians on both sides of the aisle stuck by it.

While Democrats fended off anti-accountability voices on the left, Republicans fended off local control zealots on the right. At the time, I was running a local school system and I didn't like federal oversight any more than anyone else, but I knew it was important for kids, parents and educators to be open and honest about achievement gaps and work to address them.

Once I was in Washington, we were handed a historic opportunity to drive change. The 2007–8 recession prompted Congress to pass the American Recovery and Reinvestment Act (ARRA), which included $100 billion in additional funding for public education.

Tucked into the ARRA was $5 billion for two competitive grant programmes we developed aimed at prompting states and districts to adopt high standards, loosen up restrictions on school choice, take steps to improve underperforming schools and create innovative, evidence-based strategies. In a matter of months, nearly every state in the country adopted the Common Core learning standards in order to compete for the grants. Many states and districts also revised local school choice policies. Our work was celebrated across the political spectrum.

In one of the more unusual pairings – suggested by President Obama himself – I spent a few weeks on the road touring school districts with civil rights icon Al Sharpton and conservative firebrand Newt Gingrich. The media ate it up. At the same time, I worked with superintendents and union leaders across the country to implement these reforms.

Among the reforms I'm proudest of, and remain an advocate of, was an effort to bring accountability from the school level down to the individual teacher level. Economists like Harvard University's Raj Chetty had proved that just one effective middle-school teacher could boost the lifetime earnings of a classroom of children by hundreds of thousands of dollars. From my work in Chicago, I also knew that teacher quality and teacher effectiveness were absolutely critical to improving schools. Great teachers could become master teachers and mentor teachers to train the next generation of educators. They are our most precious resource and we underutilise them, in so doing harming children and undermining the profession.

Eventually, partisanship hit education policy too. It really struck me one night over dinner with Tennessee's Republican Senator Lamar Alexander. He had previously served as Tennessee governor and as secretary of education and was widely seen as a voice of moderation and bipartisanship. He told me that our policy on teacher evaluation was 'the holy grail of public education', but he could not support it because it violated his conservative principles around the limited federal role in education. No matter how much Senator Alexander agreed with our reforms and, despite the fact that, like me, he had actually led the US Department of Education, he could not support change driven from Washington.

I resigned at the end of 2015 and returned home to Chicago. I was proud that we helped expand pre-kindergarten programmes, and even prouder that high school graduation and college enrolment rates in every subgroup of students rose on our watch. But I also knew how much more work there was to be done and I left Washington with a worry that partisan politics would be an obstacle to progress in education reform in the years ahead.

For the last seven years I have been working to reduce gun violence in Chicago, but I have stayed abreast of education policy debates and I'm mostly disheartened by what I see. Education debates are dominated by right-wing extremists while the reasonable centre is quiet. A recent survey from the Pew Research Center found widening disparities between Republicans and Democrats on a whole range of education issues, from what kids should be learning to how schools should be governed and the role of the federal government. Sadly, that most illiberal of practices, banning books, has come back to life.

For the sake of our children's education we need to work to swing the political pendulum back to the centre and support elected officials who will ask the foundational question that should power any education reform anywhere in the world: are the children learning? Answering that question should be at the core of any centrist education policy.

For example, we know that students all over the world suffered severe learning loss during the pandemic and we know that school systems, for the most part, have done a poor job helping them catch up. We don't know the long-term consequences of the pandemic, but in the short term there are clear signs of emotional trauma and educational stress.

We know that the education sector is facing an acute labour shortage, especially in areas like STEM, special education and bilingual education. We should pay teachers better and pay great teachers even more, including those who take on the hardest of assignments. And, given the stress of the pandemic, provide more mental health support to both teachers and students. So there are important, unaddressed issues that could unite us in the years ahead if leaders come together and put the education of our children first. This isn't just the right thing to do, it's also a smart investment for nations.

I recently accepted an invitation to chair the board of the Hunt Institute, founded by and named for the legendary North Carolina governor Jim Hunt, who had always believed education should be the ultimate bipartisan issue. My vice-chair is the former Republican governor of New Mexico, Susana Martinez. Together we're hoping to chart a bipartisan path forward in the USA around core learning issues, from early childhood education and reading and maths proficiency to access to rigorous high school courses and affordable post-secondary options.

There should be nothing polarising about giving more children access to pre-school, increasing high school graduation and helping more people complete college. If you want to build a strong middle class, this is the best way to do it. This is nation-building work and we should all be in it together.

16

A CENTRIST APPROACH TO PROGRESS: INNOVATION AND INCREMENTALISM

Haley Stevens

Throughout much of the last 120 years, Michigan, the region I am humbly proud to represent in the US Congress, has been responsible for world-shaping industrial innovations.

The mass-produced automobile, the first practical snowplough, the first four-way electric traffic light, the first superhighway with eight lanes and a divided median – these innovations of a century ago constitute our built environment and changed how people work, live and play. The industrial systems of the twentieth century improved human life through revolutionary advances in medical care, education, human rights and working conditions.

The growing understanding of the environmental impacts of industrialisation over the last quarter-century, and even more recently their human toll, however, highlights the massive challenges of industrial policy, infrastructure and work we as a civilisation face for the remainder of this century. In many respects, as groundbreaking as they were at the time, the inventions of the early twentieth century were easier to build than the type of innovation we need today.

The challenges of the industrial and infrastructure innovation needed for this century, and the centuries to come, are best framed by the analogy of a home remodel. Now we must renovate rather than rely on the opportunity to build from a blank slate, so what are the costs and impediments that don't exist in a new-build? How do we get there in steps that allow us to continue to live in the house as we reshape it for our modern needs? Renovating our industrial economy to achieve the paradigm shift we need can practically only be accomplished in incremental steps. This embodies modern-day centrism: incrementally doing what needs to be done to usher in newfound solutions. We can neither afford to stagnate nor demolish everything that we've built and start again. We need to 'fix the damn roads', as the governor of my state, Gretchen Whitmer, famously said; *and* we must create a new green, industrial economy that focuses on both workers and the planet.

Centrism is the *and*. We can fix our roads and build high-speed rail. We can catch up on semiconductor manufacturing and invest in quantum computing. Centrism in public policy, especially fields as important and complex as infrastructure and industry, is the embrace of incremental steps that get us to the grand vision – in this case, a decarbonised infrastructure and industry. Building, not just envisioning, a decarbonised industrial economy that brings everyone along – including the workers who built our modern world – is the path of centrism. And centrism rooted in achievable incremental goals is what makes this future not just achievable, but achievable in our lifetimes.

Mobility is a particularly important area of change and innovation. My home state of Michigan is the heart of the USA's automotive industry where new mobility has been invented, reimagined, updated and built for generations. And now Michigan finds itself at the heart of America's green mobility transition. This shift, however, has not been without its challenges. We have wide-open stretches of road and infrastructure built over a century to get petrol-powered cars across the North American continent. But we must overlay electric vehicle infrastructure on the infrastructure for combustion engines while millions of people gradually transition from one type of vehicle to another. An incremental approach will be what gets us to a mobility future that doesn't rely solely on internal combustion engines. Policymakers can provide funding and incentives to make sure every community has charging infrastructure; we can encourage companies to develop other non-electric, no- and low-carbon mobility options; and, crucially, we can fund the scientific research that will yield new lower-carbon options we cannot yet imagine. As Rachel Pritzker writes in her essay on global energy needs, we need new green technologies that are affordable for the developing, not just the developed, world. We can't fight climate change by decarbonising only the USA and its wealthy allies.

Government must also implement policies that mitigate the pain of transition. That begins with a genuine understanding of the sacrifices and fear felt by working families who see entire industries under threat from technological advances or proposals for transition to a new type of economy. We need to understand them and fight every day to make sure they're never left behind. That's not only the role of elected representatives, it is also smart policymaking.

It is also important for policymakers to appropriately address the challenges and costs of moving to a new green economy. We need to make sure that auto-manufacturing jobs remain the well-paying, middle-class jobs that sustain working families. In an electric vehicle future, workers who produce our mobility solutions must be paid good middle-class wages, just like their predecessors who built internal combustion engines. While transitioning away from carbon is critical to future liveability, we must also make sure that people have dignified work that allows them to buy into the promise of this future. That's why I meet with workers on production lines in Michigan almost every Monday. I spend time sitting in meeting rooms with engineers, testing out equipment with lab techs, and on factory floors with workers to see what they're inventing and building. Not only do the companies I visit build great products that solve real problems across the entire world, but they also provide the jobs that allow people to live middle-class lives with a sense of pride and dignity. These jobs are not just a pay cheque, they pay dividends to democracy.

I hear time and again that people don't just want a job, they want a good job that rewards them for their hard work and lets them pay the bills, not with ease but with security. In the industrial heartland of the USA, our workers are the steady drumbeat of success ploughing through whatever obstacles they face. And with that comes the economic imperative to yes, work hard, but also have a good life, affordable housing and the opportunity to retire. That's what the modern worker movement represents: making sure that everyone, not just the wealthy and well-connected, can move, generate savings and get ahead. When political leaders become distracted by divisive social policy, we frankly lose sight that the primary concern of our citizens resides in the anxiety of a quality job that provides meaning, often contributing to something bigger than oneself. Getting distracted by manufactured social politics means we lose sight of tangible issues that impact people's lives, and everyone pays the consequence. Good jobs empower people to participate in their communities and buy into the vision that democracy and prosperity can coexist.

In a world trending towards the seemingly easy answers of authoritarianism, shoring up middle-class jobs in democracies is critical in ensuring that all people have access to the dignity of a decent pay cheque. Recent political tumult across the democratic world has been fuelled by people from all walks of life who feel the deep economic frustration of working all day without a horizon for progress, or fear that something will be taken from them. They can't save up enough to purchase a home, or send their kids to college, or buy the cars they build. They look back to their parents' generation and sense that their own situation is worse, not better. Or they have done well but feel it slipping, or sense that forces in society are going to strip them of stability. People want a guarantee, and they want governance they can trust.

A healthy economy that empowers workers to participate is also the best tool we have to champion democratic ideals worldwide. We not only want entrepreneurs in the new green economy to be able to provide good jobs domestically, we want to be able to sell better products globally. We want innovators to have ownership of their ideas

– if an innovator has a good idea, they should be able to make money off it. That basic idea drives innovation, creativity and a free-market economy.

Innovating and bringing the best of the future to market is also a key tool in countering the technological and advanced manufacturing ascendance of authoritarian states like China. If we don't build it, if we don't create it, if we don't export it – our adversaries will. That's why I was so proud to play a hand in passing the USA's first industrial policy in a generation, the CHIPS and Science Act. This legislation is a $50 billion investment of taxpayer dollars in microchip manufacturing design, production and shipment, intended to bring good jobs back to the USA and ensure we can build the technology to improve life in the twenty-first century. The CHIPS funding of foundational research also plants the seeds of the next invention that can help us deal with the challenges of the modern world and provide tomorrow's workforce with the same opportunities we're working to create today. Centrists, as noted elsewhere in this book, are hopeful about the future and understand the need to plan for the long term. The results are rarely immediate (and neither is the political reward), but in a world of complex, interdependent and long-term challenges, centrists offer complex, interdependent and long-term solutions.

The 'and' that is centrism, however, also means that we must recognise the necessity and benefits of positive peer trading relationships. We must work with allies and those who share our democratic values to make sure that the transition to a new green industrial world lifts all boats. The CHIPS and Science Act, for example, also prioritised fair trade with our allies and 'friend shoring', or building our trade capacity with nations with whom we share democratic values. As we build our new knowledge-based green economy, companies from democratic countries need access to markets on a level playing field. The next twenty-five years will be determinative in the battle for the future of liberal democracy and the future of our planet. We must invest in the people, global partnerships and scientific progress that strengthen liberal democracies and make green economies possible for everyone.

Centrism is the path to addressing the interconnected challenges that we face in creating a just, green and liveable future. As an elected official, I must champion policies that make sure that democratic governance, dignified work, a healthy environment and human rights thrive in our modern world. We want workers to be able to afford the things they build, own a home that is safe, put healthy food on the table and ensure the education their children need for a better future. To invoke the well-worn adage, the long journey to this vision starts with a single step.

A centrist approach to seizing the opportunities of our next industrial revolution means bringing everyone along, even those who don't agree with us. The goal of incrementalism is to get to the next step, not to stop. It is to make progress without losing sight of the past. It is to strengthen our communities without losing their unique identities. Rather than condemning us to a world of seemingly insurmountable challenges, incrementalism allows us to tackle concrete problems and work with people who may have a different perspective on many broader topics but agree on the need to solve the problems right in front of us. Incrementalism and centrism are about action and not just words. It's about the 'and' of chipping away at immediate concerns while building towards a more productive, inclusive tomorrow. Folks in Michigan, and across the world, want their leaders to secure tangible results on the issues that directly impact their daily lives *and* build a better future for generations to come.

17

A CENTRIST APPROACH
TO COUNTERTERRORISM

Jonathan Evans

Terrorism evokes perhaps the strongest emotional and political reaction of any challenge faced by a government, as it typically involves the use of violence against innocent victims and is a deliberate and illegitimate challenge to the established political order. Consequently, there is a temptation to demand tough, immediate and uncompromising responses to terrorism with the aims of stamping it out, demonstrating political strength and expressing moral outrage. Terrorism does require a tough response, but we need to recognise that terrorist motivations differ and can be a deliberate provocation to lure governments into over-reaction. Therefore, the response of democratic governments to terrorism must be multidimensional and sustainable, focused on clear outcomes, and it must avoid unintended consequences. More than perhaps any other area, it requires the pragmatism and embracing of complexity which define political centrism and are articulated throughout this book.

An uncompromising and one-dimensional security response might be emotionally satisfying, and even effective in the short term, but there is little evidence that it works in the long run. To take a UK example, the security crackdown in the early days of the Northern Ireland Troubles, which included widespread detention of terrorist suspects without trial, is generally judged to have been ineffective and, in the longer term, counterproductive. It created several problems.

First, given that intelligence is never comprehensive nor wholly reliable, some of those detained were the wrong people and, since they were denied a proper trial, the case against them could not be independently tested. Second, since many of the real terrorists were not detained, the terrorism continued but the perception of injustice and incompetence by the state took hold. This hardened attitudes among parts of the community whose support the state needed if the terrorists were to be isolated. Third, arbitrary action by the state played into the hands of the extremists by suggesting that their characterisation of it as an unjust and unprincipled occupying force was correct. This created a political and diplomatic problem for the UK for decades and the damage to British interests that it caused greatly outweighed the tactical advantage of detaining at least some of those involved in terrorism.

Some similar criticisms can be levelled against the US War on Terror after the 9/11 attacks. While the USA was undoubtedly justified in wanting to bring the attackers to justice and to prevent Al-Qaida from mounting similar attacks elsewhere, the war paradigm, which limited the application of due process and emphasised military solutions, led to some serious mistakes by the USA which undermined its moral authority and international political leadership. Specifically, the detention without trial of many suspects, the use of torture and mistreatment on a wide scale, and the extrajudicial and extraterritorial killing of terrorist suspects were all in contradiction to the values that the USA claimed to stand for in the world, and which had been an important part of its soft power.

So, if an unconstrained security response is not the right approach to terrorism, what is?

The alternative is *not* insecurity for the population and impotence by the state. It is a more sophisticated and integrated approach that recognises terrorism as a symptom of deeper causes and that bases strong security measures on law, accountability and human rights, thereby

117

creating a moral and political foundation for a strong security policy and helping to ensure that it is sustainable.

The first step in countering terrorism is to articulate an overall strategy with a clear and deliverable goal. This will help all those involved to come together within a strategic framework. Terrorist problems do not arise in a vacuum but in specific political, social or religious contexts. We need to understand what lies behind any particular manifestation of terrorism. The root cause might be a genuine injustice that is experienced by a specific ethnic or social group. It might be rooted in religious doctrine. It might be a form of revolutionary violence aimed at a political outcome and exploiting perceived injustices to this end. Some terrorism, seen recently in the West, might be driven by individual grievance and sometimes mental instability. We cannot respond to all these different sorts of terrorism in the same way. Therefore, a successful counterterrorist strategy needs first to understand who the terrorists are and why they are using terrorist violence. Understanding what motivates terrorists is not to justify terrorist acts, as some on the political right might suggest, nor does recognition of an underlying injustice mean that there cannot be a forceful response to terrorism, as some on the left might conclude. But without understanding we cannot develop a sensible response.

Once we understand who the terrorists are and what their motivation is, we can decide rationally how to respond. If there are genuine injustices involved, can they be addressed, both on the basis of natural justice and to stop them being exploited by the terrorists? Where this is not possible then at least the state needs to do what it can to isolate the terrorists from the community from which they come, so that they draw less support. If there are religious drivers of terrorism, how can these best be challenged, and by whom? If a terrorist problem is to do with personal grievance or mental instability, what is the best response? At an absolute minimum, the state must avoid counterterrorist tactics that make any of these underlying problems worse. Recognition of the underlying causes of terrorism, and addressing those causes where it is just and feasible to do so, is not 'giving in to terrorism'. It is acknowledging that terrorism thrives where it can feed on actual or perceived grievances: we need to deny terrorists this opportunity.

The operational aspects of terrorism – hunting down the terrorists, reducing the vulnerability of potential targets and recovering quickly from attacks – are vital but they need to be part of a wider strategy and to run in parallel with attention to underlying causes. In all this, we must be realistic about how quickly terrorist problems can be brought to an end. Any successful counterterrorist strategy will take time to deliver, so it needs to be durable and sustainable. Populists in particular will offer simple solutions that promise to bring terrorism to an end in a matter of days or weeks. To quote H. L. Mencken, 'For every complex problem there is an answer that is clear, simple, and wrong.' A centrist approach recognises the need to balance the competing tensions that lie at the heart of counterterrorism strategy.

One such tension is in the relationship between security and human rights. It is much debated and I addressed this in my maiden speech in the UK's House of Lords in 2015, after completing my term as head of the UK's Security Service:

It is sometimes suggested that there is a zero-sum game between security on the one hand, and civil liberties and human rights on the other – that this is some kind of see-saw and that if one end goes up the other will inevitably go down. That seems to me to be fundamentally mistaken. I believe that a country that has a strong basis of civil liberties and human rights is likely then to be able to draw on that as a form of resilience in the face of extremism and violence; in that sense our civil liberties and human rights are a very important component in the struggle against extremism. Conversely, inadequate security will breed vulnerability and fear, and that in turn will tend to limit people's ability to contribute to civil society, will provoke vigilantism and will diminish people's ability to exercise the very civil liberties and human rights that we wish to sustain . . . security and civil liberties and human rights are mutually supportive.

Respect for human rights does not stop the state from using intrusive surveillance where it is necessary, nor does it stop terrorists from being hunted down and imprisoned, or even killed in extreme cases of an imminent threat where there is no alternative. Human rights, such as the right to a fair trial and protection against torture or arbitrary detention, are not incompatible with strong counterterrorist policies. Indeed, in my experience the fact of bringing suspects before the courts, like any other criminals, can be a very effective way of demonstrating that those detained have indeed done the things they are accused of, and that their claims to be treated as political prisoners are nonsense.

The right to privacy, like several other rights articulated in the European Convention on Human Rights, is a qualified rather than an absolute right. This means that it can be restricted in certain circumstances where it is necessary and lawful. The UK's Investigatory Powers Act 2016 is a good example of how this works. For historical reasons, the UK has strong intelligence capabilities for investigating the activities of those suspected of terrorism. By definition, the use of these capabilities entails severe intrusion: for instance, placing microphones in suspects' homes, following them around and hacking into their computers. But the 2016 Act places these capabilities onto an explicit statutory basis. No one can complain that they did not know their privacy rights might be breached if they started planning a terrorist attack, and by placing these powers in statute law they are consistent with international human rights agreements. The corollary is that the state must be able to demonstrate that the powers are only being used against the right people and that there must be a remedy if the powers are misused. This is achieved under the 2016 Act by requiring that both a senior government minister and an independent judge authorise the use of intrusive techniques. Moreover, anyone who believes that they have been wrongly put under surveillance can complain to an independent judicial body, the Investigative Powers Commission, which looks into the complaint and can order redress.

These arrangements mean that it is possible to mount extremely intrusive investigations into suspected terrorists which would, in other circumstances, be a serious breach of their human rights. Since the powers are used in a foreseeable, lawful and accountable way, with appropriate remedies against misuse, respect for human rights is maintained. Rather than ignoring human rights components, it harnesses them for a more effective counterterrorism strategy. Human rights are not in conflict with strong investigative powers: you can have both.

Even more controversy surrounds the use of torture or mistreatment to obtain counterterrorist information. Some campaigners try to avoid the issue, taking the easy way out and saying that you cannot trust the information obtained by torture or mistreatment. This is not self-evidently true. Some information derived from torture might well be accurate, so we cannot avoid the moral, political and practical question of whether we should permit the use of torture at all.

Irrespective of any moral revulsion, torture is not the right response to terrorism. Its use is unnecessary. Most developed countries get by without permitting torture, including many that have faced significant terrorist problems, such as the UK and Israel. In my experience, intelligence and security services that rely heavily on the torture and mistreatment of detainees are usually those that have limited intelligence capabilities and fall back on torture for want of better options. Moreover, it is hard to imagine anything more likely to undermine public and political support for a counterterrorist campaign than the widespread use of torture. In the long term such abusive behaviour is likely to spawn a new generation of terrorists determined to punish or overthrow the state that has abandoned the moral basis of its own actions. Here, too, a centrist approach is not to simply reject the use of torture (although it should) but to ensure that stronger and more effective alternatives are put in place.

Even if human rights issues are well managed, countering terrorism will take time. Quick solutions are unlikely to work and can be counterproductive. Terrorism usually occurs in the context of long-standing social or political problems (though individual terrorists might be radicalised quickly) and our strategic response must recognise this. Perseverance and patience are key. We should not allow tactical errors (and in an area of policy this complex tactical errors will occur) to undermine our strategic goal. Addressing underlying issues exploited by terrorists will take time, counter-radicalisation is not instantaneous, building resilience is complicated, developing intelligence coverage is incremental. But nation-states have been around a long time and have significant resources: financial, moral and political. Most terrorist groups are not so lucky. We can use sustained effort and strategic patience as an asset and bear down on terrorism over the long term. It took nearly thirty years to bring the Provisional IRA to the point of a final ceasefire. It was nearly ten years after 9/11 before Osama Bin Laden was killed. The Greek terrorist group November 17 operated for over twenty years before being destroyed. But in each case the ultimate staying power was with those countering terrorism and not with the terrorist groups.

A counterterrorist strategy is most likely to succeed if it acknowledges the complexity of the problems it must address, leverages the advantages of the state, uses strong security measures but also recognises that a narrow security response alone will not be enough. The balance of competing principles, the embrace of complexity and the rejection of simplistic solutions are all the hallmarks of a centrist approach.

18

A CENTRIST APPROACH
TO GLOBAL ENERGY POLICY

Rachel Pritzker

Climate and energy policy is an area ripe for a centrist, pragmatic approach. To make durable progress on climate and energy issues, the world needs fewer extremists committed to ideological warfare and more pragmatists committed to policies that are both politically viable and effective at solving these challenges. A pragmatic agenda recognises that climate change is a global issue, with political and policy implications that vary in wealthier and poorer countries and cannot be addressed by one-size-fits-all approaches. It takes seriously the perils of climate change while also acknowledging that abundant energy is fundamental to human flourishing, enabling developing nations to move their populations out of poverty and developed nations to maintain and expand high living standards.

Energy abundance

It is a common belief of many on the left that to effectively address climate change we must significantly cut energy consumption. Yet global electricity demand keeps growing and is, according to the International Energy Agency, expected to expand by 75–150 per cent by 2050. Vast disparities in energy access – *Our World in Data* shows, for instance, that the average American uses eighty-six times more electricity than the average Nigerian – mean that while those of us in rich countries already use tremendous amounts of energy, people in poor nations still aspire to even modest consumption. Despite growing alarm about climate change, none of us seems inclined to diminish our quality of life – in fact, quite the opposite.

The problem on the right is the inverse. In the USA, sections of the Republican Party are *still* sceptical of climate science, and many right-wing parties around the world view the left's climate approach as unwarranted catastrophism. The chants of 'drill, baby, drill' still resound as tangible proof that many on the right value energy abundance with little regard for the climate consequences.

Neither of these approaches is viable. The goal of pragmatic energy policy, then, should be to produce abundant clean, cheap energy that allows the world to mitigate climate change while also enabling people across the globe to live fulfilling lives.

The idea of using less energy may sound appealing, but that is only because few of us can actually imagine life without it. Abundant, reliable energy is vital to modern life. Energy powers conveniences like washing machines and freezers, runs our factories and hospitals and enables the innovations required to improve lives, address environmental challenges and drive economic growth. That is why in rich countries like the USA the idea of using less energy is deeply unpopular across the political spectrum. In poor countries, asking people who already use so little to remain in energy poverty is immoral and poses geopolitical risks.

Indeed, energy abundance is particularly vital in addressing a range of important issues in developing countries, first among them poverty. As Todd Moss, executive director of the Energy for Growth Hub, has written: 'No country in human history has ever become wealthier without steep increases in energy consumption, both at home and especially in the wider economy.' More energy for poor countries would improve health outcomes by powering refrigeration for vaccines and machinery for complex surgeries. It would improve educational outcomes by enabling schools to use computers and other modern technologies and by ensuring that children have light by which to read at night. Abundant energy would provide protection from extreme weather events, including allowing people to run air conditioning on hot days and powering the fabrication of sturdier building materials to withstand major storms. It would enable greater economic mobility by creating more jobs and housing in more places and fuelling motorised transportation that can take people over long distances.

Energy also matters deeply for geopolitics and national security. The Russian invasion of Ukraine, which led to the cut-off of natural gas to the entire EU, is the latest demonstration that where countries get their energy from matters for both national security and global stability. This applies as equally to poor countries as it does to rich ones. Yet global development agencies, led by wealthy nations, generally restrict support for energy projects abroad to renewable technologies such as solar and wind that remain incapable on their own of providing sufficient reliable energy to power modern societies. This often leads countries that want to invest in fossil fuels – or even other carbon-free energy sources such as hydropower or nuclear power – to turn to non-democratic countries like China and Russia for financing and partnership.

Energy policy in rich nations – and the international financial institutions they dominate – must balance climate considerations with the priority of providing energy abundance for all. Any policies that seek to limit human needs and economic growth in the name of climate change are likely to be politically fraught and thus short-lived. Meanwhile, trying to limit the energy use of people in nations that did not cause climate change while we in the developed world use dramatically more energy is deeply wrong. Developing countries need increasingly clean energy abundance, yet they must be able to decide their own energy futures with the help and support of rich countries and multilateral agencies like the World Bank.

Changing our approach to climate change

Pragmatic climate policy, therefore, must enable people to use more energy from cleaner sources rather than focusing on restricting or reducing energy consumption. This will require a shift from the traditional environmentalist stance of preventing development (including, ironically, on-the-ground opposition to renewable energy projects occurring across the developed world) to a politics of building more.

In the USA, we need reform to enable the timely construction and deployment of power plants, transmission lines, electric vehicle-charging stations and other clean energy-related infrastructure. Conservation restrictions are likewise preventing the deployment of clean energy across the developed world; while conservation matters, we must strive for balance across these priorities. And wealthy nations need to change their export and investment policies to help create global systems to fund, construct and remove barriers to carbon-free energy projects abroad. Such policies will also have the added benefit of bolstering democracy by ensuring that fewer poor countries become reliant on authoritarian nations for their energy needs.

Several pragmatic movements and philosophies have emerged over the past decade to drive this much-needed shift in environmental politics. Ecomodernism, led by The Breakthrough Institute, believes that technology is the key to addressing climate change and calls for significant public investment in technological innovation as well as policies that enable commercialisation of a range of new energy technologies. Supply-side progressivism, championed by the *New York Times* columnist and podcast host Ezra Klein, argues that the left needs to focus on reforming government to make it easier to build energy infrastructure, housing and other public goods, including revising or eliminating regulations that prevent important projects from getting built. An aligned philosophy, the abundance agenda, sparked by Klein's co-author Derek Thompson of *The Atlantic*, calls for boosting living standards through investment in innovation, regulatory reform and production of essential goods and services.

Pragmatic climate policy involves spreading our technological bets around rather than putting all our eggs in one basket. Instead of closing off options through policies that favour one set of technologies over another, we should support policies that advance a broad range of climate interventions, including solar, wind and hydro, alongside nuclear power (one of the densest and cleanest forms of power generation), deep geothermal (extracting heat generated within the Earth), and carbon removal (taking carbon out of the atmosphere). We should also invest in developing and deploying carbon capture and sequestration (catching carbon at the point of emission and putting it into the ground rather than the air), accelerating the coal-to-gas transition (responsible for the largest drop in carbon emissions to date) and researching solar radiation management (mimicking natural processes that reflect sunlight back into the atmosphere in order to cool the planet). Centrism, as essays throughout this book argue, must embrace science and technological development. In energy policy this should be no different.

All energy and climate mitigation technologies have their benefits and drawbacks, and none works perfectly in every situation. There are no bumper sticker solutions. Pragmatic policymaking requires weighing risks and rewards and analysing how technologies work together in the context of whole energy systems and in relation to the alternatives, including inaction. And it requires continued investment in innovation even while we deploy current technologies at scale. These investments will likely lead to improvements in the performance of existing technologies and to even better ones in the future.

Finally, pragmatic climate policy should focus on the end goal of decarbonisation, prioritising imperfect compromises over stubborn inaction, technology agnosticism over preferences for particular energy sources, and 'quiet' policymaking over efforts to 'raise awareness'. In a politically divided nation like the USA, we are unlikely to see major future climate legislation labelled as such. Indeed, the most important climate legislation in US history was the 2022 Inflation Reduction Act (IRA), not the sweeping and much-touted Green New Deal, which was never even introduced as a bill. And the IRA is a model of pragmatic climate policy, with massive public investments in a swathe of clean energy technologies. Every country will face its own political context and pragmatic leaders will find the most effective way to implement these policy approaches in their own countries.

Moving forward, wealthy nations are likely to have greater sustained policy success by focusing on discrete challenges in service of larger climate and energy aspirations rather than aiming for society-wide transformation. For instance, while dozens of firms are developing advanced nuclear reactor technologies to help provide abundant clean energy and at the same time reduce many of the downside risks typically associated with nuclear power, we must update the nuclear regulatory process. For example, in the USA a pragmatic approach would discard the process designed more than fifty years ago and replace it with a balanced approach that takes into account society's need for clean energy as well as safety and cost. Likewise, pragmatic climate policy would focus on removing barriers to domestic critical mineral production, which is necessary for developing clean energy technologies to meaningfully scale electrification and decarbonisation. These bite-sized, and often boring-sounding, policy matters may not feel like big wins to climate activists, but they are critical to mitigating climate change and are less likely to become polarised precisely because they're not particularly exciting or controversial to most people. In other words, they are much more durable.

Conclusion

Centrist, pragmatic climate and energy policies will look different in the developed and developing worlds.

In wealthy countries, climate has been a prototypically polarised issue, with one side claiming the world is about to end and the other that climate change is barely a problem worth acknowledging. Unfortunately, these dynamics are mutually reinforcing, and the result is a political and policy environment that lacks nuance and fails to build enduring support for climate and energy policies. Policies favoured only by one side of the ideological spectrum are especially vulnerable when the government changes hands. Pragmatic policymaking can avoid the trap of polarisation by balancing climate change and energy abundance priorities, steering clear of environmental shibboleths such as opposition to development and attachment to specific energy sources, and focusing on incremental progress. By charting a pragmatic course, we can remove political barriers to genuine progress and create solutions that are effective and politically feasible. Nothing is more likely to lead us to climate catastrophe than paralysis due to political intransigence.

In most poor countries the politics of climate change are much less polarised, as the trade-off is clearer between prioritising a climate issue they didn't create or the energy needs that will allow their citizens to improve their lives in the immediate term. A pragmatic policy agenda for the developing world is one that prioritises human and economic development needs alongside climate imperatives, and that responds to national interests instead of imposing the environmental priorities of wealthy nations.

19

A CENTRIST APPROACH
TO THE CHALLENGE OF TECHNOLOGY

Jamie Susskind

The great political controversy of the twentieth century concerned the relationship between the state and the market. One side argued that the state should have an extensive – perhaps even dominant – role in shaping and overseeing economic activity. The other said that market forces, left largely to themselves, would better allocate benefits and burdens. This debate prompted wars and revolutions. It divided blocs of nations. And within them, it separated left from right.

That debate has not disappeared. But it may soon be eclipsed. A particularly likely source of dispute in the next few decades is digital technology, i.e. non-human systems with the growing ability to exert power, affect the democratic process, define the limits of our liberty, decide questions of social justice and move basic resources around society. Such systems are becoming increasingly capable and increasingly visible, but you won't find them analysed in the great works of political theory that make up the Western canon. Those works are from a different time. In the future, political scientists will have to reckon not only with the invisible hand of the market and the great clunking fist of the state but with a new political force: the power of computer code, which will influence more and more of the actions, interactions and transactions that are the basis of human sociality.

The great political question of this century is shaping up to be something like this: to what extent should our lives be governed by powerful digital systems, and on what terms?

It is possible to imagine the answers that might be given to this question by those on the traditional left and right.

On the left, it might be said that the primary aim of digital policy should be to prevent the immense power of digital technology from becoming concentrated in the hands of private corporations and their shareholders; and to ensure instead that the means and benefits of technological development are regulated, socialised and redistributed by the state. That way, everyone can share in the wonder of digital technology, not just economic elites.

The right would counter that the most important aims of digital policy should be, first, to create conditions which ensure that the wonders of technological innovation are actually unleashed as soon as possible, free from the dead hand of regulation; and second, to ensure that innovation takes place *here* rather than *there* – so that technological, economic and geopolitical power can be combined in a thriving *domestic* tech industry. The way to achieve both ends, to the rightward-inclined, would be an unfettered market economy.

These sketches are caricatures, but there are attractive elements in both. And they share some assumptions: that tech is likely to continue to improve at an accelerating rate, that it can be a force for good, that it can give power to those who own and control it, and that policy levers can affect the nature and geography of technological change.

But – and you might expect this in a book on political centrism – neither the traditional left nor right can offer a satisfactory answer to the central question posed above. This is partly because some of the old left/right assumptions have aged poorly. For instance, we know that a truly laissez-faire economy is unlikely to be as innovative as one with a responsible and active state. Countries which aspire to tech superpowerdom need high levels of basic and advanced education, a skilled and healthy workforce, sound infrastructure, an efficient judicial system free from corruption and a serious industrial strategy. These cannot be achieved in a trickle-down system. We also know that, although regulation can be stultifying, it can also be energising. A viable anti-trust regulator, for instance, is an important part of a dynamic tech ecosphere. For these reasons and more, the dusty playbooks of the last century do not offer an adequate guide to the debates of tomorrow.

The old left/right dichotomy is unsatisfactory for another reason too. Debates about digital technology are not like traditional debates about the ownership and control of economic resources (even important resources like land, machinery and other forms of capital). This is because digital technology is not merely an economic resource; it is an instrument of political influence. Every line of code that determines what we can and cannot do, what we can and cannot say – that is political. Every algorithm used to allocate things of social importance like jobs, credit, insurance, housing and social security – that is political too. Every social media platform that influences an election, every bot used to spread a political message – these are political. And every time technology gathers data about a person, so that it can be combined with the data of millions of others and used for surveillance, or influence, or social prediction – that activity is inescapably political. So the question of who owns and controls the most powerful digital technologies is not merely a question about the distribution of *economic* power; it is about the distribution of *political* power. Some call this a 'fourth industrial revolution', but in truth it is a political revolution too. The digital is political.

What's more, digital systems are not 'objective' or 'scientific' in their operation. They should not be treated, either by political theorists or policymakers, as merely commercial in nature. Almost every socially important digital technology is shot through with biases, prejudices and priorities, whether its creators know it or not. Every digital artefact, every line of code, is engineered according to a set of values, whether explicit or implicit. Technology has the power to mould the moral character of society, for better or worse. That power is quintessentially *political*. And it is growing.

What, then, is the *centrist* answer to the great political question of the twenty-first century? It is not a splitting of the difference between left and right, though it should seek to incorporate the best of both. Nor is it a technocratic fudge which ignores the roaring social fissures that digital development is likely to expose. Instead, the centrist approach should seek to jettison the ideological baggage of the left/right axis and start with a more fundamental series of questions: why do we regulate things at all? What is the purpose of regulation in a free and democratic society? Why regulate technology?

I cannot hope to do any more here than sketch out the beginnings of an answer to these era-defining questions. My suggestion lies in a doctrine that is older even than the notions of 'left' and 'right', and cannot be claimed by either.

Start with an attempt at diagnosis: what is the problem that we are trying to solve? I believe this can be answered in two words: *unaccountable power*. In short, the growth in technology's power has not been paired with corresponding growth in legal or political responsibility. The consequences of digital technology are at the very least *political* – affecting democracy, freedom, justice – and in the long run could even be *existential*, affecting the very survival of human civilisation, at least in its current form. It will not be adequate to govern the development and deployment of these technologies through consumer decisions about what to buy. That is not how we regulate other powerful agents in society, like doctors, lawyers or politicians. Tech is the anomaly. Yet history teaches us that unaccountable power, left unchecked, can gnaw away corrosively at the body politic. It undermines the capacity of democratic institutions. It shrinks our liberty and stains our dignity. And it does so without anyone really meaning for it to happen. Societies weaken when powerful people fail to wield their power wisely – not necessarily because they are evil, but because they are human, and humans make mistakes, especially when faced with difficult problems to which there is no easy answer. The centrist answer is not to lament the flaws of particular people or corporations, but to build robust systems of accountability that hold things together in good times and bad.

Pausing there, you might think that this diagnosis, while claiming to be untainted by left/right dogma, is more leftish in flavour than it likes to admit. One can imagine twentieth-century socialists nodding vigorously at the notion that concentrations of corporate power (whether enabled by digital technology or something else) ought to be dismantled, or regulated, in the name of the common good. But the traditional leftist response is problematic. Put simply: any solution which tries to fix the problem of privately held digital power by simply transferring that power into the hands of the state is not a solution at all. While the modern democratic state is more accountable than a business corporation, it is nevertheless 1) the most formidable concentration of power ever known to human civilisation; 2) usually imperfect in its operation; and 3) though some might not accept it, perfectly capable of acting as a kind of agent with its own interests, not merely as a vessel for the will of the *demos*. Concern about private power is arguably left-wing; concern about state power is arguably right-wing. What unites the two is concern about power – and that is a useful place for a centrist to start. To the centrist, all concentrations of power should be treated as potentially problematic, whether they occur in the public or private sector.

So if unaccountable power is the diagnosis, what is the cure? Well, we undoubtedly need new laws and institutions; new regulators, rules, and standards, and so forth. While this may make the libertarian right (and big tech companies) feel uncomfortable, these are the instruments of accountability. They can be used to expose the workings of new technologies, test their reliability and suitability, and if necessary impose remedial steps. But the wise centrist should be wary of leaping into the role of lawgiver before the underlying *principles* of any legislative action have been made clear. That is to say, it would be wrong to take action in any field of technology governance without first achieving clarity on the guiding principles. As developed at more length in my book *The Digital*

Republic, here are four which ought to govern centrist efforts to answer the question: to what extent should our lives be governed by powerful digital systems, and on what terms? These principles would not work in every context, but should provide a starting point for countries which are democratic and enjoy the rule of law.

1. In the face of powerful new technologies, the law must first preserve the basic institutions necessary for a free society (such as a functioning democratic and judicial system).
2. The law should then reduce the unaccountable power of those who design and control digital technology, and keep that power to a minimum.
3. The law should also ensure, as far as possible, that powerful technologies reflect the moral and civic values of the people who live under their power.
4. As a check on the first three principles, the law should restrain government too, and regulation should always be designed in a way that involves as little state intrusion as possible.

These principles are new, but they are inspired by much older ideas. I derive them from a set of beliefs that have come to the fore at many of history's inflexion points – wars and revolutions, declarations and constitutions – just like the one we are living through. In particular, they are inspired by the doctrine of *republicanism*. This chapter is not the place to provide a history of the idea of republicanism, or how it differs from the modern US political party that bears its name (hint: a lot). But I do think it is possible to outline a centrist approach to the governance of digital technology that is inspired by republican tradition. Call it *digital republicanism*. Or call it *digital centrism*. You can even call it common sense: the point is that the old ideologies will no longer do, and this terrain is fertile for new seeds of thought. We aren't ready – legally, politically, intellectually – for the world we are building, and centrist ideas will have a key role to play.

20

A CENTRIST APPROACH
TO FOREIGN POLICY

Yair Zivan

On 13 October 2021, an informal, intimate and off-the-record dinner took place between the US secretary of state, the foreign minister of the United Arab Emirates and the foreign minister of Israel at the home of the Emirati ambassador in Washington DC. The three statesmen had brought only two advisors each, myself among them, leaving nine of us in the room. The atmosphere was relaxed, the food exceptional and the conversation flowed easily.

Hours earlier, the same three ministers had sat in a much larger room, with far more members of staff, formality and protocol. They had exchanged largely pre-written thoughts on the issues of the day and given a joint press conference. It was an important show of the closeness of this unique relationship that continues to reshape the modern Middle East, but in truth the real conversations had happened elsewhere.

At dinner, the discussions were far more open and honest, and that was what led to an innovative idea. While discussing geopolitical challenges in the Middle East, the three leaders decided to form a new international organisation to work on strategic projects. It would be small, what diplomats call a mini-lateral forum. As the discussion flowed freely about the scope of the new group and the type of projects it could take on, Alon Ushpiz, then director general of the Foreign Ministry of Israel, suggested adding India (where he had served as ambassador), to the group. None of this was pre-planned, there was no protocol or work done in advance, and at that moment, outside that room, no one else knew of the forum's conception.

Within a week, India had agreed to join the group, which came to be known as I2U2 (Israel, India, USA, UAE). The foreign ministers from all four countries met for the first time a week later in a video conference. Since then it has met multiple times, including summits at presidential and prime ministerial levels. It has launched a number of cross-regional projects. And it might never have happened through official channels.

To many people, foreign policy often seems remote from their day-to-day lives, and surveys consistently show that it ranks low on their list of priorities when thinking about which way to vote. It certainly ranks lower than the quality of their children's education, the health care that's available to their parents or their chances of finding a well-paying job to provide for their family.

But it remains an essential part of national security and economic policy, two areas that directly affect lives, and so a clear centrist approach is needed. When considering the core tenets of that approach, we need to consider three main questions:

1. Should the focus be on national interests, bringing tangible benefits to our country such as improved trade relations or beneficial alliances, or should it be on the broader global good, attempting to improve the future of humanity as whole?
2. Should centrists embrace the complex web of the international community, with its thousands of agreements, laws, bodies, agencies, norms and treaties, or try to work directly with preferred partners, circumventing international bureaucracy where possible?
3. What should the balance be between preserving the traditions and ceremony of international diplomacy on the one hand, and embracing the opportunities for rapid, informal and direct communication offered by the modern world on the other?

Throughout my time serving alongside Foreign Minister and Prime Minister Yair Lapid, I became a firm believer in the power of diplomacy and foreign policy, but recognised the need for dramatic changes in the way it was carried out. Centrists should approach foreign policy as a way to strengthen our place in the world, to build new diplomatic structures that advance our agenda, to take a moral stand, to define our identity and to bring economic benefits to our people.

The first moral responsibility of a political leader is to the security and prosperity of their people. That should rightfully impact decisions at every level. National interests can align with international ones and every effort should go into making that happen, but any political leader who sacrifices their own people's national security for the great global good will have a short political life, and rightly so.

Foreign policy doesn't need to be either isolationist or naive. Playing an active role in global affairs comes with benefits. International cooperation builds relationships, it creates mutually reinforcing loyalty and, when done well, it projects strength. Those benefits aren't always immediate but they pay dividends, whether that's through international efforts on women's rights, drug smuggling, climate change, international trade, scientific cooperation or securing critical supply chains. Some problems simply can't be solved alone, some opportunities can only be maximised through collaboration. Isolationism, the preferred approach of many on the libertarian right, doesn't work in an interconnected world.

The potential benefits of international involvement don't, however, lead us directly into the arms of the existing structures of the international community. The United Nations and its myriad of agencies are too often slow and ineffective. Peacekeeping forces in troubled regions often disappear when hostilities actually begin. Cultural and health care organisations are subjected to political pressure. The Human Rights Council is an abject joke: people are rewarded with chairs of subcommittees on issues where they are often the worst culprits.

While the United Nations Security Council might be the best we've got, it is still a body in which a country can invade its neighbour, as Russia did Ukraine, and retain a veto right. This is not a call for centrists to reject the international order; its benefits outweigh its costs. It is useful to have international legal norms through which countries can try to govern their affairs before resorting to pressure tactics or violence. The rule of law only works when people agree to play by the rules or the consequences for refusal are clear and consistent. In a complex world with a multitude of bad actors, that clearly isn't always the case.

For larger countries, particularly those with a global impact, the challenge is greater. They are often forced to choose when, where and how to intervene on both moral and pragmatic grounds. If intervention is deemed necessary, they must then decide how far it should go, from diplomatic pressure to economic sanctions and, ultimately, military action. Centrists have traditionally been associated with liberal interventionism, unwilling to look away from genocide and horrific abuses of human rights. However, every centrist leader will admit to prioritising between cases and countries. The world is full of terrible regimes doing terrible things to their own people and to others; when and how to intervene is never straightforward. Cases are prioritised according to how egregious they are, how wide-ranging and strategic their impact is perceived to be and, crucially, how impactful you can be with the available tools. It is the same agonising but necessary choice which centrists must take in every policy field.

Where the traditional bodies fail, isolationism is unable to meet modern challenges and purely bilateral relations between countries are too limited, centrists should embrace modern alternatives.

The new mini-lateral organisations are a classic example of centrism in action. They take the best of multi-lateralism and leave behind all its worst traits. I2U2 is one example; another in which I was directly involved was the Negev Forum.

Initiated by Israel's Yair Lapid in 2022, the Negev Forum is comprised of Israel, Egypt, Morocco, Bahrain, the UAE and the USA. Its creation was perhaps the clearest example of centrist foreign policy in action during my time serving in government. Rejecting the binary choice between either bilateral relations among states or unwieldy international organisations, it created a mini-lateral forum of countries that share a similar vision and purpose for the Middle East. It built on the Abraham Accords, a 2020 agreement between Israel, the UAE and Bahrain, as well as on the normalisation agreement with Morocco, to strengthen relations in the Middle East and provide a platform for cooperation on a whole range of issues.

The inaugural Negev Summit was put together through a series of direct phone calls between the foreign ministers. The usual diplomatic channels would have taken months: the negotiations over protocol would have derailed the whole thing. In this case, from conception to the opening of the summit, the whole process took under a week. Once the initial understandings were secured, the work of the diplomatic corps made it all come together. Flights, visas, security, logistics – none of that can be achieved through informal communication alone.

We arranged for all the delegations to stay in the same hotel, in the desert, far away from distractions, and on the opening night planned a dinner for the six foreign ministers alone, no staff, no protocol, no interruptions. That set the tone. The leaders met and created genuine connections, there were countless informal meetings and conversations, senior staff drank tea together at night and ate breakfast together in the morning. Peace, regional cooperation and geopolitics were all on the table during the discussions. By the end, the six foreign ministers had agreed on an annual meeting and the creation of working groups focused on creating tangible outcomes for the people of the region in fields like health, food security, energy and education. It's actually not at all surprising that effective diplomacy happens in informal settings; it is a mirror of ordinary life and human instincts – business meetings are complemented by dinner and drinks, friendships are solidified outside school or the workplace. While foreign ministries across the world still use diplomatic cables to transmit information to one another, modern foreign ministers have long ago switched to WhatsApp and Signal.

The centrist answer, then, is clear – informal interactions and direct communication which respects traditions but is never beholden to them. In the debate between the old ways and the new, push hard for the modern approach. If a defining feature of centrism is an embrace of progress, then a centrist foreign policy can be no different. There is value in tradition and in protocol, but not at the expense of effectiveness. There is a role for symbolism and ceremony, but the emphasis must be reversed – it is tradition that must be the supporting act to the modern approach.

Alternative structures must be built alongside the existing ones to make sure they are effective, pragmatic and driven by outcomes. They can be ad hoc or lasting, but they should be driven by a shared purpose and vision.

Most importantly, morals and values make us stronger, not weaker. Morality is not a zero-sum game; decisions come with costs, and the primary responsibility of a centrist foreign policy is to weigh up those complexities rather than run from them, deliver for the country's own people and make sure the public knows why it matters.

21

CENTRIST ECONOMIC POLICIES AND IDENTITY POLITICS

Andrés Velasco and Daniel Brieba

What kinds of economic policies should centrist reformers pursue? The standard answer is that they should pursue innovation-driven economic growth while at the same time doing more to ensure a fair distribution of income.

Leaving aside for a minute the boilerplate nature of the answer, there is also the pesky question of feasibility. Achieving those goals simultaneously would be hard under normal circumstances; it is harder still in our current climate because of the clash of identities that is threatening to tear many societies apart.

The conventional wisdom on this topic makes a risky claim about politics: distribute income fairly and identity warfare will fix itself. But that claim gets the story backwards. Unless we first address the angry identity clash, spurring innovation and cutting income gaps, not to mention improving public services and curbing climate change, are just pipe dreams. It is too late for oblique strategies. Today, we must address the political problem head on.

Yes, low growth and income inequality are serious problems in many countries. But priority number one should be policies to ameliorate identity warfare.

Identity lenses filter citizens' experience, so that even when a government serves them well, they might not appreciate it. Conversely, citizens who identify strongly with a government can celebrate policies that range from the mediocre to the dismal. Here are a few examples.

In 2023 in the USA, job creation was strong, unemployment reached record lows, and inflation came down fast (from an admittedly high peak). Yet Joe Biden had a lower approval rating than Donald Trump at the same point in his term, and in the summer of 2023 consumer sentiment hovered around the same level as in mid 2008, smack in the middle of the global financial crisis.

So maybe it is not the economy, stupid, but the politics. Both Democrats and Republicans view the economic situation more favourably when their party is in office, but one study finds that 'the magnitude of this partisan bias is roughly *two and a half times* larger for Republicans than for Democrats'. Partisanship explains a third of the gap between observed economic sentiment and what economic circumstances would predict.[1]

Or take Emmanuel Macron. In recent years French unemployment has come down sharply and France's economy has grown faster than perennial rival Germany's. Macron's decision not to close nuclear plants – again in contrast to Germany – looks wise now that we know what Vladimir Putin is capable of doing to European energy supplies. Foreign investment has been pouring into the country. Yet at the end of 2023, a whopping 68 per cent of the French population disapproved of how Macron is doing his job.

Again, the problem is identity. Back in 2018, when the French president proposed hiking taxes on diesel, the *gilets jaunes* took to the streets in protest. Macron, said their leader, worried about the end of the world, while they just worried about getting to the end of the month.

Examples of the opposite syndrome – that of voters worshipping politicians who implement bad policies – are also easy to come by, and exist on both the left and the right.

In Mexico, economic growth has been anaemic despite growing integration with the USA. President Andrés Manuel López Obrador grossly mishandled the pandemic. Then he tried to weaken the national elections watchdog, prompting thousands to take to the streets in protest. Yet López Obrador remains wildly popular – at the end of 2023 his approval rating was nearly 70 per cent – and his party's candidate is the clear favourite for the June 2024 presidential election (López Obrador cannot stand for re-election).

Or consider Turkey, where in May 2023 Recep Tayyip Erdoğan confounded conventional wisdom in the West by winning re-election against a candidate of the united opposition. This was in spite of ruinous economic policies, which had caused inflation to reach over 80 per cent in late 2022 (admittedly, Erdoğan mended his policies somewhat after the election).

Donald Trump's 'import tariffs on Chinese and other foreign goods had neither a sizable nor significant effect on US employment in regions with newly protected sectors', a study reported, yet the trade war 'appears to have benefited the Republican party'.[2] Residents of regions exposed to the import tariffs, the authors of the study show, became less likely to identify as Democrats, more likely to vote for Trump in 2020, and more likely to elect Republicans to Congress.

What do López Obrador, Erdoğan and Trump have in common? Their skilful manipulation of political identities. All three have managed to be perceived as 'men of the people', allegedly standing in contrast to the elites who traditionally ruled their countries.

Given this state of affairs, what is to be done? If the problem is political, part of the answer is also surely political. This begins with candidate choice: leaders who are elitist and aloof will correctly be perceived as such by the electorate. There is also room for policies to play a role, but they must be targeted at the identity gap.

It is key to convey one basic message to voters: the centrist leader has your back. He or she is working for *you* – not for elites or friends in the party establishment. However big the shocks might be – whether wars, pandemics or financial meltdowns – working together we can lessen the pain they cause.

Several economic policies potentially fit that bill. We will look at four promising ones.

Government as insurer of last resort

Becoming ill or losing one's job and then finding there is no one around to lend a hand is one of life's bitterest experiences. Whoever goes through it is likely to become a political cynic, sceptical of mainstream politicians, dismissive of government and potential fodder for populists and demagogues. In most cases the answer is insurance. You get fired or get sick, and the insurer (whether private or publicly subsidised) pays the bills. That is why Obamacare was so important: between 2013 and 2021 the number of Americans without health insurance went from 45.2 million to 28.2 million – a drop of 38 per cent.[3]

But many risks are not insurable. And in circumstances like the 2007–08 financial crisis or the COVID pandemic, insurance markets break down. That is why one of us and Ricardo Reis argue in a recent paper that government should be the insurer of last resort.[4]

When it comes to unemployment insurance, for instance, good policy predictably raises the coverage and generosity of benefits once a recession begins. The furlough scheme in the UK, and similar programmes elsewhere, allowed businesses to survive the pandemic downturn while shedding relatively few jobs.[5] During the 2022 energy crisis triggered by Russia's invasion of Ukraine, the new insurance activism was evident in the novel transfer programmes targeted at the most badly affected households.

A related goal is to sustain markets when they are near collapse. According to this logic, fiscal interventions ought to be triggered by the infrequent (but potentially very costly) meltdown of certain markets, especially financial markets. The 2007–08 financial crisis provides an example: governments, including treasuries and central banks, provided emergency credit, subsidies, public guarantees, asset purchases and capital injections to keep markets going.

145

The politics of such interventions is tricky, to say the least. Demagogues can always point an accusing finger and claim that Wall Street gets a free ride while Main Street foots the bill. And the reason why such an argument rings true is that in several historical episodes there has been a grain of truth to it.

Keeping the financial system from melting down is in everybody's interest – and yes, that includes Main Street (readers who do not believe it should conjure just two words in their minds: Lehman Brothers). But ensuring that the average citizen understands this point and gets to enjoy some tangible benefits – for instance, via debt reduction – is just as crucial. Mian and Sufi argue convincingly that during the financial crisis US policy accomplished the first goal but not always the second one.[6] This is a matter of both policy and communications.

This new fiscal activism comes with a caveat: to spend more in bad times, government needs to retain access to credit at reasonable interest rates. That means spending less (or taxing more) in good times and preserving the special status of public debt. Fiscal activism for insurance purposes is not synonymous with fiscal profligacy. This point, too, has to be explained to the public in a way that does not alienate the residents of Main Street.

Jobs, jobs, jobs

In Western Europe and North America after the Second World War, the golden decades of rising trust in democratic institutions were also decades of strong employment creation – a period of good jobs at good wages. The wave of democratisation in East Asia and Latin America in the 1990s and early 2000s was also underpinned by job growth, often but not always in exports.

The years since have been very different. Most advanced countries have experienced declining job stability, growing underemployment and a declining labour share.[7] In emerging and developing countries, the Asian miracle based on the growth of manufactured exports looks increasingly hard to replicate. Service jobs (the one fast-growing category) often involve low productivity and high rotation.

And in all countries, rich and poor, the spectre of job destruction from automation and AI haunts workers. Whether such fears are exaggerated or not is politically beside the point: the mere fear of being rendered unemployable fuels polarisation and identity-driven divisions.

'One of the fundamental problems of contemporary capitalism is its failure to produce adequate numbers of good jobs to sustain a prosperous and growing middle class,' write Dani Rodrik and Stefanie Stantcheva.[8] In response, they propose a strategy aimed at increasing the supply of good jobs in the economy.

A possible way out is the 'active' labour market policy pioneered in Scandinavia and adopted elsewhere in Europe. It includes skills re-training, pro-employment subsidies and helping with job searching. The goal is to increase the chances that everyone – including people with few skills and little experience – can land a decent job. The emphasis must be on the kind of employment that provides people with good wages and a sense of pride.

If increasing social cohesion and lessening identity divides is the goal, then supplying jobs is much better than handing out a universal basic income (even if the latter were affordable, which it probably is not). Good jobs can provide links to the community, a sense of self-worth and hope for the future; sitting at home checking social media while waiting for a government handout cannot.

Policies of place

Not too long ago, if a country had pockets of prosperity alongside de-industrialised regions where businesses had shuttered and unemployment was high, the standard advice to the unemployed was 'pack your bags and leave'. In the language of mainstream economics textbooks, people should move from high- to low-unemployment areas until wage rates are equalised.

Today we understand that is questionable advice. People are reluctant to move, and for a very good reason: they prefer to live where their community, family and friends are. That is where a good deal of their identity, rootedness and sense of self-worth comes from. Centrists who do not understand the point should watch the films *The Full Monty* and *Los Lunes al Sol*.

And when some young and enterprising people do move away, it is bad news for the communities they no longer call home. Social bonds break down, local productivity declines even further, and businesses also pack up and leave.[9] We know from the American Midwest, the north of England, certain regions of France and Spain, and many other places, that citizens who feel left behind are easy prey for populists and nasty identity politics.

As the experiences of Italy and the UK (two countries with a north–south divide) show, providing effective help for the heartland can be tricky. Levelling up is a good campaign slogan and a hard policy to implement. But the fact that it is hard should not keep centrist leaders from trying.

The key is to move away from transfers and income support, towards a 'big push' that expands the supply of goods which can be sold elsewhere and creates demand for services that can be sold locally. Cooperating with local companies to identify the public goods and services they need, easing the assimilation of productive know-how, and helping train workers in new technologies – those are among the components of a successful strategy.[10]

Another lesson is that some of the standard tools of economic and financial analysis should only be applied in conjunction with a generous dose of political good sense. Well-run governments compare alternative public investment projects and then choose those with the highest social rate of return. But what happens in the UK if, using this rule, almost all the public transport investments end up in London or the south of England, and very few in the north? Or, in an example from our country of birth, how do you explain to citizens in Chile's relatively poorer south that the lion's share of 'allowable' infrastructure projects will be built in Santiago, the nation's capital? Citizens who live on a road filled with potholes and served by few buses, whether on the outskirts of Sheffield, England, or Temuco, Chile, will have every reason to think that politicians have forgotten about them.*

Common sense on immigration

Most centrists are liberal, and liberals have good reasons to welcome the mobility of people and ideas across national borders. Communities that are open to the world are likely to be more creative, more productive and freer. And rich countries that receive migrants can help counter the undesired effects of a falling birth rate.

Both authors of this essay have been migrants more than once. We do not need to be convinced of the potential benefits of transnational migration. But we are cognizant – as are many centrist leaders – of the potentially deleterious political side effects of mass inward migration, the costs and benefits of which are unequally distributed across people and regions. This is an area where centrists and liberals should avoid hubris. Not everyone who worries about the impact of immigration on the fabric of local communities is a racist or a xenophobe.

The right migration policies will differ from country to country. But they must have one element in common to avoid becoming fodder for the populist monster: those policies must make intuitive sense to voters. A democracy is a community of people who have agreed to grant one another some rights (including economic and social rights)

---

* There is an additional twist to this argument. Because the population of cities like London or Santiago is huge, per capita infrastructure investment is often not that high. The reverse happens in sparsely populated faraway regions. But what residents of these regions see is gleaming new train lines in the capital, and none at home.

and to expect the fulfilment of some mutual responsibilities. It is not wired into the common sense of most voters that those rights should be automatically extended to anyone who wishes to cross the border, no questions asked and regardless of the volume of people wanting to come in at a given time. There is nothing wrong with regulating migration – nor with expecting that migrants will come to share some of the core political principles of their new nation (what John Rawls called the 'overlapping consensus'), learn the language and make an effort to integrate into society.

* * *

Donald Trump's slogan 'Make America Great Again' is the marriage of two interconnected promises: not only will America be great again, but Americans (of a certain kind) will make it great once more. 'Take back control', the slogan of the 2016 Brexit campaign, was even more explicit in its focus on willpower. What mattered was for Britons to seize the steering wheel. To take the country in which direction? That was left unsaid. The key was control.

Contrast that narrative with the standard centrist approach. A factory worker has lost his job? That is the inevitable result of impersonal market forces operating globally. Food prices have spiked? Well, that is the unavoidable impact of the Russian invasion of Ukraine.

The rhetoric of populists is all about will. The response of non-populists is all about the limits to the exercising of that will. Some might say the emphasis on limits is sound realism. Perhaps. But it is also very bad politics. Saying 'Sorry, but there isn't much we can do about it' just won't do.

And it need not be good economics, either. Healthy economic arrangements are all about risk-sharing. Not every risk can be shared, but many can be if centrist government leaders remain on their toes and govern creatively. Just as national security is too important to be left to the traditional right, economic security is too important for it to remain the exclusive domain of the traditional left.

We are in it together – that is the narrative these policies convey to the average voter. This is a government you can *identify* with. A government that works, first and foremost, for you. They are messages that voters need to hear. Otherwise, there is little hope of beating back nativist populism and the identity divides it feeds on.

SECTION 4

CENTRISM AROUND THE WORLD

For centrism to be a genuine political movement, it must apply beyond the narrow confines of a particular moment or a particular geographical boundary. If the principles, ideas and policies laid out so far are worthy of serious consideration, then there should be ways to apply them across the democratic world. This section looks at a selection of case studies and the broader lessons that can be learned from each of them.

Europe offers numerous examples of where centrism can succeed. Strong centrist parties exist both within the EU and across the continent. As Stéphane Séjourné and Sandro Gozi and Matteo Renzi articulate in their respective essays, Europe has become stronger, healthier and more prosperous due to those centrist influences.

With much of the writing on centrism coming from the UK, the USA and Europe, this section shines the spotlight on the role of centrism in some of the world's other large and most important democracies. In India and Brazil, polarisation has left people with fewer choices, a trend that both Simone Tebet and Dr Shashi Tharoor argue threatens the political stability in their respective countries. They both offer clear alternatives.

Across Latin America, countries too often veer from one extreme to another, holding back the potential for progress. There are centrist success stories here too, and a model for more. Centrist approaches have offered solutions to problems that plague Australia and Japan and the rest of the democratic world. Dr Tomohito Shinoda highlights the centrist approach through the prism of the unique Japanese debate around national security. Malcolm Turnbull takes the Australian example and eloquently uses it to explain the value of compromise, a point that comes through time and again across the pages of this book.

There is one thing missing from this section. I was unable to find African leaders willing and able to write about political centrism. The African leaders and writers I reached out to felt that centrism didn't apply to the politics in their country or were unsure about attaching the label to themselves. The failure to find those voices is mine, and it is a challenge that has to be addressed by centrist thinkers and writers going forward. I believe centrism has a role to play in African politics and can help nations across the continent improve the lives of their citizens and the long-term growth of their countries. Something about the message of centrism isn't resonating for them and we need to do more work to find out why.

Centrists can do much more to learn from one another. There is an enormous amount of collective wisdom and experience in centrist parties and organisations across the world. Using a political approach that embraces change and learns from failure, we should build on the success of others and learn from where they went wrong.

22

CENTRISM AND THE AUSTRALIAN MODEL: THE VALUE OF COMPROMISE

Malcolm Turnbull

For some years now, the voice of William Butler Yeats has been running on a loop in my mind:

> Turning and turning in the widening gyre
> The falcon cannot hear the falconer;
> Things fall apart; the centre cannot hold;
> Mere anarchy is loosed upon the world,
> The blood-dimmed tide is loose, and everywhere
> The ceremony of innocence is drowned;
> The best lack all conviction, while the worst
> Are full of passionate intensity.

He wrote 'The Second Coming' in 1919, a prelude to an apocalyptic foreboding. The world war was over, but the chaos and the bloodshed were not.

We are not living in the wake of a world war, although we may be on the eve of one. But whether we are given to forebodings of apocalypse, poetic or otherwise, Yeats's lines, more than a century old, seem to sum up the political problems of today.

Liberal democracies work best when the rivals for power have similar goals and ambitions. They work best when the side that is in government will be disappointed, but not overly anxious, when their opponents take their turn at the helm. Democracy, in other words, needs to operate at the centre where sensible people can reach compromises in the national interest.

A liberal democracy, which is what we understand to be a democracy in the Western tradition, both empowers and constrains the majority. An electoral system should ensure that the leaders or parties supported by the majority of voters are entrusted with government and authorised to set policy – until the next election. The rule of law should ensure that the majority, no matter how sweeping, cannot use that power to disadvantage or oppress the minority or to fundamentally change the rules of the game.

The first, majoritarian, element in democracy is well understood. The second is not only less well understood but increasingly no longer adhered to by some leaders in democratic systems. Donald Trump's attempt to overthrow the 2020 election result, and most of the Republican Party's support for him since, causes many people to question whether the GOP, the party of Abraham Lincoln, is still committed to the rule of law.

Many self-styled US conservatives profess great admiration for Viktor Orbán's 'illiberal democracy'. Mr Orbán is a regular guest on Fox News, a favourite of Tucker Carlson, and speaks at the CPAC conferences of *soi-disant* conservatives. His illiberal democracy, of course, is nothing more than a systematic attempt to ensure that power can never freely shift to another party.

In too many countries today, especially the USA, the political discourse is filled with angry and violent language. There is less debate on substantive matters of economics, national security or education and more and more on issues of culture and values which are most able to anger and divide people.

Some of these issues are genuinely about values, but increasingly matters that should be the subject of objective analysis are being embroiled in the culture war. The goal of those who promote them is more often not to build a healthier society which tackles complicated cultural issues, but to use them to divide and push the public away from the centre to the extremes. It is why centrists should be, and often are, the fiercest opponents of these culture wars. Centrists reject the extremist positions and binary nature that typifies the discourse populists are so eager to stoke.

A person can say, reasonably, that they believe in lower taxation and smaller government or higher taxation and bigger government. There is a perfectly reasonable argument to be had about the best model of education or health care for a country. People can also have differing opinions about sensitive cultural issues like gay marriage and abortion. But to say you believe, or disbelieve, in global warming is like saying you believe or disbelieve in gravity. Global warming is real. The climate is changing as a consequence. The policy debate can be about the best way to tackle that challenge. Political leaders are free to argue that we shouldn't tackle it (a position I suspect will be radically unpopular), but instead many populists choose to deny its existence all together.

Political rhetoric has become more vicious, more personal, more hateful. Those in a different political camp are to be despised. They are no longer political opponents but enemies. Trump set out to demonise Hillary Clinton and his cry of 'lock her up' was matched by an increasingly frenzied flood of claims that Clinton and her Democrat colleagues were satanists and paedophiles.

And if you have persuaded yourself that your political rivals are not decent people with a different political agenda but deeply evil, traitorous enemies of the state, how can you compromise? And if by some mischance these evil people win an election, how can you accept the outcome?

As Adam Kinzinger, a former member of the US Congress, observed to me, if you believe your political opponents are indeed satanists, don't you have a constitutional duty to take up arms to stop them taking office? The USA's founding story is, after all, one of armed insurrection against illegitimate government. But not even the most fervid American revolutionary contended that George III was a satanic paedophile.

The commercial reasons for this hyper-polarisation are obvious. Anger, hatred, fear – all the negative emotions – are more powerful motivators than positive ones. As they used to say in the television news industry, 'If it bleeds, it leads.' So whether it is a cable news service like Fox or social media platforms like X, YouTube or Facebook, the way to keep people engaged with the platform (and its advertisers) is by making them angry, fearful, hateful. This is the world of 'angertainment'.

There has always been a strong element of this in politics and media. But the digital age has seen at least two profound changes.

The cost of communications has been dramatically reduced. Each of our smartphones has the ability to broadcast a live video stream to a global (or very local) audience. In other words, these tiny devices have a capability that a generation ago was limited to only the largest media corporations and governments.

At the same time, it is now viable not only to monetise narrowcasting to tiny audiences that were in years past too small to commercially address but also to personalise media to individual consumers.

The consequence is that we are losing the shared factual reality that enables us to engage with each other in constructive political discourse. If citizens are in silos of differing realities – Trump's alternative facts – how can they collaborate to address national challenges?

So the commercial objective of many, if not most, of our media platforms, mainstream and social, is to maximise engagement with negative emotions that have the effect of dividing society and turning citizens against each other.

This type of division undermines democratic parliamentary government. It undermines the ability to build consensus, to compromise where necessary. It undermines the political centre which poses the most serious challenge to the political extremes.

Australia's parliament is bicameral, and as prime minister I had a generally supportive majority (albeit slender) in the House of Representatives. But, like most governments, we did not have a majority in our Senate, and as prime minister I was often accused of 'horse-trading', doing deals with the opposition, more often the crossbenchers, to get legislation passed by the Senate. Compromising was routinely denounced as a sign of weakness. But, as I often pointed out, our parliament is designed for compromise.

A previous prime minister, faced like I was with a Senate in which he did not have a majority, would berate the opposition and the cross bench, telling them to 'get out of the way' and respect his electoral mandate. That cry is often heard by those trying to emulate the illiberalism of Viktor Orbán. It is majoritarianism dressed up as democracy. Unsurprisingly, it didn't work in the Australian context. As I found out, a little compromise, some charm (if you can muster it) and genuine respect works much better. The parliamentary system is designed to bring people together for the purpose of compromise. It isn't a necessary evil but a fundamental and positive part of our political system. Compromise creates smarter and sustainable policy, and, in the end, that should be the goal of government.

Politicians from Westminster-style parliamentary systems like the UK and Australia used to remark on the loose party discipline of the US Congress and how often compromise could be effected by representatives and senators working across the aisle. But that was a long time ago. Nowadays the antagonistic partisanship is too intense. Similar trends are found in other democracies. Part of the role of centrists in modern politics is to build those relations, whether through centrist parties or collaboration across party lines, and enable compromise. If we are able to do that, we will improve political outcomes, increase trust in politics and push the populists back to the fringes where they belong and can do the least harm.

While we are not immune from these trends in Australia, they are less marked. For that we can thank not just our good sense, but a century-old electoral system that has three features which work to bring the political contest into the centre.

For a century, voting in national elections has been compulsory. A citizen over the age of eighteen is obliged to register on the electoral roll and to vote. We estimate that 97 per cent of Australian adults are on the electoral roll and, typically, around 93 per cent of them vote in parliamentary elections. Australians are habituated to voting. In 2017 in a rare, voluntary, national plebiscite on same-sex marriage, 79 per cent chose to vote (and 62 per cent voted to legalise it). Compulsory voting means that parties and candidates do not need to run off to the extremes to fire up their base and get them out to vote. Successful campaigns are waged by persuading the swing voters in the centre to go one way or the other. That creates a different type of political discourse and a healthy incentive for politicians.

A second feature is preferential, or ranked-choice, voting. Voters have to number each candidate in their order of preference. If one candidate secures a majority with his or her first preferences, then they are declared the winner. If not, the candidate with the lowest number of first preferences is eliminated and their preferences are distributed until one candidate has secured an outright majority. This also brings politics back to the centre, as was graphically illustrated at the 2022 federal election. Following my resignation as prime minister in 2018, the Liberal Party (Australia's largest centre-right party) was regarded by many of its traditional voters to have swung too far to the populist right on several issues and especially in its response to climate change.

In a number of very safe Liberal electorates (including my old seat of Wentworth in Sydney's affluent Eastern Suburbs), small-l liberal Independent candidates ran on a platform of climate action, integrity in government and respect for women. All were women and most of them won. As a result, there are now nine historically ultra-safe Liberal electorates represented in the House of Representatives by small-l liberal Independents – all women.

The preferential voting system allowed them to win. In most of these seats the Liberal candidates would have traditionally won easily with more than 50 per cent in first-preference votes. However, in 2022 the Liberal candidates' primary votes dropped to 40 per cent or less as traditional Liberal voters defected to the Independents, who also picked up votes from Labor and Green voters. So the first-preference result saw the Liberal incumbent with a primary vote of 40 per cent and the Independent with, say, 30 per cent. In a first-past-the-post system, as in the USA or UK, the Liberal, with a plurality, would have won. But in our system the preferences of Labor and Green voters were distributed, enabling the Independent to overtake the Liberal candidate and win on preferences.

In the USA, for example, a Republican voter who is uncomfortable with the Trumpification of the party can hold his or her nose and vote Republican, hold it a little tighter perhaps and vote Democrat, or simply stay at home. In Australia's system, our voters cannot stay at home (without paying a modest fine), but they can support a middle path and vote for an Independent centrist candidate.

Preferential voting is practised at the federal level in Alaska and Maine, and in both states the Republican senators and representatives elected are closer to the centre of politics than most of their colleagues. Liz Cheney stood up to Trump and lost her Republican primary in Wyoming. If she had run as an Independent Republican in the general election, and if ranked-choice voting had been applied, she would likely have won on Democrat preferences.

The message to the Liberal Party is clear: you cannot take your centrist liberal voters for granted. And in a House of Representatives of just 151 seats, it is very hard to get to 76 if nine of what had once been your safest seats are in the hands of liberal Independents, each of whom has built up a formidable local grassroots organisation.

The third element in our electoral system that supports a more centrist approach is that our electoral boundaries are drawn by an independent Australian Electoral Commission. There is no gerrymandering. This means that more electorates are contestable; a party membership may lean far-left or -right, but if they select candidates that reflect extreme views they run the risk of losing the seat altogether.

In the USA especially, widespread gerrymandering has meant that most Congressional districts are not genuinely contestable and can only be won by one of the two major parties. And so that means that the real contest is not the general election between Democrat and Republican but rather the party primary, where the choice is made by a smaller number of often very ideological party loyalists.

The Australian experience is that the design of the electoral system matters. A successful electoral system allows for a true reflection of the will of the majority, but also forces that majority to compromise, to take into account the minority and to build consensus. As others in this book argue, compromise and moderation are core elements of centrism. They are also fundamental to representative democracy – compromise, negotiation, horse-trading, if you like, is not a bug but a feature of liberal democracy.

However, wherever democracy is struggling, where the parties cannot compromise, where corruption is endemic and administration inefficient, in those circumstances some will look to 'the strongman' who can sweep all before him.

Tyrants have this in common with democratic governments – they invariably disappoint. But unlike democratic governments, removing them generally involves bullets rather than ballots. The last decade has reminded us once more that our democracy cannot be taken for granted. To defend it we must ensure it delivers the opportunities and security our citizens expect, and it is best able to do that when we work together.

In a frenzied world, the respect, compromise and moderation at the heart of political centrism are the best guarantees that our democracies will endure.

23

EUROPE AT THE CENTRE

Matteo Renzi and Sandro Gozi

The European, and indeed global, political landscape is undergoing profound changes. At a time when traditional parties are being called into question and democracies are suffering a crisis of representation, conservatism and populism on both the left and the right appear to be gaining ground. The participation or support of extreme right-wing movements in the governments of Italy, Poland, Hungary, Sweden, Latvia and Finland and the growth of the Rassemblement National in France and the AfD in Germany illustrate this worrying trend. At the same time, part of the European left seems to be radicalising, like the Nouvelle Union Populaire Écologique et Sociale (NUPES) dominated by La France Insoumise in France or the leftish drift of the Italian Democratic Party, casting doubt on their ability to govern. What extreme parties have in common is that they exploit people's fears and frustrations. The ideas they promote undermine political and economic stability as well as social cohesion. They seek conflict, not solutions; they emphasise identity politics, not building a shared identity.

In this context, centrist politics is the main bulwark against the rise of extremism, because it aims to bring together different political players and fosters a culture of compromise. We want to overcome the traditional divisions that no longer correspond to the real needs and new challenges of our societies.

In Europe, the different centrist movements and initiatives seek to build new public policies and concrete solutions by overcoming the traditional left/right divisions, which are more and more extreme, and offering a coherent and forward-looking alternative. Our initiatives are based on a clear set of values including individual freedom, equality of opportunity, confidence in individuals and new technologies, bold economic reforms, European sovereignty and power, strong countries with a renewed commitment to multilateralism, and an unwavering commitment to civil rights and the defence of minorities. Our centrist approach is not an old ideology but rather a political philosophy based on these values and on a different approach to government.

It is about harnessing and implementing good ideas, be they new or even if they come from the left and the right, to be as effective as possible. Embracing the best ideas of others is not a political weakness, it is a necessary strength. Modern centrist politics is therefore pragmatic and rooted in reality. In the face of authoritarian excesses, centrist politics is emerging once again as a responsible alternative that cultivates dialogue and cooperation between political persuasions to unite a country around a common vision. With the debate becoming increasingly polarised, different centrist parties need to cooperate. This approach can convince the majority of voters, insofar as it offers credible solutions to their concerns. Governing from the centre allows political leaders to maintain stability and national cohesion while implementing pragmatic and effective policies. Centrist political parties emerge as unifying and responsible forces, seeking to transcend artificial, and increasingly violent, polarisation by looking for concrete solutions based on evidence and pragmatism.

Centrist political parties have demonstrated their ability to create political and economic stability while avoiding extremist tendencies. In an unstable world, that is both a political and policy necessity.

But centrist politics is not always 'moderate': sometimes it must be very radical and disruptive, which means taking a clear direction and making clear-cut choices to reach the identified goals, as centrists are doing with the digital and green transformations. There is no place here for splitting the difference between right and left or searching for consensus based on the lowest common denominator. Strong centrist politics sets a clear path for owning the future and developing radical new solutions to radically new problems.

There is one area where centrism is still lagging behind our conservative and progressive rivals. While so-called 'National Conservatives' or the 'Socialist International' offer strong international networks, centrists are yet to build this new transnational dimension of politics. It is crucial to take back control of the complex and interconnected problems facing our societies such as climate change, technological innovation or migration issues, which all require experience-sharing and strategy at the European and global level.

To this end, centrist politics must grow beyond national boundaries and promote new transnational political movements which are absolutely indispensable in increasing the legitimacy and accountability of new European and global initiatives. And this is essential also to shape a more democratic and successful globalisation. In light of the last thirty years' experience and of the new challenges which have emerged, our response cannot be to close ourselves within national borders but rather to better choose with whom we want to share trade and welfare, under which conditions and through which structures.

At the European level, the influence of centrist political forces such as Renew Europe, the new alliances between European democrats, liberals and France's Renaissance Party, is crucial to preserving the cohesion and effectiveness of the EU and to building up a new sovereign and democratic European power. Centrist networks will strengthen centrist politics and also the countries and institutions in which they serve. Centrism has become a bulwark against excessive divisions that could weaken the democratic world's position on the international stage.

In the different European states, the example of Emmanuel Macron and his *En Marche!* movement, now renamed Renaissance, allied with the Democratic Movement of François Bayrou, testifies to the positive impact of central strategies in mobilising citizens around a shared vision for the country; in overcoming the deeply rooted resistances to change; and in seeking a centrist way that aims to both unleash energy and protect our fellow citizens.

To actively promote centrist strategy it is essential to promote new political alliances among like-minded parties, open to all those who share a common project for the country, for Europe and for the world, notwithstanding their previous affiliations. If parties are willing to change, if they are willing to share our principles and approach to politics, we should embrace them.

We are strongly committed to encouraging this new development, favouring a nuanced and thoughtful approach based on dialogue, tolerance and the search for common solutions to the future challenges facing individual countries and our continent. Centrism is sometimes accused of arrogance; this is the opposite. It requires modesty and a genuine willingness to take the best that others have to offer while seeking to balance the complicated values involved in running a modern country.

In conclusion, modern centrist politics is emerging as a positive and necessary political alternative in overcoming divisions, fostering dialogue and finding pragmatic responses to the complex challenges of today.

By embracing this path of balancing competing tensions and, crucially, of progress, we will shape a better future for countries and for the global community in which they operate. Centrist politics offers the opportunity to build a more united, prosperous and forward-looking society, overcoming the divisions that have hindered progress to date. By adopting a pragmatic, dialogue-based approach we can tackle the complex challenges of the twenty-first century while preserving our fundamental values and, in our case, our European identity, building the way to a better future for Europe and the world. Elections everywhere can and must be won at the centre.

24

HOW THE EU EMPOWERED CENTRISTS ALL OVER EUROPE

Stéphane Séjourné

There is a political drama that most Europeans are acquainted with: European Council summits, the quarterly meetings of the heads of state of governments from the twenty-seven member states of the EU. It is here that the biggest decisions are made on the future of the European continent: enlargement, new policies, and goals for the 450 million EU citizens. As in any international summit, an official photo marks history. In a way, it is a screenshot of the power dynamics of European politics, capturing the mood of the European electorates.

Browsing through those official photos from the 1960s to the early 2010s, the informed observer will be struck that almost all the participants were either Socialists or Christian Democrats or their equivalents. Just two decades ago, most household names were exclusively from these two families. On the right, Sarkozy, Merkel, Aznar, Berlusconi. On the left, Hollande, Zapatero, Kok, Persson, to name a few.

The same observer would also remark upon the stunning difference in these photos more recently. Close to half of the participants are no longer from the two old political families. Centrists and radical conservatives (and sometimes, but rarely, the radical left) have made their way to this temple of continental politics. Voters seemed to have had enough and have been ready to elect leaders outside the duopoly between traditional left and traditional right. That explains why President Macron of France, Dutch Prime Minister Mark Rutte and Estonian Prime Minister Kaja Kallas have become familiar faces at those events since the 2010s.

This reality is even more striking in the EU, where after sixty years of uninterrupted reign, the duopoly of centre-left and centre-right has given way to a three-party coalition where the centrists of Renew Europe, the political family that I led, are kingmakers.

So what happened? How have the two major forces that shaped a political debate across decades retreated so easily?

From my experiences in both French and EU politics, I would name one key factor: the EU. The EU has been a defining body for centrism, and that has led centrists to define the future of the EU.

European integration has been one of the most defining political adventures of our recent history, though it is constantly underestimated as a structural theme of our public discussion. This underestimation is what led to the fall of Social Democrats and Christian Democrats. They never fully succeeded in embracing a clear *and* consistent vision. Their hesitation led to their decline. Voters want a well-defined agenda for Europe. For more Europe or for less. But certainly not an unintelligible in-between.

Let's be clear: few citizens vote according to one's position on institutional reform and Byzantine debates about what the EU is or should be, and certainly not on the details of the EU's famous treaties. But the EU has embodied a choice of society. Open versus closed. Decisions based on knowledge and expertise or on outdated ideology. A willingness to influence the world or isolationism. Liberal democracy or electoral autocracy. Ukraine or Russia. The list is long and the ill-fated debate that led to the Brexit referendum in the UK highlighted the fundamental choices. Electorally, the EU is more than the EU. If you are not clear on the EU, you are likely to be unclear on other issues as well; its citizens sense that, no matter which side of the arguments they are on.

Ironically, European integration is first and foremost the creation of the two left and right blocs. What we call the 'founding fathers of Europe' are exclusively Christian Democrats or Social Democrats. But there has always been a part of their members – between a quarter and a half – that mistrusts the EU. The moderates of both those families fought hard to keep the EU moving forward in spite of the pressure of their more radical elements. In many ways they succeeded, but the public grew more and more uneasy to see ministers contradicting their prime ministers or presidents on EU issues. Many were puzzled as leaders yielded to the demands of their Eurosceptic wings – the British Conservatives were masters of this art. The most famous gift to their Eurosceptics was the Brexit referendum and the result that we're all still living with today.

In the meantime, centrist forces all over Europe have been consistent even when it was not so popular to be staunchly pro-European. For liberals, democrats and centrists, the free market and rule of law were better guaranteed at the European level than only within national borders, where dominant parties could be tempted to reverse those accomplishments.

It pays off hugely. In France, for example, the 2005 lost referendum on the European Constitution shaped the country, but the old political structures survived for more than thirteen years. Eventually, we created the alternative to represent and inform a new reality.

This referendum was my first active campaign as a young member of the Socialist Party (which was at the time relatively centrist). Like many citizens on the pro-European side, I felt I had much more in common with moderate centre-right pro-EU campaigners than with my own political comrades, who were against the European Constitution. After this hard-fought campaign, life continued like nothing had ever happened. Bipolarisation pretended that there was no such thing as a pro-European centre beyond party lines, and even worse, that if it existed it was a sideshow. For the old guard, EU politics was secondary, though everything indicated it was much bigger and the public understood that faster than its old leaders.

Thirteen years later, the candidacy of Emmanuel Macron ended, possibly for good, this artificial polarisation. Centrists from left and right found a home led by a man who did not hesitate to wave the EU flag at his own political meetings. The electorate appreciated this clarity and ambition, and France entered a new age when a centrist leader could actually govern and be re-elected. A first.

Did the big guys from the two dominant forces attempt to stop this process? Not really. In many ways they were afraid to pick a side, to reshape the political landscape. Form became more important than content. The old parties should survive, even if it meant that they were not ideologically consistent on the most pressing issues of the moment.

The appeal of Macron's candidacy was also based on the capacity to be indifferent to party structures. Citizens resonate first with ideological affiliation, then look at which forces represent them. Left and right in France thought – wrongly – that the electorate was captive and wouldn't dare to innovate at the polling station.

It is also a double-edged sword. At the same time that centrists rise as a clear alternative to the ruling parties, the same dynamics embolden extreme-right parties, which are also more consistent on the EU – just in the opposite direction. It is another classic case where the strongest opposition of the extremes is the centre.

These events are of course fascinating for European centrists, but they also offer a wider perspective for every centrist force in the world. The combined success of centrists and the EU present interesting ideas that can be summarised in three concepts: consistency of approach, embracing political innovation and always favouring content over format. Interesting, these counter some of the most common criticisms of centrism.

Consistency of approach

Centrism thrives on consistency, as it allows for trust-building and predictability among voters. Centrist politicians who articulate and uphold a consistent vision and policy framework can establish themselves as reliable leaders. By embracing the EU, centrists gained the advantage of presenting a unified approach to governance, reinforcing their credibility and electoral prospects. Their fundamental promise, that Europe is here to protect us, became tangible to voters in terms of vaccine development, the COVID-19 recovery plan and the response to the war in Ukraine.

Embracing political innovation

The EU's integration process has necessitated political innovation, creating opportunities for centrists to adapt to new challenges and ideologies. Centrist politicians, through their engagement with the EU, have been exposed to diverse policy approaches and perspectives, enabling them to refine and innovate their political platforms. This flexibility and willingness to adapt has allowed centrists to respond to changing societal dynamics, capturing the electorate's attention and support. It is particularly the case with the green transition. Though not the strongest suit of classic liberalism, environmental policies are now a core of European centrism. Centrist parliamentarians have battled day and night in order for EU legislation on climate neutrality to pass. European centrism is proving that green transition is better accepted and operated with technological solutions and progressive time frames than by the radicality of the first 'environmentalist parties'.

Favouring content over format

By prioritising political content, focusing on policy outcomes rather than rigid political structures, centrism's strength stems from its ability to provide a platform for implementing policies that address contemporary issues effectively and efficiently. What trapped the old left and the old right was that, while the EU was emerging as a key voting factor, they refused to see the consequences of this and preferred to keep their old structures and political spaces. It is no mystery, then, that most new parties that emerged in Europe, in Italy, in Bulgaria, in Slovenia or in Estonia, were born in the political centre. The old parties refuse to adapt and clarify their policies, leaving plenty of room for newcomers.

Of course, no reality is eternal. Even though I am convinced that the best days of centrism are still ahead of us at the European and global level, there will be also a time of reconsideration for our political family.

In the meantime, I will continue to advocate that centrism can succeed not by being a moderate halfway point between two old political adversaries that have exhausted their own electorates but by embracing a political 'radicality of consistency'. Centrism can be the alternative and a lasting governing majority if it has the courage to impose its own vision of the real choices we have to make collectively. Centrism does not have to jump into 'already-seen, already-made' culture wars to win. It can create its own holistic vision for society. Centrists should not fear to 'make their own kind of music', even when it looks electorally risky. This consistency and nuanced approach are the way to win the trust of voters in the long run.

For European centrists, the EU has been that differentiating backbone. Every centrist should ask themself what this foundation can be for them.

25

JAPAN'S POLITICAL CENTRISM IN NATIONAL SECURITY POLICY

Tomohito Shinoda

The Liberal Democratic Party (LDP) has been the predominant political party in Japan since its inception in 1955, in government except for two periods: 1993–4 and 2009–12. While the party is often considered to represent post-war conservatism, that analysis misunderstands Japanese politics. The domestic policies of the LDP have been more inclined towards a centrist liberal approach and the party always had a focus on the weakest in society, supporting them, reallocating wealth from urban to rural areas and pursuing economic growth. As a result, the opposition on the left had difficulty showing any distinct differences from the government when it came to domestic policies. It is this economic success of the post-war experience that has long kept the LDP in power.

Japanese politics during the Cold War era was often referred to as 'the 1955 system'. The ruling LDP and the largest opposition party, the Japan Socialist Party (JSP), were ideologically split, predominantly around national security. While the LDP was in favour of promoting close security relations with the USA and maintaining the Self Defence Forces (SDF), the leftist JSP was against these and hoped to establish an unarmed neutrality. The JSP was strongly influenced by the public-sector unions with a militant Marxist stance who supported it.

The LDP itself was never a solid, single entity but a coalition of factions which had different political and policy goals. These factions were often divided on how to deal with major foreign policy issues.

173

For example, in the 1970s the LDP was seriously split between pro-Taiwan and pro-China groups. The party even contained a group of right-wing nationalists who wanted to seek an independent national security policy. Interestingly, both the rightists and leftists shared a view that security reliance on the USA diminished Japan's sovereignty.

The centrist thinking within the LDP during this Cold War period was the so-called Yoshida Doctrine, designed by Prime Minister Shigeru Yoshida. This basic foreign and national security formula of depending on the alliance with the USA enabled Japan to focus on economic recovery with minimal military rearmament. The framework continued even after the 1960 revision of the Japan–USA security treaty which confirmed the asymmetrical nature of the alliance. The USA pledged to defend Japan, while Japan provided US forces with the use of its bases for the defence of Japan and the security of the Far East.

Japan's centrist national security policy, articulated by the Yoshida Doctrine, significantly contributed to its economic growth during the Cold War era. In 1968 Japan became the second-largest economy in the world. Its GNP reached 15 per cent in 1990, compared with less than 3 per cent in 1950.

Although the Yoshida Doctrine provided Japan with significant security and economic benefits, the subordination of its security policy to the USA negatively impacted Japan's national pride and international respect. Nations must consider three essential factors in the choice of national security principle: security, economy and independence. Centrists understand that smart policy demands a balance of competing values: it is impossible to maintain all interests all the time. Japan's centrist national security framework satisfied aspects of security and economy, but sacrificed its national security independence. Japanese leftists tried to pursue an unarmed neutrality which would be economical and independent, but would not provide Japan with real security.

The autonomous defence preferred by Japanese right-wing nationalists would have also offered more independence in foreign and national security policy, but would have sacrificed Japan's economic growth if it had pursued the capacity to defend without the security cooperation of the US forces. The centrist approach understood that, taking into account the geopolitical context and Japan's situation, abandoning either security or economic growth would have devastated the country. Those two interests had to be the priority, even at the cost of some impact on national pride and independence. It was a perfect example of centrist thinking in action.

Throughout the 1960s and 1970s Japan managed to maintain the centrist Yoshida Doctrine, and pursued liberal national security policies. After the 1960 revision of the Japan–USA security treaty, Prime Minister Hayato Ikeda further advanced the Yoshida line of an economy-first foreign policy. In 1973, Prime Minister Kakuei Tanaka made Japan's energy security a priority and pursued a pro-Arab policy, supporting Palestinian self-determination at the UN despite US opposition. Tanaka's successor, Takeo Miki, strengthened the arms export ban to stop the trade of virtually all military technology to any nation and introduced a ceiling on defence spending of 1 per cent of GNP. Prime Minister Takeo Fukuda announced the Fukuda Doctrine during his 1977 trip to Southeast Asian nations, and declared that Japan would not be a military power. His successor, Masayoshi Ōhira, introduced the concept of comprehensive security which emphasised diplomatic efforts for food, energy, environment and social security.

In the late 1970s, when Cold War tensions escalated, Japan's political centre shifted slightly to become more realistic and adapt to a changing reality. Washington pressured Tokyo to assume a more important role in the bilateral alliance. In 1978, Japan signed the Guidelines for Japan–US Defence Cooperation which provided a framework for bilateral defence cooperation plans in the immediate defence of Japan. The US government pledged to provide Japan with nuclear protection and offensive projection power, and to protect Japan's sea lanes in the Southwest Pacific and the Indian Ocean. In return, Prime Minister

Zenkō Suzuki promised to protect the sea lanes of the Northwest Pacific, north of the Philippines and west of Guam. Suzuki's successor, Yasuhiro Nakasone, further strengthened Japan's security role. He announced that Japan would serve as an 'unsinkable aircraft carrier' for US forces against Soviet aggression, improved anti-submarine warfare capability, and approved a defence budget which exceeded the 1 per cent of GNP ceiling.

After the Cold War was over, the asymmetrical nature of the alliance was questioned. As the Soviet military threat disappeared, the apparent value of the US bases in Japan decreased. Simultaneously, Washington expected Tokyo to begin to play a more significant role for international security. The 1990 Gulf Crisis became the first post-Cold War challenge to the alliance and to the Yoshida Doctrine.

The Japanese government could not find any legal basis to provide the personal and equipment assistance requested by the USA. Instead it provided a total of $13 billion of financial contribution to the multinational forces, but this was not appreciated by the international community and was even criticised by the US media as 'too little, too late'. The label of 'chequebook diplomacy' traumatised Japan's foreign policy establishment.

After the Gulf War was over, centrists in Tokyo voiced the need to contribute manpower to international security, and the government dispatched minesweepers to the Persian Gulf in April 1991. It was highly appreciated by the international community, and widely supported by the Japanese public as well. According to a newspaper poll, 74 per cent responded positively to the SDF being dispatched overseas for this mission. Building on this support, the Japanese parliament (Diet) passed the Peacekeeping Operation legislation to dispatch the SDF for UN peacekeeping activities in Cambodia and Angola. The operations by the SDF were widely regarded as a great success, and Tokyo could show its willingness and capability to contribute to international peace and security, rather than just throwing cash at the problem.

The second challenge to the national security concept was the North Korean Nuclear Crisis. In 1993, North Korea threatened to withdraw from the Nuclear Non-Proliferation Treaty, and conducted a test launch of a missile vehicle into the Sea of Japan. The US forces in Japan requested Japan's assistance, and their request listed as many as 1,900 items, ranging from grass-cutting at US bases to supplying fuel, material and weapons and using the SDF to sweep mines and gather intelligence. The Japanese government set up a task force to establish what it would be able to do, but once again found nothing under the existing legal frameworks.

Fortunately, the June 1994 visit by former president Jimmy Carter led to an agreement with Pyongyang to avoid a military confrontation. But officials in both Tokyo and Washington felt that it would be a disaster for the alliance if another crisis happened on the peninsula and Tokyo could not provide anything more than 'chequebook diplomacy'.

As a result of this experience, Prime Minister Ryutaro Hashimoto and President Bill Clinton made a joint declaration on security in 1996 to begin an extensive review of the bilateral defence cooperation guidelines. An agreement was made the following year to enable Tokyo to provide support to US forces during peacetime, during contingencies and during an armed attack on Japan and areas surrounding Japan. They included cooperation in search and rescue operations, inspections of ships during enforcement of economic sanctions, minesweeping, rear echelon support and the evacuation of non-combatants. The new defence guidelines strengthened the bilateral alliance, significantly reducing its asymmetrical nature. Centrists once again adapted to a changing reality while maintaining the basic principles of sacrificing the independence factor.

A further strengthening of the alliance came when Prime Minister Junichiro Koizumi swiftly reacted to the 9/11 terrorist attack by preparing legislation to dispatch SDF vessels to help the USA in collecting intelligence, shipping supplies and providing medical services and humanitarian relief. The bills were drafted and approved by the cabinet within three weeks, and enacted after just three weeks of deliberation in the Diet, an amazingly swift procedure for such a major, historically significant decision to send Japanese forces overseas to a combat situation for the first time since the Second World War. Japan showed its willingness and capability to contribute to international security.

The third challenge came under the government led by the Democratic Party of Japan (DPJ) in 2009. Prime Minister Yukio Hatoyama published an op-ed article in the *New York Times* in which he stated that 'as a result of the failure of the Iraq war and the financial crisis, the era of USA-led globalism is coming to an end', and he outlined his ambition to establish a more autonomous foreign policy strategy and develop closer relations with Asian neighbours to build an East Asian community. The DPJ government stopped the SDF refuelling activities for the multinational forces in the Indian Ocean and created a deadlock on the relocation of the Futenma air base. Some US experts saw these actions as a major setback and dubbed them a 'strategic disappointment'.

As soon as Prime Minister Abe recovered power for the LDP in December 2012, he moved again to improve the bilateral relationship. In 2014, the Abe government made a cabinet decision to reinterpret the Constitution to enable Japan to exercise the right of collective self-defence. The following year, new security legislation was enacted to expand the geographical area in which Japan would assist the US forces, to create a legal framework to exercise the right of collective self-defence, and to enable greater contribution to international security and multilateral cooperation. The new Japan–USA defence guidelines now account for seamless bilateral cooperation from peacetime to contingencies, and addresses cooperation in new domains such as cyber and space. They also provide a more effective alliance coordination mechanism and enhanced information-sharing, including information on defence equipment and military technology. As the geopolitical reality has shifted, so too has the approach to national security. Changes in the national security arenas demand reassessment, and it is an area where those bound by old ideologies struggle to adapt while the centre is able to create forward-looking policy.

In summary, while the rightists wanted to achieve autonomous defence and the leftists armed neutrality, Japan's centrists chose to rely on the alliance with the USA. During the Cold War era, the centrists preferred the economy-first policy under the Yoshida Doctrine. After the end of the Cold War, with serious challenges to the national security approach, the Japanese political centrists responded by gradually making the alliance less asymmetrical, dispatching SDF for peacekeeping operations, resuming refuelling activities in the Indian Ocean and helping with the reconstruction of Iraq, and playing a more dynamic role to maintain international peace with the new security legislation.

The centrist approach requires a balance of competing values, a realisation that in a complex world with complex challenges the answer is rarely simplistic. In Japan's case, the need for security, economic growth and national pride came into regular conflict. The centrist approach has been, and remains, to balance these competing interests, with the focus shifting depending on the context. This is the strength of centrism and why it remains the path forward for Japan. To pretend that national security policy can remain stagnant after dramatic changes like the end of the Cold War or the 9/11 attacks on the USA is to attempt to create a national security policy that is by definition out of step with reality.

As we look forward, Japanese centrism will have to offer a coherent approach to the major global and regional challenges we face. The return of great power competition between our closest ally, the USA, and our close neighbour, China, demands a balance between our security and economic needs. We cannot choose a binary approach that favours only our alliance with America or only our economic interests with China. Likewise, Japan must continue to play an active role in tackling global challenges like climate change and technological advances.

The isolationism or aggressive nationalism supported by some of the extremes in Japanese politics is unfit for the reality we face.

By charting a successful path forward on the critical issue of national security, centrists can continue to dominate Japanese politics and offer a roadmap for democracies across Asia on both domestic and international policy. That will lead to a stronger Japan and a stronger democratic Asia.

26

CENTRISM IN INDIA IN A TIME OF POLARISATION

Shashi Tharoor

This is a curious interregnum in world history. From the rise of Trumpism in the USA, Netanyahu in Israel, Orbán in Hungary and Erdoğan in Turkey to the gains made by the right in Germany, Austria, the Netherlands, Greece and France, we are seeing a striking rise in the popularity of populism, predicated on a resentment of globalisation, immigration and cosmopolitanism, and topped off by the cultural grammar of hyper-nationalism. The mere existence of groups like QAnon in America, or the neo-Nazi 'Third Path' in Germany would have been unthinkable even as recently as the end of the Cold War. When Francis Fukuyama wrote of 'the end of history' and the world waxed eloquent about the victory of liberal democracy as the time-sanctified supreme form of social, political and economic organisation, few anticipated the destructive potential of the backlash to the very consensus that was seen as the harbinger of global prosperity.

The trends that became apparent in the second decade of the century were reaffirmed in the atavism of the COVID-19 pandemic – when the time came for the world to stand in solidarity and cooperate to overcome a truly global health emergency, what we saw instead were tribalist, chest-thumping proclamations prioritising sovereignty over multilateral cooperation, all meant to play to domestic audiences. Countries rushed to procure and hoard protective equipment, medications and vaccines, vastly in excess of their own population's needs, leaving the less fortunate to fend for themselves. Remember also the assertion of xenophobic English nationalism underpinning Brexit, or the backlash against immigrants in many parts of the West, the very part of the world that had championed human freedoms and given birth to multiculturalism. Parties and leaders, combining nationalist fervour with popular prejudices, have made nationalism the default model of national self-definition. It is a far cry from the centrist heydays of Clinton and Blair, who steered their parties closer to where their opponents had been in order to reassure voters that they had moved away from ideological extremism. Today it comes as no surprise that liberal centrism – inclusive, non-judgemental and accommodative – is in decline in most parts of the world, while ideological extremes are precisely where many politicians believe their voters wish them to go.

Western critics decry liberal centrism for having 'left people behind'. More severely, its denouncers on the left argue that the 'centrist' approach to governance has historical ties to imperialism and colonialism, harbouring scepticism towards democracy and workers' rights while serving as a guise for capitalist exploitation. Throughout central and eastern Europe, several democracies that arose in the aftermath of the Cold War have undergone a significant shift towards majoritarian regimes. In these countries, political opposition is vilified; independent media, civil society and impartial judicial systems have been stripped of their power; and the leadership's primary goal is to defy external pressures to adopt Western principles of political diversity, government openness and acceptance of dissenters and minority groups. While the 'old democracies' still have plenty of room for centrism – Macron in France, Rutte in the Netherlands, and even Biden in the USA being prime examples – a look at the 'newer democracies' of Europe confirms that we are far from the golden age of political centrism.

It is in this strained global context that I turn to India. Indian politics has long been consensually centrist. The Indian National Congress, the liberal nationalist movement that dominated Indian politics for several decades, was a 'big tent' party that found room for all political tendencies, ranging from Marxian to feudal, within it, and still struck a golden mean. It was first challenged from the left by vigorous Communist and Socialist parties and then gradually from the right, by two dissimilar parties, the pro-free-market Swatantra and the Hindu-chauvinist Bharatiya Jana Sangh. Both disappeared, for different reasons, in the 1970s, merging into larger centrist formations, but the Jana Sangh re-emerged in 1980 as the Bharatiya Janata Party (BJP). The BJP then embarked on a steady rise in its electoral fortunes on a platform of Hindu revivalism and an end to the 'appeasement' of minorities. In 1996 it formed a short-lived minority government that collapsed in thirteen days. In 1998 it returned to power at the head of a coalition of twenty-six mostly regional parties, and stayed in power till 2004. In 2014 it won an emphatic victory at the polls, which it repeated in 2019. It has since embarked on a mission to reshape India in its own image – assertively Hindu, socially conservative, culturally reactionary and economically a curious admixture of welfare populism and crony capitalism. (It is called 'right-wing' by commentators, but not all its beliefs qualify as 'right' in the West's understanding of that term.) At any rate, it governs India from a standpoint that, in departing from previously well-established norms, is anything but centrist.

Since then polarisation has increased substantively in India, and from public discourse to dinner-table conversations the greys have given way to Manichean blacks and whites. The marriage of the BJP's Hindu nationalism or 'Hindutva' with Prime Minister Narendra Modi's cult of personality has given birth to a brand of politics I call Moditva. Moditva's route to populism, based on a vilification of the religious 'other' and a lionisation of ethnic nationalism, has struck at the very heart of the Indian consensus built around the centrism of the Congress Party. Though the Indian National Congress has witnessed considerable erosion in its strength and numbers in recent years, including several breakaway factions in different Indian states, most continued to adhere to its essential convictions – that there was room for everyone in the national consensus and that a multiplicity of ideas of India should be enabled to flourish.

One could, of course, argue that polarisation is merely a natural consequence of the pushes and pulls that are inevitable in a democratic polity. But the Indian discourse has taken on extreme hues that imperil both democracy and centrism, with the centrist opposition denounced as 'anti-national' and the prime minister repeatedly calling for a '*Congress-mukt Bharat*' or 'Congress-free India'. In October 2023 the ruling party even issued a social media meme depicting Congress leader Rahul Gandhi as the demon-king Ravana, the embodiment of evil whom the blessed god-king Rama had to destroy. Can centrism even be possible amid such a venomous political discourse, when opposition to the ruling party is literally demonised?

The Overton Window of political mobilisation (in other words, what is considered acceptable in the political arena) has become more vengeful, driven by resentment and an obsession to expiate past wrongs. Social media has emerged as an important tool through which the political benefits of this polarisation are reaped. The prime minister's obsessive attention to self-promotion – public relations optics, advertising and the spreading of fake news as a means of government propaganda – has become a key feature of Indian public life, while objective journalism is at a low ebb, with many mainstream media houses cajoled or cudgelled into craven submission. Incendiary WhatsApp forwards have been known to provoke violence in multiple instances, and most of these cases have involved stereotyping or vilification of Indian Muslims, who regularly find themselves under fire in Modi's 'new India'.

This polarisation is deliberate, orchestrated and has been a long time in the making. The 1990s was when these events came to a head: while the boons of liberalisation created an emerging middle class that anchored India's growth story, the successful agitation that ensured reservations, or quotas, for 'backward classes' in government jobs, university admissions and the like, increased opportunities for the underprivileged and so deepened India's democracy. The politics of religious identity reached its zenith with the demolition of the Babri Masjid in Ayodhya by Hindutva fanatics. The growth of India's middle class led to rising support for polarising Hindu nationalist narratives, and years of coalition government created a 'leadership anxiety' that turned to Modi's strongman persona for succour.

Modi scores as an avatar of development, epitomised by India's rapid progress in infrastructure development (highway construction and airport renovation are visible evidence of this) and the creation of a high-tech 'India stack' in digitisation that has turned Indians into internet users and experts at transferring money from their mobile phones. But the ruling party still seeks votes, and promotes political mobilisation, on a politics of bigotry, prejudice and overt Hindu chauvinism. To its credit, the motley opposition has not flocked to the other extreme itself. Instead, twenty-six opposition parties have converged into a centrist grouping, the Indian National Developmental Inclusive Alliance, or INDIA, to take on the ruling party.

This is all the more necessary since, with the concentration of power since 2014, polarisation is being employed to attack the crux of Indian democracy – its institutions. The highest levels of our autonomous institutions, from financial regulators like the Reserve Bank to institutions of accountability like the Central Information Commission, and even hitherto sacrosanct bodies like the Election Commission, have witnessed a striking dilution of their independence. The judiciary and even the free press are widely perceived as insufficiently clear of the government's influence. Think tanks have had their sources of funding slashed and their motives put under the microscope; harassment by tax officials is often the preferred route to rein in dissident voices. The Nehruvian parliament of old was premised on a reverence for institutions and institution-building. The erosion we see today of that legacy is manifest in routine disruptions of parliament (sometimes engineered by the ruling party itself!), skewed coverage of parliamentary debates, unwillingness to discuss issues of national importance (the border dispute with China and ethnic violence in Manipur being standout instances), and the comfort that the ruling party seems to find in passing bills amid the din. One can see how pitiful a situation this is by the fact of the opposition tabling a no-confidence motion just to get the prime minister to speak in parliament on a burning issue he has preferred to remain silent on.

As long as Modi remains dominant, dissenting voices within the ruling party are not heard in public, though many mutter *sotto voce* that they are not happy about these developments. Given that, in addition to the vocal and visible Hindu chauvinists in the party, the BJP includes a smattering of technocrats and former bureaucrats whose instinct would normally be to govern from the centre, one could well ask if it might be possible to create broad agreement between them and the opposition. But in the Indian political context today, electoral logic prevents any of the positive forces in the BJP who lean towards centrism from jumping ship. In other democracies it is possible to hear centrist voices in more than one party, but the few in the BJP are either muffled or silent, preferring to stay on the 'winning side' or biding their time for more propitious circumstances. Mercifully there are no 'extremists' in the opposition who might deter the emergence of a progressive centre. But the national polarisation has gone so far that the very prospect of cooperating with the BJP is anathema to the rest.

In their 2023 book *The Civic Bargain: How Democracy Survives*, Brook Manville and Josiah Ober argue that democracies that survive in the longer term do so because of their adeptness at negotiating a civic bargain – a political pact about who is a citizen, how decisions are made, and the distribution of responsibilities and entitlements. For India, that civic bargain was always centrist – embedded in the Constitution's commitment to balance the sanctity of individual rights with the social attachment to communal norms. The Moditva-directed change in the nature of political discourse, threatening the rights of citizens of other faiths to consider themselves as Indian as any Hindu, undermines that compact, for it dubs any accommodation of minorities or attempt to reach out across the aisle as 'vote-bank politics' and 'appeasement', and any dissent as 'anti-national'. The disdain for a centrist opposition has made the creation of political common ground suspect, thereby stiffening the challenge of reviving centrism.

Where then, in this age of polarisation, does Indian centrism find the space to define itself?

This is where one must take refuge in the past. I defer to the chairman of the Indian Constitution's Drafting Committee, Dr B. R. Ambedkar, who was deeply perceptive of the conflicts that could mar the Indian constitutional project he was launching. In the contestation between the wielders of power and the drafters of law, Ambedkar carved a triumphant place for enabling change through democracy and legislation. He birthed the concept that helped anchor Indian centrism – 'constitutional morality'. Ambedkar realised that it 'is not a natural sentiment. It has to be cultivated.' It was 'a commitment to constitutional means, to its processes and structures, alongside a commitment to free speech, scrutiny of public action [and] legal limitations on the exercise of power'. In his view, constitutional morality could only be realised through an administration which is in tune with the spirit of the Constitution, and through the cultivation of constitutional values among the masses. This constitutional view of centrism assumed that it is not merely neither-this-nor-that, nor is it avoidance of activist politics. It rejects the extremes of ideological excesses on both sides but actively pursues an engaged middle course. Of course, as the saying goes, the risk of being middle-of-the-road is that you could be run over by traffic from either side! For Ambedkar it was a constitutional duty to defeat the forces of feudalism, casteism, bigotry and parochialism. This was centrism as action.

To note the application of this uniquely Indian spirit of centrism, you have to look no further than the Directive Principles of State Policy

– an unusual feature of the Indian Constitution not found elsewhere. The principles confirmed that 'whoever captures power will not be free to do what he likes with it'. Beyond being 'directive' in that sense, they also acknowledged that reform and social transformation (though radical in nature) can be successful only through incremental steps. Accepting that reform has to be both top-down and bottom-up, the Constitution infused the idea of Indianness, so brilliantly articulated by Jawaharlal Nehru and his acolytes, with an extra dimension through Ambedkar's lens of social justice for those who had been oppressed and marginalised for millennia. Political scientists Alfred Stepan and Juan Linz call India an example of the 'state-nation' model, in contrast to the European nation-state model. While a nation-state aligned the boundaries of the state and nation, a state-nation allowed for a multiplicity of 'imagined communities' to coexist beneath a single democratic roof by recognising that citizens can have multiple, overlapping identities that need not detract from a larger sense of national unity. Thus emerged the civic nationalism of the Constitution, which occupied the centre by balancing the rights of the individual (as championed by the West) and the rights of the community (flowing from the Indian attachment to communal norms).

Given that the 'state-nation' predicates national allegiance on values and not on religious or ethnic identity, India's very foundation is amenable to centrism. Unlike European nation-states of the nineteenth century, the only commitment Indians need to make to qualify as Indian is an allegiance to the values enshrined in a markedly liberal Constitution. The spirit of accommodating the idiosyncrasies of the plethora of identities Indians have is in itself centrist. Thus, progressive centrism is embedded into the anchorage of our constitutional democracy, the revival of which is complementary to democratic revival in a polarised India.

Similarly, the construction of an Indian nationalism capable of surviving the vagaries of a hostile and uncertain post-colonial world included taking the 'middle path' too. Neither did India choose to lose itself in reveries of past greatness and glorifying everything pre-colonial, nor did it choose to reject its heritage entirely and conform to the Western ideal of what a nation should look like. Today's BJP nativism, tracing every modern achievement to an imagined Vedic precursor in ancient India and asserting that everything worth celebrating in human civilisation had already been anticipated by our Hindu forebears, has moved far from that consensual centre.

The centrist understanding of the Indian project is all the more necessary because too many scholars and commentators have remained impervious to the contribution a centrist approach added to our nationalist imagination. Any roadmap to revive progressive centrism in India must be sensitive to the cultural, socio-economic and political specificities that make the Indian context unique. For instance, India does not strictly abide by the European political spectrum of 'left', 'right' and 'centre'. Many Western outlets refer to the BJP as the 'Hindu right wing' when, in fact, the basis of much of their claims to economic glory has been their strengthening of the welfare schemes introduced by the Congress government (leading one Indian journalist to call the BJP the 'Hindu left'!). Those seeking to resuscitate the centre must first coalesce on what that project means for them, before they chart out how to garner popular sentiment for it.

In India, the centre will also have to tilt slightly leftward because of our very large population of poor people, marginalised communities and minorities, who need the government's help. Making policy choices in a democracy with a majority of poor voters (living below $2 a day) predisposes electable politicians to focus on the needs of the poor. While we proudly enjoy the fruits of economic liberalisation, we must also be sure to make the distribution of those fruits a primary priority. The Congress-led United Progressive Alliance government did so in the form of redistribution of enhanced government revenues, with an eye on those who were excluded from the direct benefits of liberalisation.

A liberal economy with an emphasis on social justice is, in essence, centrist. A strong and credible foreign policy with a robust national security capacity is centrist. An emphasis on pluralism and inclusion of all, and a rejection of majoritarianism and communal bigotry, is centrist. It's high time to forge a consensus to revive that progressive centrism in India.

India is a country that is much more than the sum of its parts – where citizens can disagree on everything, as long as they agree on the ground rules of how to disagree. In this central understanding are the seeds of reviving progressive centrism in India: the promotion of consensus, a moderating constitutional influence through the restoration of checks and balances in our institutions, a pluralist ethos and free media and civil society. It is to that kind of political centrism – to paraphrase Tagore – that we must unite to let our country awake.

The author gratefully acknowledges the assistance of Armaan Mathur in the preparation of this essay.

27

THE FUTURE OF LIBERAL DEMOCRACY IN LATIN AMERICA: IN SEARCH OF A CENTRE

Mauricio Cárdenas and Eduardo Levy Yeyati

Much has been said about the growing political discontent throughout Latin America, where a declining percentage of the population is satisfied with democracy – even in countries where social indicators have been improving such as Chile, Colombia or Peru.

The symptoms of this malady are well known: a mistrust of the system; a disenchantment with traditional politics and politicians; a social fatigue prone to explode into civil unrest and massive demonstrations that conflate multiple social demands (on immigration, fiscal transfers and income support to the poor, identity politics, access to quality public goods and services) from increasingly vocal groups; and the rise of outsiders with a vague anti-system rhetoric catering to, and further fuelling, ideological extremes and antagonistic polarisation.

These symptoms are not new, only this time the sentiment of frustration is channelled through leaders who operate within the system, rather than outsiders trying to emulate the Cuban Revolution as in the 1960s and 1970s. And caution is needed not to overly generalise a phenomenon that differs across countries, with leaders who may share little more than a few selfies and communiqués and use a common rhetoric but are immersed in their own domestic political struggles.

But the most prominent Latin American faces of today's 'politics of emotion' – Jair Bolsonaro, Nayib Bukele, José Antonio Kast or Javier Milei on the right; Andrés Manuel López Obrador, Gabriel Boric or

Gustavo Petro on the left – do have some things in common. They have blossomed as a direct challenge to traditional politics, exposing the fissures of liberal democracy and hollowing out the distribution of voters to the extreme positions of outsider populism. A salient feature is anti-establishment rhetoric and the constant clash with liberal technocracy, dividing society into two antagonistic groups: 'the pure people' and 'the corrupt elite', to use the words of Cas Mudde.[1] The politics of 'us' vs 'them' is what has taken hold in Latin America.

What's wrong?

There is a paradox that goes as far back as the nineteenth-century work of Alexis de Tocqueville: social frustration often grows as social conditions improve. We've seen this in Chile, where demands for better public services have been renewed and refined as a result of social progress over many years. Colombia is another illustrative case: the worst wave of street unrest in recent history took place right before the pandemic, as the country was closing two decades of significant reductions in poverty rates. Tocqueville was right: social progress in Latin America has finally created the need to break with historical forms of discrimination and exclusion.

But that view, if anything, is certainly only a small part of the story. Perceived (and often actual) unfairness in access to public goods and services (education, transportation, housing) or the social glass ceilings of a 'caste society' are seen as hampering the promised social progress. The prevalence of socio-economic origin and connections over human capital and effort, if not corruption in the form of interest groups, revolving doors and cronyism, reveals a society of privileges that betrays the balance between opportunity and merit that is at the root of the modern liberal credo.

And there is more.

With a few exceptions, there is in the region a rising awareness of an economic underperformance relative to the rest of the world today, or to the region's golden years. Talk of 'lost decades' has been common-place in Latin America and is the present sentiment, with no hope of a brighter future ahead. Rather than resorting to the politics of modera-tion, voters seem more willing to revive 'caudillos',[2] strongmen with almost unlimited power, hoping that they perform a magical trick – or, in the more likely case that they bring another round of disillusion and unfulfilled promises, they will at least take the establishment down with them.

There are also the long-standing shortcomings that revamped social policies were supposed to fix, but did not. Take, for example, social exclusion or, more generally, the insider-outsider divide in our soci-eties that mirrors the dual formal-informal structure of labour markets. There is also a growing population dependent on fiscal transfers in many countries, which does not help to attenuate the perception of unfairness. Season this with the diminished expectations from a dec-ade of stagnant social progress, even reversals in some countries, and a weak economic outlook, and the negativism that may initially seem a subjective Tocqueville disappointment starts to look more like a very objective pessimism.

Overpromising and underdelivering have been the main fuel of dissatisfaction. The benefits of free trade, deregulation, privatisation and many other reforms were oversold, generating not just fatigue but distrust. The backlash is not against the Washington Consensus, but against everything that sounds technocratic. More than counter-reforms, the new leaders promote revisionism, empowering those who have been historically marginalised and discriminated. At the other end of the spectrum, rather than empowerment of the marginalised what is visible is the use of national security as a political tool.

What's next is uncertain, and probably frustrating, but there is a silver lining: it could be an opportunity for a revival of centrism, if democratic institutions are not undermined in the process.

The middle-class mirage

Latin America's middle class doubled in size between 2001 and 2015, reaching almost 200 million, or one in every three individuals according to a study by the Washington-based Brookings Institution in 2015. This unprecedented expansion was driven by rising commodity prices coupled with pro-poor policies, especially conditional cash transfers. The growing middle class played a role in driving demands for progressive tax policies (which did not materialise) and greater social spending (which accelerated during the boom years but then fell to historical averages).[3]

The growth of the middle class was seen as a potential catalyst for development, including political stability. Unfortunately, these expectations did not materialise, for two main reasons. First, the end of the commodity boom meant a loss of household income and government revenues. By 2018, poverty had risen above the levels of a decade earlier. A second blow came with the COVID-19 pandemic, which in some countries increased poverty rates by more than 10 percentage points, reversing much of the progress made since the early 2000s.[4]

Second, there is a qualitative difference between a society with a growing middle class and a middle-class society. Higher incomes do not always translate into a higher quality of life, since a large part of household consumption includes publicly provided goods and services. Think, for example, of a new middle-class worker who enjoys a higher real income but suffers a two-hour daily commute on packed trains or buses, purchases private health insurance to escape the long lines in under-resourced hospitals, and pays for private education to avoid decrepit school buildings operated by a strike-prone public education system. One growing trend in the region is the reliance on privately provided forms of security. No wonder why Nayib Bukele in El Salvador or José Antonio Kast in Chile build their support on the need for a public safety overhaul.

These limitations in public services can be seen as the flip side of a fiscal structure where direct subsidies and transfers have crowded out investment in public utilities, transportation or security, and where government revenues have remained relatively stagnant.

But there are other reasons behind the middle-class disappointment. A middle class that does not save (and hence does not accumulate wealth) is by definition unstable as it can easily slip back into poverty (as the COVID-19 pandemic dramatically illustrated). And things can be worse, as one of us pointed out in a World Bank report,[5] when surveys suggest that middle-income families favour the consumption of depreciating durable goods such as cars and televisions instead of investing in real estate. This vulnerability is compounded if those purchases are financed by credit, which allows consumption to rise faster than incomes at the expense of larger debts that may leave households worse off in the end – an irony often missed by promoters of financial inclusion as an indiscriminate access to credit.

Another aspect to consider is that cash transfer payments are not seen as a reliable and secure source of income. Recurrent fiscal crises, changes in macroeconomic conditions, or even changes in governments have made households aware that social programmes expand and contract overnight, without notice. Volatile and unsecure transfers cannot be the basis of a middle-class society.

Thus, there are good reasons to argue that manifestations of this discontent can be attributed in part of the downfall to a frustrated middle-income miracle.

It's the politics

Lack of investment in resilient state capacities might seem an obvious shortcoming that governments would readily sort out. But there are political reasons why they do not. Voters tend to credit increases in minimum wages, pensions and social transfers to the government that provides them, and punish those that try to increase taxation.

By contrast, the benefits of public investments are slower to be felt, and their beneficiaries are more diffuse. Politicians operating on short electoral cycles inevitably target public spending at potential backers.

Put all this together and there is no surprise that the new and fragile middle class was the first to express discontent and embrace polarisation. Instead of owning and anchoring the system and preferences that support moderation and centrism, it has disowned it.

Moreover, this state of affairs has feedback effects: polarisation begets uncertainty which has a clear impact on economic performance, as the pendular nature of polarised policies may deter investment. Thus, a vicious circle emerges: a weak economy creates the conditions for the voting base of populism to strengthen. Populist leaders then undermine and weaken the institutions of the state which are needed to build and implement effective policies. Weakening institutions is also functional for populists to remain in power even when economic conditions deteriorate.

And traditional politicians are not taking notice.

To the previous list of 'demand' factors we need to add an important 'supply' consideration: the obsolescence of the political class. Professional politicians repeating tired speeches like Warren Beatty's Bulworth are pushed to retirement by new generations with broader interests and a natural rejection of patronising clienteles, using activism, social media and confrontation as a substitute for bureaucratic and budgetary power.

The very presence of outsider populists embodies the drivers of anti-politics and the shortcomings that need to be addressed to revive the basic social contract of our democracies. It is clear that policymaking and politics are not delivering what society is expecting: the traditional 'rational' swing between centre-left and centre-right looks unappealing and its agenda sounds dated.

The real question, then, is: can we restore the politics of moderation, the use of evidence, the blending of markets and state, without revitalising a 'political class' (however it is defined) that is tone-deaf, indifferent or unable to rebuild trust? Traditional political parties are perhaps necessary for this transformation, but that does not mean traditional politicians. How can the current cast of political players be renewed – or, at least, revamped? Where to start?

This book in part tries to identify the beliefs that characterise centrism. Words like balance, moderation and pragmatism come to mind. The problem with these concepts is that, in isolation, they do not mean anything concrete and, even when they do, they remain unappealing to many audiences, especially the young, who see them as synonyms for the status quo.

Another relevant part of the centrist identikit is the propensity to negotiate a solution between diverse interests. The ability to compromise also has negative connotations where it is interpreted as continuity or, even worse, back-door dealings. Centrists are democratic reformers and know that deep changes need broad, albeit partial, approval. In that sense, they differ from populists who, typically uncomfortable with the division of powers, the right of minorities and the search for agreement, tend to favour policy referendums as a shortcut to autocratic processes.

So how can terms like moderation and negotiation be refreshed? What should be included within them to make them attractive again? What are the psychological underpinnings of the revenge-thirsty polarisation that need to be addressed by politics, before policymaking addresses the real challenges?

Whatever the answers to these questions are, there is no point in criticising polarisation or whining about the newcomers; they are just filling the void left by old-fashioned politics. Until it is replaced by a new narrative that is viable and inspiring enough to compete with the three-chord punk of outsider populism, a reform agenda that meets the new expectations and brings voters back to the centre will struggle to find an audience. There are, however, examples where this narrative can succeed.

What should this narrative look like?

There are no silver bullets in this effort. The new centrists need not only to innovate (in their priorities, strategies and communication approach); centrism should become a new political movement, not a return to the past.

Indeed, a crucial starting point is to reinvigorate the centre with a new breed of politicians willing to break with the practices of corruption, nepotism and clientelism that have for so long characterised politics in Latin America. The centre cannot be a home for the recycling of insiders, masquerading as a transformation. The goal should not be to resuscitate the centre but to reinvent it.

Any *gatopardismo* or bogus staff change would be easily noted, only feeding back into further mistrust.[6] While not every experienced politician is of the same mould, as they are often perceived to be, new centrists, and even old ones, would need to get out of the 'politician' stereotype where years of – sometimes warranted – typecasting have cornered them. A strong rupture with traditional politicians is mandatory. Short-term opportunistic alliances will only undermine the viability of the political project.

This new brand of centrism will also need to master the novel communication tactics that populists have excelled at, such as the use of direct and simple messages and an appeal to emotion (positive emotions of hope rather than negative feelings of rage and fear) without falling into the trap of polarisation or unfounded promises that will inevitably lead to disappointment. It will need to be unapologetic about its beliefs and unafraid to take on the populists and the myths that they sell to the public. Crucially, those tactics must be governed by a strategic direction: moderation and balance should not be confused with tolerance.

Last but not least, new centrists need a new policy agenda. True, they will still have to break with the region's pervasive manifestations of inequality and exclusion, and the resulting diminished expectations behind the non-cooperative, every-man-for-himself attitude that often characterises outsider populism. And they will need to promote policies that improve living standards in the short term without compromising long-term sustainability. In other words, new centrists have to yield tangible results while avoiding the unattractive 'short-term pain, long-term gain' rhetoric that breeds frustration and scepticism, ultimately empowering the populists. Inclusiveness, transparency and sustainability should be the keywords of the new call to action.

But a new centrist agenda also requires a deep change in political habits, a shift from quantity to quality, from the old-fashioned, passive distribution through fiscal transfers that make up for the failure of the welfare state to modern, proactive policies that prioritise labour training and access to quality public services, and a leaner and more efficient state. Actions that prove that politics is at the service of the people and not the other way round, as often perceived. In short, policies for fairness.

Finally, a new centrist agenda is bound to be a broader and younger one, covering the new inescapable challenges: environmental care, technological innovation, migration and demographics, security, and the ever-changing balance between labour and leisure. This could be critical to engage with younger constituencies that will soon become the decisive majority in most Western democracies – not only as an opportunistic gesture: representatives need to represent more than just their own age-specific concerns.

Centrism has the answers to many of Latin America's problems. Centrists are capable of reaching a balance between short-term improvements and long-term results. Reforming and investing in areas that directly impact the middle class's ability to grow steadily – education and health care, infrastructure and personal security, connectivity and access to credit – while preserving macroeconomic stability has been the cornerstone of the centrist approach. However, the failure of populists is not bound to win back the lost electorate; it could send our battered democracies into a widening pendular swing between improvised right and left populism for a number of years in a negative-sum polarisation game.

To avoid this democratic undoing, we need a true regime change within the political tribe: a new breed of politicians that translates a broad and rejuvenated policy agenda from technocratic programming into a political platform with a sense of mission, including concrete actions in the areas that matter the most to voters. If a crisis is also an opportunity, we are facing the opportunity of the century to rewrite the political centre, the backbone of Western liberal democracies.

28

THE CASE FOR A DEMOCRATIC CENTRE IN BRAZIL: OVERCOMING POLARISATION

Simone Tebet

In recent years, elections in Bolivia, Brazil, Chile, Colombia, Honduras, Mexico and Peru have given the impression of a 'new pink tide' in Latin America – the name some analysts gave to a wave of newly elected leftist leaders in the early and mid-2000s. The new stream of political change in the 2020s appeared even more prevailing than the original pink tide two decades ago, which radically altered politics in the region. But the state of play now is distinct in some very important ways.

People tend to look to the current political landscape in Latin America as a rigid dispute between right and left. Yet what has recently characterised politics in the region – and Brazil in particular – is a concern with political instability and the rise of authoritarianism. In a region that has been a haven for democracy and diversity, some countries had to put up a fight just to safeguard their institutions.

Brazil's presidential election in October 2022 was an emblematic moment. President Lula da Silva, an icon of the original pink tide, narrowly defeated his far-right rival, Jair Bolsonaro. I was a candidate during that election, representing the Brazilian Democratic Movement Party. My decision to run – in what I considered a crucial moment for Brazil's history – was motivated by my strong belief in the democratic centre and in its capacity to pacify and unite the country, as well as to provide much-needed public policies to rebuild Brazil from the devastation caused by the pandemic.

For the unfamiliar reader, let me introduce myself: I was born in Três Lagoas, in the state of Mato Grosso do Sul, an agricultural power-house in Brazil's Midwest region – home to one of the most important biomes in South America, the Pantanal. I started my professional career as a law professor in 1992. In 2002, I was elected for a seat in my state's legislative body. In 2004, I was elected mayor of my home town – and re-elected four years later. After serving as lieutenant-governor, I was elected in 2014 to Brazil's Senate for an eight-year term.

In Brazil's Upper House, I was the first chair of the Committee to Combat Violence Against Women, created in 2014. I also served for two years as chair of the Constitution and Justice Committee – the first woman to lead this important board, through which all bills must pass prior to a floor vote. After the 2022 presidential election, then President-elect Lula da Silva invited me to be a member of his cabinet, as minister of planning and budget.

Coming from a Brazilian Midwest state, I have always championed the values of free enterprise and limited government. And I understood that these goals were inseparable from an unswerving commitment to equality of opportunity and the rule of law. Growing up in Mato Grosso do Sul made me a first-hand witness to the importance of Brazilian agriculture and livestock towards a green and sustainable world. My experience as a law professor – and my understanding of Brazil's Constitution – made me an advocate of social justice, particularly gen-der equality. As minister of planning and budget, I have also advocated that Brazil – a country which suffers from serious inequality – needs a functioning, fiscally responsible state capable of providing a strong social-safety net: health care, education, sanitation, environmental pro-tection and income distribution.

Above all, my political career has been marked by a basic prin-ciple: that democracy is an irreplaceable instrument for ensuring human dignity and justice. My party – the Brazilian Democratic Movement (MDB) – is one of the most traditional political parties in Brazil. It was established in 1966 to unify nearly all the opposition to the military dictatorship (1964–85). It led the struggles to re-establish democracy in my country, such as the reinstitution of political rights to persecuted individuals (amnesty), the return of direct elections to the presidency of the republic (*Diretas Já!*), and the formation of a constituent assembly in 1987, which resulted in Brazil's 'Citizen Constitution' of 1988 – our modern-day version of Magna Carta.

Today, the MDB still has the greatest political representation throughout Brazilian municipalities, with the highest numbers of mayors and city councillors. It was the party of four former presidents since Brazil's re-democratisation. The MDB is one of the few Brazilian parties to have maintained a consistent political profile since its founding. It is a centrist party with a fundamental commitment to democracy – its core principle. The inspiration of the party's programme has always been the *democratisation* of Brazilian life – on the political, social and economic levels. As a member of the party throughout my political career, I have echoed, and helped shape, this commitment.

The MDB came about in a moment of Brazil's history marked by authoritarianism, governmental inefficiency and intolerable social exclusion and injustice. But it was also a moment for the awakening of a people, amid brutality and disappointments, in a collective call for democracy, citizenship, equality and justice. In 2022, I believe we went through something similar.

Prior to the 2022 presidential election, my participation in the Senate and, specifically, in the Parliamentary Commission of Inquiry to investigate Jair Bolsonaro's disastrous response to the COVID-19 pandemic – which killed more than 700,000 Brazilians – made me well known to the Brazilian public. With indignation, I saw a president turn his back on science and endanger the health and lives of his fellow citizens.

I was part of an exhaustive and detailed investigation into why Bolsonaro's administration promoted ineffective treatments such as hydroxychloroquine; why three health ministers were removed during the pandemic; what caused a devastating health-care collapse in the Amazon (when, in January 2021, hospitals ran out of oxygen and patients died of asphyxiation); and what led to the delay in the acquisition of vaccines. The final report of the Parliamentary Commission of Inquiry was weighty, providing nearly 1,300 pages of robust evidence against the former president and many of his officials.

But the mismanagement of the COVID-19 pandemic was not the only malaise afflicting Brazil in recent years. Political polarisation in the country was shockingly severe. In many democracies around the world, the rise of deep political divides has many causes, but one stands out: a loss of confidence in political institutions and in their capacity to act for the benefit of the people. This loss of trust in politics crippled efforts for legislative compromise, eroded behavioural norms and encouraged politicians to pursue their aims outside of gridlocked institutions. The crisis of confidence, which preceded the pandemic, was a fertile ground for the rise of authoritarianism. In Brazil, what started with indignation at corruption and economic stagnation evolved into radicalism and destruction.

Destructive polarisation leads to the division of society into mutually distrustful political groups. Ideological partisan identities can drive the public away from social norms that support a deliberative democratic system. In a politically divided society, it becomes easy to characterise the other side as fundamentally twisted or evil. Polarisation is also fuelled by the deliberate promotion of fear and uncertainty, through the mass creation and circulation of misleading news, rumours, conspiracy theories and lies, which can be widely disseminated through social networks – making the very openness of democratic societies a tool to be exploited by its enemies.

As difficult as it can be, I firmly believe that democracies can depolarise. In my view, the institutional crisis that many democracies face today is the direct result of a political crisis. But the solution to this crisis does not lie outside politics. Engaging in political conversation is the most effective way to re-establish trust and break the gridlock. And the best position to engage in that critical dialogue is from the political centre. I believe that no strong democracy can flourish without a big centrist movement capable of promoting the alliance of all democratic forces, especially in times of crisis. Democracy is at risk when there is no political association that constantly seeks to close the gaps opened by exacerbated polarisation and build moderate alternatives.

In 2022, the restructuring of a centrist movement in Brazil was not a mere option designed to run for the October elections. It was, in fact, a call from the country itself. A call from a significant part of the population who were fully aware of the risks that polarisation posed to our democracy. My candidacy was embraced by the population in general and by women in particular. It seemed very clear to me that, without women, a centrist political movement could not achieve its goals. Women's political participation results in tangible gains for democracy, including improved responsiveness of policymaking, increased cooperation across party lines and greater concern for the needs of women as well as those of marginalised voters. These are lessons that can be applied by centrist movements everywhere and they benefit from having women front and centre.

Female representation in politics remains a problem in Brazil. Although women constitute 53 per cent of all Brazilian voters, politics in my country is still dominated by male voices. In 2022, only ninety-one women were elected as House Representatives, which corresponds to 17.7 per cent of the total of 513 seats of Brazil's Lower House. The Federal Senate started the current legislature with only ten women out of eighty-one members (12.3 per cent). The share of women in the national houses of parliament in OECD countries stood at 33.8 per cent in early 2023 – and even that is far too low. Worldwide, the average is at 25.4 per cent. Women's political representation in Brazil is far below what it could and should be. Brazil is placed 131st out of 187 countries regarding women's participation in parliament. I had to demonstrate that the democratic centre in my country not only had a coherent and consistent plan for government, but also had a woman's face and voice.

With the campaign motto 'With love and courage', I fought the good fight. I tried to make the case for a more just and fully democratic country. I got almost 5 million votes, placing third in the presidential race. I didn't make the second round, but I delivered – in a short period – a message that there was an alternative to radicalisation and to the lack of trust in our institutions. But being part of the democratic centre did not mean that I had to remain *neutral* in the political dispute that was about to come.

My strong commitment to Brazil's democracy was the reason for my immediate support for Lula da Silva in the second round. My differences with President Lula's platform during the campaign were mainly focused on the economic agenda: his programme had a state-led focus while mine was based on market-oriented reforms. Although I had some areas of disagreement with President Lula, I recognised in him an indisputable commitment to the values of our Constitution that I held so dearly – and did not recognise in Jair Bolsonaro.

I understood that many supporters of Jair Bolsonaro – even when they stormed government buildings on 8 January 2023 – thought they were protecting Brazil's democracy. But their perception was based, in large part, on lies, hyper-partisanship, fake news and hate. Bolsonaro himself was responsible for spreading false information about our electoral system. His political career was boosted by radical rhetoric in defence of authoritarianism – praising, for example, the military dictatorship that many people in my party and in my family fought against. In 2020, Bolsonaro's culture secretary even used parts of a speech by Nazi Germany's propaganda chief Joseph Goebbels in a video, sparking outrage.

The values that I have always stood for would never fit with neutrality. At the age of fourteen, in the last phase of the military dictatorship in Brazil, I asked my parents for permission to go to the streets to fight for direct elections to the presidency – the *Diretas Já* movement. My conscience told me that, at a crucial moment in our history, staying neutral would mean betraying not only my trajectory in public life, but also my principles. The same principles without which there could be no centre, no left, or no right – for there would be no democracy.

29

A CENTRIST APPROACH TO DEVELOPING COUNTRIES: EXPAND OPPORTUNITIES

Ann Bernstein

This essay makes the case for a new way of conceiving how developing country policymakers should think about the goals of development, providing content to the aim of inclusive growth. In societies characterised by poverty, unemployment and inequality we should strongly uphold the ideal of equality of opportunity. Within that ideal, developing countries should emphasise the importance of focusing on the fastest and most effective possible expansion of opportunities for the poor. We should focus more attention on eradicating poverty than on programmes that ameliorate poverty. Instead of radical redistributive proposals, developing countries should build on what works; focus less on inequality and far more on how to expand dramatically the opportunities available to poor people.

In seeking to deal with large-scale poverty, governments often look for solutions that compensate the poor for their exclusion rather than pushing for the labour-intensive and fast economic growth that would include them. Redistributive interventions of this sort can often help reduce poverty in the short term but do very little to empower individuals to move out of poverty. Doing that requires a relentless focus on expanding employment.

Growth is the key to inclusion

Job-rich growth was the dynamic that explains the single most important fact about global development of the late twentieth and early twenty-first centuries: the rapid decline in the proportion of the world's people living in poverty. So rapid was this that the Millennium Development Goal of halving poverty by 2015 that was set in 1990 was achieved five years early.

The main cause of this astonishing improvement in human welfare was economic growth. The economies of the three regions of the world that are home to the vast majority of the world's poor had all grown rapidly: at 8 per cent per year in East Asia, 7 per cent in South Asia and 5 per cent in Africa. This era of global economic growth saw the first fall in global inequality of household income since the early nineteenth century.

Notwithstanding this vast reduction in global poverty, more and more attention is devoted to issues of inequality by policymakers and opinion leaders across the world. One reason is that, while inequality has fallen, if one looks at humanity as a whole and between nations of the Global North and those of the Global South, inequality has risen within many countries, both developed and developing. The political salience of rising inequality in the developed world influences the way in which political and economic issues are shaped in all countries. In this context, the issue of inequality has become increasingly important in framing policy debate in developing countries too.

It is, however, strange that rising inequality in North America and Europe should be a more significant determinant of global debates about how to tackle poverty in developing countries than the remarkable fact that poverty rates have fallen from 90 per cent to below 1 per cent in China in the last fifty-five years. That income inequality may have risen in China seems considerably less relevant than the reality that hundreds of millions of Chinese people are now living vastly more prosperous lives, as indicated by the massive jump in the mean daily income of China, from $1.18 in 1981 to $14.17 in 2019.

Despite the scale of poverty reduction across the world, many people remain in desperate circumstances. In 2019, 659 million people lived on less than $2.15 per day. In India, 10 per cent of the population of 1.4 billion remain at this level of absolute poverty. In an upper-middle-income country like South Africa, a shocking 20.5 per cent out of a population of 55 million lived on less than $2.15 per day in 2014, and the situation has deteriorated since then. Large numbers of people also live just above the poverty line and are vulnerable to falling back.

Too often, the response to poverty in developing countries like India, Mexico, Brazil, South Africa and elsewhere has the wrong emphasis. Governments focus on increasing grants and other redistributive programmes rather than on growing their economies. As development economist Ricardo Hausmann argues, '[Frequently] they compensate people for their exclusion, rather than focussing on poor people's inclusion.'

Of course, societies should provide direct assistance to poor people, but we should not exaggerate the impact of these efforts or assume that this can be easily done. Helping people cope with poverty is clearly necessary, especially in the most unequal and poor countries. But it is important to appreciate that poor countries do not have many resources, so it is vital that this help reaches as many people as possible (not just political 'clients') and is not captured by better-off people (an enormous problem in India, for example).

However, policymakers' goals need to be considerably more ambitious. They should aim to permanently change the circumstances of millions of poor families for the better and be held to account for this by their societies and electorates.

Expanding access to formal-sector jobs

In any society, finding employment is the most effective route out of poverty. Jobs can transform societies. The 2013 World Development Report put it well:

Jobs are the cornerstone of economic and social development . . . development happens through jobs. People work their way out

210

of poverty and hardship through better livelihoods. Economies grow as people get better at what they do, as they move from farms to firms, and as more productive jobs are created, and less productive ones disappear. Societies flourish as jobs bring together people from different ethnic and social backgrounds and nurture a sense of opportunity. Jobs are thus transformational – they can transform what we earn, what we do and even who we are.

The key to expanding opportunities and including millions of the excluded is expanding formal employment, even if this is initially largely in low-productivity, low-wage sectors, to which the limited skills of the existing workforce are suited.

Middle-income countries are particularly susceptible to placing significant hurdles in the way of the creation of low-wage jobs, and northern governments and northern NGOs often encourage this. These regulations benefit the insiders who already have jobs, and the well-educated middle class qualified for high-tech jobs. They leave out in the cold the large number of uneducated or unemployed people with no experience of working. These economies must stop creating jobs mainly or only for the skilled workforce they wish they had; they have to create jobs for the workforce they actually have.

By ensuring that available jobs are subject to basic health and safety standards and are not dead-end informal jobs or 'make-work' public-sector ones, a more labour-intensive approach to economic growth will immediately contribute to rising productivity and skill levels. Employed people learn on-the-job skills and earn the steady wages that will allow them to invest more substantially in their children's education.

Critics who label internationally competitive low-skill employment as a 'race to the bottom' make the mistake of assuming that low wages are forever, but they are wrong. Individuals can take advantage of opportunities for social mobility through employment experience and training. Some factory workers can learn new skills and move to better jobs: from making T-shirts to supervising others making them, or graduating to making more complex garments. Other workers will save money and move out of low-skill factory jobs to establish small firms of their own.

The firms involved acquire new capabilities, access new markets and become more productive. They move up the value chain, creating new opportunities for themselves and their workers. And, because factory workers will have resources and opportunities to educate their children (especially girls) for longer, the next generation of workers will enter an economy that offers more opportunities than the one their parents faced, and with the ability to take advantage of them. Getting this process right can reap rich rewards, as demonstrated in many societies in Asia and elsewhere. That is how medium- to long-term progress is made.

The alternative to low-paying jobs isn't high-paying jobs, it's no jobs at all. Ernesto Zedillo, former president of Mexico, argues: as people move from agricultural and informal jobs to low-paying manufacturing jobs, they find that 'these jobs are a step towards better opportunities. It is progress that matters the most when considering the standards of a given country.'

In many countries, high minimum wages and inflexible labour regulations make it difficult for the economy to generate a rapid expansion of formal-sector jobs. Limiting the creation of low-skill, low-wage jobs harms poor people the most. Nobel laureate Paul Krugman has written: 'In a substantial number of industries, low wages allowed developing countries to break into world markets . . . [and] wherever the new export industries have grown, there has been measurable improvement in ordinary people's lives.'

Countries seeking to expand the opportunities of the poor need, first and foremost, to pursue the fastest possible rate of economic growth. That means building institutions and adopting policies that help firms to thrive and force them to innovate.

Apart from finding oil, labour-intensive export-oriented activities – especially in manufacturing – are the one tried and true method for developing countries to escape poverty. They are the vehicle for prosperity, and the principal source of opportunities for hundreds of millions of people. The only real question is whether policymakers embrace this fact or ignore it. If politicians and policymakers of the centre are serious about doing away with poverty, they need to adopt policies based on evidence. The history of countries that have moved from poverty to a better life for all demonstrates the benefits of avoiding a short-term, populist focus on redistribution. Those countries that have succeeded have instead expanded opportunities for the poor by focusing on sustained periods of growth and massive job creation.

Creating cities of hope for the poor

If formal-sector jobs are one key to expanding opportunities for the poor, the other is the building of cities that work much better for them.

Nobel laureate Paul Romer argues that successful development is driven by marrying two critical phenomena: the market and the city. The city brings scale to economic activity, allows for an extensive division of labour, and enables goods, ideas and innovations to travel rapidly through networks of people. Competitive markets ensure that goods and inputs are used as efficiently as possible.

The link between prosperity and high levels of urbanisation is one of the strongest correlations in the social sciences, with the relationship rooted in the all-but-magical effect that dense agglomerations of firms, workers and consumers have on productivity. Historically, most countries moving up the income ladder have done so in concert with the development of strong cities that generate incomes and jobs and, if well connected, these growth dynamics spread to intermediate-sized cities and urban peripheries.

There is, however, nothing inevitable about urbanisation and the achievement of greater prosperity. The existence and growth of poor megacities – urbanisation without industrialisation – has cast doubts on this relationship. As Harvard's Ed Glaeser argues, 'the demons of density must be dealt with: congestion, crime, disease, unaffordable land and housing prices if cities are to deliver on their enormous potential'.

There are too many 'reluctant urbanisers' – governments, politicians, leaders from civil society – who think that cities shouldn't grow and the rural poor should not urbanise. This is a huge mistake, and one that will be leave future generations much worse off than they might otherwise be. Much more sensible would be investment in the needs of expanding cities and urban populations.

National policy and investment priorities need to catch up with the increasing reality of urban-led societies. Large and important urban centres with capacity need to have some direct control over revenues and crucial functions. They require greater accountability and authority for public safety, transport, skills, labour markets and more. Investment in infrastructure, especially basic services and affordable, reliable public transport, is vital for successful cities of hope for the poor.

There is no proven alternative to urban-led economic growth. Rural areas are generally in much deeper, more unbreakable poverty traps. Partly this is caused by the proliferation of low-productivity, small-scale, usually family-based farming often coupled with landlessness in remote areas where few non-agricultural jobs are available.

Danny Leipziger of the Growth Dialogue argued in 2015 that 'Many politicians ignore increasing urbanisation since it requires long-term planning and multi-year expenditures, coordination between different levels of government, engagement with the private sector and significant improvements in governance.' In his view, countries that have managed urbanisation well, such as South Korea and Malaysia, have thought long-term and have used strong political leadership to connect the growth of cities with national development plans. Seeing the rural poor become the urban poor is a bad development outcome;

yet without an increased focus on the urban agenda and a change in policy direction this is quite likely.

Governments should not limit the rate of urbanisation. Instead, the movement of poor people out of rural and into urban areas should be regarded as a positive dynamic, and governments concerned to expand opportunities for the poor should remove barriers and artificial incentives that keep people in rural areas. Here too, centrists have an opportunity to craft successful policies. Rather than giving in to populist pressures for wholesale land expropriation, or the redistribution of income or unrealistic projects in rural areas mired in poverty, they should focus on empowering rural people through better education, better health care and public investments in rural infrastructure and its maintenance.

Concluding remarks

Most developing countries have had harsh histories of racial discrimination, colonialism and worse. Policymakers need to take this into account: ignoring the specific context of a country is a recipe for disaster. Extreme proposals on the left (expropriation of property, destruction of institutions and worse) and fundamentalist proposals on the right (minimisation of the role of the state, unfettered capitalism and a refusal to see the strong barriers preventing participation by the poor in moving out of poverty) will often not help people trapped in terrible circumstances. There are realistic and achievable policies that centrist politicians can adopt with real hope of delivering ladders of opportunity for millions of poor people. This is the only way to get rid of multi-generational poverty.

Achieving equality of opportunity for everyone in a society is an important ideal and benchmark. However, the pragmatic here-and-now focus in developing countries should be on dramatically expanding opportunities for poor people. This essay has focused on the two most important mechanisms in the route out of poverty – mass employment and managing cities well to cater for expansion and inclusion. There are many other policy areas in which this approach can be applied, from quality education and skills provision for the poor to housing policy close to urban economic opportunities, and ensuring competitive space for new and small firms.

Improving the lives of the poor and expanding dramatically the set of opportunities to which they have access should be the core goal of a successful government. Anything else is a recipe for failure.

SECTION 5

CENTRISM AS THE WAY FORWARD

The final section of the book looks forward, exploring both how to build successful centrist parties and governments but also how centrism can help us to build better societies. From the first essay in the book, we've been reminded that centrism can't stop with the role of the state or the market, it has to take into account wider society. Issues of culture, heritage, identity and narrative aren't peripheral to the political world, they lie at its centre. Ignoring them is to ignore the intrinsic identities of the people centrists seek to represent.

The approach in this section varies between structural and behavioural modifications. There are better models for governance, as Michael Bloomberg argues from his experience as mayor of New York, where he rejected partisanship and demanded policies that were based on facts. Charles Wheelan advocates for reforming electoral systems, particularly party primaries, to support the push away from polarisation by forcing politicians to cater to the entire electorate and not a narrow political base. Polly Bronstein has developed a uniquely centrist way to approach creating policy, offering a series of practical models in her essay, while Josef Lentsch presents the way forward for centrist political parties looking to adapt to the modern world.

And there are also ways for centrists to improve engagement with wider society, tackling polarisation not only at the political level but from the grassroots. It starts with encouraging and lifting up moderate voices, not allowing the extremes to dominate, frame and distort the debate. Centrists can't afford to ignore this part of the work.

This section is centred on hope. It completes the picture of the centrist approach by offering a set of pragmatic solutions and inspiring ways of thinking about the political realm we inhabit.

30

GOVERNING AS CENTRISTS

Michael Bloomberg

I have never put much stock in labels. I've worked closely and productively with Democrats, Independents and Republicans. I suppose it hasn't hurt that I've *been* a Democrat, Republican and Independent.

No party has a monopoly on good ideas. I saw that throughout my twelve years as mayor of New York City. But that simple truth is denied every day by most elected officials – if not in their words, in their actions or lack thereof. In the US it has become increasingly common for elected officials in each party to view the other as a plague to be avoided. That kind of hyper-partisanship is weakening our nation, by limiting our ability to solve difficult problems and by fostering a culture of animosity and hostility that is bleeding into so much of public life.

In the US, increasingly, people are self-segregating by party – in the communities where they live, in the places where they worship and even in the people they marry. Fifty years ago, most parents didn't care whether their children married a member of another political party, but they didn't want them marrying outside their race or religion, or inside their gender. Today, thankfully, polls show a strong majority support for interracial, interreligious and same-sex marriage – and that is great progress. Unfortunately, however, the percentage of parents who don't want their children marrying outside of their political party has doubled.

The more people segregate themselves by party, the harder it becomes to understand the other side, and the more extreme each party grows. Studies show that individuals become more extreme in their views when they are grouped together with like-minded people. That's how smart and well-informed people can be so quick to excuse actions that are ethically wrong and defend statements that are blatantly untrue – and even threats to the preservation of democracy.

Globally, we see the consequences of extreme polarisation all around us. When ideology and party loyalty replace reason, logic, facts and data, nations suffer – and special interests win. Here in the US I've seen it on issue after issue: gun violence, education, public health, and even one that threatens our life as we know it: climate change. Progress depends on a dialogue that treats these issues not as pawns in a political battle but as problems to be solved.

From my experience, centrism does not mean splitting the difference, so everyone gets a few crumbs. It means enlarging the pie, so everyone gets more. That requires the creativity to break out of tired old left/right debates and find new ways of drawing parties into partnership. Centrism demands pragmatism. It's looking for the best way forward, no matter which party suggests it or which party would benefit. It's grappling with the best available data, no matter how politically difficult. It's bucking the party line whenever truth and progress require it, no matter how fierce the special-interest reaction might be. It's leading from the front, not following the crowd. It's listening to opponents with an open mind, not falling victim to confirmation bias. And it's staying focused on problem-solving, not public opinion polls.

That's the approach that guided my twelve years in New York's City Hall, and from my experience successful centrism rests on four main pillars: personnel, policy, partnerships and public trust.

Personnel

Most politicians view winning an election as a time to reward supporters, and they often appoint their friends and donors to plum positions. I've always found it outrageous that US presidents in both parties select donors as ambassadors. Diplomacy, which involves matters of war and peace and crisis management, should not be a pay-to-play game. Too

often, senior positions in many departments get filled by campaign supporters with few relevant qualifications.

Similarly, elected officials rarely hire people from outside their party.
After being elected mayor, I never asked any job applicants what
party they belonged to or whether they had voted for me. I knew that
some, if not many, had supported my opponent, but that didn't bother
me in the least. I wanted the most talented and qualified people. I
hired senior staff members who were liberal Democrats and conservative Republicans. They didn't always agree, of course – and that was
the point. Their differences made us less susceptible to partisan traps,
made our policies sharper and stronger, and made our government more
reflective of the political diversity of our city. This approach to personnel, when combined with open and constructive working environments,
challenges confirmation bias and promotes genuine debate.

Policy

There's a saying in the private sector that also applies to government: 'In
God we trust. Everyone else, bring data.' What can't be measured can't
be managed, at least not well. The only way to develop truly innovative
policies and solutions is to leave your dogma at the door – and replace
it with data.

When people have accurate and timely data, they can make better
decisions. That's the main idea behind the financial data and information company I founded in 1981 at the dawn of the computer age, but
it's just as true in government today. Data doesn't give us all the answers
– that requires creativity, innovative problem-solving and hard decision-
making – but it does help anchor our thinking to reality.

For instance, when we set out to tackle air pollution in New York
City, we asked: where does most of the pollution come from? Most
people assumed the leading culprit was automobile traffic, given the
congestion in our streets. But we decided to test that assumption by
placing air quality monitors around the city, and what we found was

surprising. Across the US, automobiles account for about three-quarters of all air pollution, and buildings account for the rest. In New York City the reverse was true – buildings accounted for about three-quarters of the pollution, because so many were using old furnaces that ran on dirty-burning heating oil. We also learned that just 1 per cent of the city's buildings were spewing more soot into the air than all the city's cars and trucks combined – so that's where we first targeted our efforts.

Without data, government leaders often fail to design and implement effective programmes and end up throwing good money after bad to keep failed programmes and policies in place. This not only wastes taxpayer money, but it also diverts resources from other essential priorities. Failing to collect, analyse and disseminate data also prevents the public from holding leaders accountable for delivering results.

Whether it was reducing air pollution, grading restaurants for their sanitary practices, issuing progress reports to schools, targeting out-of-state gun sales, tackling disease or many of the other efforts we launched, data helped ground our policy debates and guide our decisions. 'Everyone is entitled to their own opinions,' New York Senator Daniel Patrick Moynihan once said, 'but not their own facts.' And not, I'd add, their own data.

Partnerships

Pragmatic centrism means more than just working across the aisle. It also means working across sectors and seeking support and collaboration from outside government.

The world has grown too complex for government to solve every problem alone. All the major challenges we face – creating good jobs, building modern infrastructure, stopping terrorism, fighting climate change, improving public health – require expertise, technology and resources that governments alone cannot supply. Too often, however, governments and businesses don't talk to each other – and that means both are missing opportunities that each would benefit from.

I've seen the power of public–private partnerships time and again. In the above example concerning air pollution, we could have simply passed a law banning all dirty-burning heating oil. But that heavy-handed and one-size-fits-all approach would have imposed high and immediate costs on many homeowners and renters. And so we took a hybrid approach: we phased out the dirtiest heating oils, while also creating a public–private programme to help building owners finance the switch to cleaner heating fuels. The programme was highly effective, and by the time I left office, New York City's air was cleaner than it had been in more than fifty years. And cleaner air makes the city a more attractive place to live and work, strengthening its economy.

The private sector can be a resource for government leaders not only domestically, but also internationally. The ties that bind nations together are more deeply connected to trade and investment than ever before, but the main channels of international dialogue were designed around governments. The more that we allow business leaders into that dialogue, the more progress we can make on the biggest issues we face, especially climate change, emergency preparedness and public health.

Public Trust

The public has a healthy scepticism about the trustworthiness of politicians, in part because they often speak through a partisan filter, making their words almost as predictable as their positions. Their party is always right, the other party is always wrong, and every problem can be solved by turning to the same old playbook. While ultra-ideological voters may nod their heads in agreement, most voters roll their eyes in exasperation.

Centrist leaders can break free from this trap by showing independence from party platforms, and by levelling with the public in direct and forthright language. This is one of the great political advantages of being a centrist: it creates an opportunity to build trust with voters across the political spectrum. And that trust starts with being open and honest with voters, including about mistakes – and respectful of other parties.

That trust is useful not only at the polls, but in governing. Voters are far more likely to accept the introduction of innovative new policies – policies that are not guaranteed to work, and that anger the special interests – if they know elected officials are acting based on the merits, not the politics. In my first year in office we raised property taxes, closed firehouses and banned smoking in bars and restaurants – all of which faced fierce opposition. But over time, voters saw that the revenue allowed us to invest in schools, parks and social services; the city became safer than ever; and bar and restaurant owners – and even more importantly, their employees and customers – benefited from clean air.

I've seen time and again how people – voters and customers – respect and reward leaders who take risks, so long as they tell it like it is. People won't always agree with you, but if they believe you are focused on getting results and not angling for votes, they will give you the benefit of the doubt – and the chance to prove that a new idea can work.

Public trust is especially important in a crisis. During the pandemic, we saw the dangers that result when public-health policies and practices get overtaken by partisan politics. In the US, the lack of pragmatic centrist leadership not only increased tensions and animosity; it cost many people their lives.

Whether it was after the attacks of 9/11, during a city-wide blackout, during a city-wide transit strike or in the run-up to and aftermath of Hurricane Sandy, I always strove to give the public as much information as possible, as clearly as possible – and to keep it fully removed from any hint of politics.

To encourage more pragmatic problem-solving, Bloomberg Philanthropies works closely with the elected officials who are closest to the public: mayors. Unlike legislators in national governments, mayors cannot get away with constructing alternate realities or playing partisan games. Every day they are responsible for the services people depend on, and their success is measured in real time: whether streets are safe, the air is clean, roads are in good condition and students are graduating from school. There is nowhere for them to hide. Through a wide variety of programmes, our foundation is helping to give mayors the tools they need – including the capacity to use data more effectively – to advance innovative local policies and programmes on a broad range of issues. And we're working to spread the most successful efforts to communities far and wide.

Public policy is not a zero-sum game, and it doesn't have to be a partisan tug-of-war. We need more leaders who prioritise adaptability and exhibit a willingness to learn from diverse perspectives, rather than adhering rigidly to a specific ideology. And with authoritarianism on the rise and democracies backsliding across the globe, this approach is becoming essential not only for executing the basic functions of government, but also for sustaining the health of free and democratic societies.

31

WINNING AS CENTRISTS: A CENTRIST GUIDE TO POLITICAL CAMPAIGNS AND COMMUNICATION

Josh Hantman and Simon Davies

'You campaign in poetry, you govern in prose.' This quote, attributed to the former governor of New York, Mario Cuomo, captures much of the cynicism associated with political campaigning, both among the practitioners and the voting public.

Indeed, political campaigns, and political communications in general, get a bad rep. Sometimes deservedly so. Grand promises distort voter expectations. Dashed hopes cause disillusionment. The prose rarely matches up to the poetry.

And campaigns today are conducted with unprecedented verse and rhyme, with hundreds of millions of dollars being spent in election cycles in developed and developing countries alike. With the tools of today, the electorate can be reached directly, frequently with little transparency or accountability behind the messaging. It's easier to create materials, easier to disseminate them and easier to hide any connection to them. This all too often encourages campaigns to push polarisation, cultivate culture wars and fan the flames of fear and fury.

Of course, riling up the masses for the benefit of a small political elite is not a new phenomenon, and certainly isn't limited to democracies. The manipulation of societal anxiety and divisiveness, leveraging perceived enemies to strengthen the political positioning of leaders, is tried and tested, from the Crusaders through to Mao's cultural revolution, from the Brexit referendum to the rise of the far right in Europe. Sadly, it works. But it comes with a cost.

Social media algorithms, online echo chambers and hyper-partisan media networks amplify the frustrations and fears which exist in all societies. Much has been written about the recent rise of authoritarian leaders on both the left and right who leverage contemporary dog whistles, translated into clickbait headlines to provoke primal anxiety, offering simplistic, divisive solutions to benefit from what is often a very legitimate and real feeling of disenfranchisement.

As societies become more polarised by the illiberal extremes, there is a sense that the liberal democratic centre is left without the means to communicate its more moderate, nuanced message. It is one of the core arguments often used against centrism: though you may be right, there is no way to sell your ideas to the public in the age of modern political warfare.

Indeed, one of the challenges for effective communication is that centrism by definition promotes a unique combination of consensus, compromise and complexity.

These three Cs on the surface appear to be the antithesis of effective political communications, which in the modern era derives oxygen from divisiveness, conflict and simplicity. So what is the solution?

The five pillars of campaigning: a centrist approach

1. Decisive not divisive issues

In any winning campaign it is imperative to probe the hopes and fears of the voters to unearth the real issues that currently, and could potentially, drive voter behaviour. Campaigns need to dive deep, through intensive polling and focus groups, into the hearts and minds of the silent majority who often have little interest in the culture wars of the extremes, and find out what voters actually want. Real issues, from money in your pocket to food on your plates, can move voters even more than identity politics and culture wars. That doesn't mean issues of identity can be ignored, but rather that they are often trumped in importance by regular, pocketbook issues.

Centrists should find the issues which will form the canopy of a broad-tent movement. And while the issues may be complex, the art is to condense them into succinct and powerful messages.

Bill Clinton's team, led by the legendary strategist James Carville in 1992, ran a broad issue-based campaign to defeat the incumbent Republican president, George H. W. Bush. 'It's the economy, stupid' would go down in history as one of the most memorable phrases in political communications.

Five years later, and Tony Blair's famous 'Third Way' in the UK offered a 'New Labour' which promised a 'New Life for Britain'. This historic campaign was accompanied by a famous five-point pledge card, highlighting five decisive issues: cutting class sizes (education), fast-tracking punishment for young offenders (crime), cutting the NHS waiting lists (health), getting 250,000 under-25s off benefits and into work (jobs), and promising no increase in income tax while cutting VAT on heating (the economy). Blair's focus on these decisive issues (but not divisive issues), combined with a message of hope and renewal, stood him apart and helped contribute to his historic landslide victory, removing the Conservatives after eighteen straight years and inflicting their greatest loss since 1906.

Fast-forward to 2020, and in the USA Joe Biden declared he stood for two major issues, 'workers who built this country' and 'values that can bridge divisions'. Instead of making the election purely about the dangers of populism, extremism or indeed the incumbent, Donald Trump, he struck a chord focusing on two issues a large chunk of American voters could unite around.

While African politics often lacks the nomenclature of right, left and centre, one presidential campaign from Zambia in 2021 stands out as an excellent example of a pragmatic centrist defeating an incumbent populist and runaway spender who had overseen an authoritarian slide, economic ruin and rampant corruption.

Wary of the deteriorating economic conditions, President Edgar Lungu did everything to make the campaign about identity politics and distract the voters from the issues truly affecting their daily lives. His campaign played on the fear of minorities, calling his opponent Hakainde Hichilema (HH), who is from the minority Tonga tribe, a 'dangerous tribalist'.

Lungu's party, the Patriotic Front, spread disinformation about HH being a so-called devil worshipper, while the president used the power of incumbency to double down on identity and religious issues, hosting days of prayer and randomly reaffirming Zambia's status as a 'Christian country' in the middle of the campaign. HH and his United Party for National Development (UPND), however, were unperturbed. Their campaign remained laser-focused on the issues Zambians actually cared about irrespective of tribe, namely jobs and rising prices; it was supplemented with an Obama-esque disciplined message of 'Time For Change'.

In the final days, HH framed the choice: 'You can vote UPND to grasp these opportunities, create jobs and lower food prices, or you can choose Lungu and five more years of empty promises and visionless government.' Zambians chose the former, as he won with a landslide victory, an almost unseen electoral outcome on the continent.

2. Hope, unity and patriotism

Joe Biden also embraced hope. Not wide-eyed, intangible optimism but hope built on a plan to bring people together to build a better, shared future. Barack Obama (albeit not originally entirely from the centre) and Bill Clinton did the same before him. And when offering hope, centrist communicators must bring an optimism which emanates from a clear, easy-to-understand plan. A hope built on the complexity of consensus and compromise, and the determination of the liberty-loving majority to find common ground.

Blair promised a 'New Life for Britain', Clinton, 'It's Time to Change America', while Joe Biden ran with the slogan 'Our Best Days Still Lie Ahead'.

Further afield, in Indonesia, Joko Widodo (or Jokowi as he is commonly known) ran two extremely successful campaigns (2014 and 2019), positioning himself – a small-town mayor from a humble background – as the antithesis of the established elite who had dominated Indonesia's politics since independence.

But Jokowi's brand of popular politics was not from the fringes; rather he focused on rallying around the flag. He built a truly broad-tent movement, unifying the people around democracy and against a candidate with authoritarian tendencies and a dubious human rights record associated with the previous non-democratic regime.

Jokowi's patriotic message was a defence of fairness, consensus, human rights and moderation. In one notable speech he noted, 'We gather here as part of a democracy that ensures participation of all people in determining the nation's future, to respect human rights, fight for justice and maintain plurality and peace.'

Likewise, Hakainde Hichilema, the aforementioned Zambian candidate, not only owned the country's patriotic motto, 'One Nation, One Zambia', but brought his Christianity to the fore throughout the campaign, pre-empting the identity politics and disinformation of the other side.

More recently in Israel, throughout 2023 a genuine mass movement has been built to challenge a judicial overhaul by the most right-wing government in the nation's history whose plan, if implemented in full, would hamstring the independent judiciary and provide unrestrained power to the government. It has been met with massive opposition.

By adopting the Israeli flag and the Declaration of Independence as their two core symbols, the protest movement's patriotic campaign stood as a clear challenge to the government's attempts to present it as a foreign-funded, extreme and even non-patriotic minority. The struggle cannot be framed as a simple one between the so-called 'left' and 'right' (much to the frustration of the government). Rather it is presented as a movement of patriotic, liberty-loving Israelis who want to protect their democracy against those who seek to undermine it. A winning message.

By being 'too sophisticated' to connect with the deep emotion of loving one's country, or ceding emotive national symbols to the extremes, centrists run the risk of alienating large swathes of the electorate for whom these symbols hold great significance and meaning.

3. Don't fear fear campaigns

Third, do not *fear* to run a fear campaign. Not all negativity is a bad thing. Just as there are wars of choice and wars of necessity, there are also necessary negative campaigns. And negative campaigns work. Fear the demagogue. Fear authoritarianism. Fear illiberalism and the erosion of democracy and basic civil liberties. But furthermore, fear the incompetence of populist rule, and how it negatively affects your personal security, your savings, your health and your day-to-day life.

Emmanuel Macron, in the infamous 'dirty debate' of 2017 in France, called the far-right Front National candidate Marine Le Pen ill-informed, corrupt and a 'hate-filled' liar. He accused her of 'feeding off France's misery' and argued that she would bring 'civil war' to France.

Biden framed his 2020 victory as a battle for the USA's soul. And while there was plenty of fear surrounding Trump, Biden and his team also focused their communications on the fear of incompetence; in particular Trump's failed handling of the COVID-19 pandemic.

So while it is natural to want to warn of the dangers of creeping authoritarianism and even fascism, such phrases can appear distant and 'unbelievable'. On the other hand, pointing out the historic incompetence of populist rulers can be much simpler and more effective. Fear can help push people away from the opponent, but it can't define you and it won't necessarily convince people you are a better alternative. If campaigns are only about fear, centrists will lose, but that doesn't mean there is no place for such campaigns at all.

4. Be a side – bold ideas

Fourth, centrist communications need to be proud, punchy and combative. Centrism is not just fence-sitting or 'taking both sides'. Rather, centrism is 'a side'. Own your beliefs, value proposition and clear set of policies. Be proudly and passionately *for* something; not just *against*.

Be *for* liberal democracy and individual rights.

Be *for* finding a balance between free markets and fair societies, fiscal responsibility and social-safety nets.

Be *for* pursuing peace while remaining tough on security.

Be *for* pragmatic solutions that will make people's lives better.

When communicating, it is perfectly possible to walk and chew gum at the same time.

On the 2017 campaign trail, Macron was at one point ridiculed for saying the phrase '*en même temps*' so many times. Translated as 'at the same time', he shot back, 'I'm going to keep on using it,' noting, 'because I choose growth and solidarity [at the same time], liberty and equality [at the same time], businesses and employees [at the same time], the best of the right, the left, and the centre [at the same time].' *En même temps* went from being a negative jab to a slogan which embodied the contradictions, complexities and nuances of a sensible centrist message, as opposed to the simplistic reductionism being offered by his opponents.

Indeed, just as governing is not a zero-sum game, neither is campaigning. Not everything is a Manichean struggle between two extremes. There is, just as the centrist movements of the 1990s put it, 'a third way', or as Bill Clinton called it, 'a vital center'.

5. Bold leaders

And finally, without stating the obvious, centrists have to find the right leader. Just as the ideas must be bold, punchy and inspiring, so must the leader.

Bill Clinton, Tony Blair and Emmanuel Macron stormed the scene with charisma and unapologetic purpose, as well as a healthy dose of audacity. Even an ageing Joe Biden ran his 2020 campaign as the char- ismatic, folksy 'Joe from Scranton' whom Americans have known and loved for decades. The African American civil rights leader and senior Democratic Party figure Jim Clyburn summed up Biden's appeal at a rally in South Carolina: 'I know Joe, we know Joe, but most importantly, Joe knows us.'

Precisely because centrism has a brand problem, the character of the leader matters so much more. Matthew d'Ancona recently noted in an article for *Prospect* magazine that 'the label "centrist dad" is only a notch or two up from "gammon" or "imperialist". To identify as a centrist is to be seen as both wretchedly outdated and ideologically craven; analogue in a digital age.' Which is why any leader owning this label must do so with confidence, gravitas, and the natural glow of a winner.

Tony Blair, Bill Clinton and Emmanuel Macron are obvious examples from the West. Yair Lapid, the former TV anchor turned prime minister, stands out in Israel. In Asia, the aforementioned Jokowi, a heavy-metal-loving former furniture salesman dubbed 'Indonesia's Obama', inspired his two campaign victories with his authentically humble charisma. In fact, in public opinion polls and focus groups the two most common traits associated with Jokowi were 'humble' and 'honest' – as refreshing as it is rare; but a lesson for centrist candidates around the world. Be real.

Elsewhere in Asia, Thailand's opposition party, the Move Forward Party, ran with the rather simple message of 'Good Politics, Good Economy, Good Future' in 2023, in a mission to finally loosen the military-royalist dominance of Thai politics. The liberal democratic party, seen as progressive in its Thai context, promised political reform to undermine the legacy of military coups while proposing deep and broad structural economic changes. But most importantly, they had a charismatic young leader. The handsome and eloquent forty-two- year-old Pita Limjaroenrat energised and engaged Thais from TikTok to town squares, eventually taking his party to a first-place finish in the general elections (though the conservative parties and military-appointed Senate, combined with a court ruling, would eventually disqualify his candidacy).

In contrast, in the recent Turkish elections there were great expectations that CHP leader Kemal Kılıçdaroğlu, running as the closest thing Turkey has to a centrist, would finally end the two-decade-long authoritarian rule of Recep Tayyip Erdoğan. And while Kılıçdaroğlu, an uninspiring bureaucrat, ran a bold and aggressive campaign, it ultimately wasn't enough to defeat the incumbent. Perhaps the missing ingredient was the X factor of the leader himself?

So while it sounds obvious, the candidate matters.

Conclusion

Centrist communications and campaigns start out with a brand deficit, something this book is trying to address. Too often perceived as an establishment, fence-sitting and inertia-driven movement to maintain the status quo, winning centrist campaigns require a bold, positive agenda led by a bold, charismatic candidate.

Straight-talking, punchy (even funny!), emotive, attention-grabbing communication is not beneath the centrist candidate; on the contrary, it's necessary to seize the initiative and dominate the narrative.

Identifying the decisive issues of the campaign early and owning them within a broad, hope-inspiring framework can help put to bed claims that centrism is merely an amorphous no-man's-land on the political spectrum.

We must not be afraid to strike fear into the hearts of the voters of the dangerous alternatives to victory, nor should we let rational, complex arguments (which must too be made) get in the way of authentic emotion. Hope, radical hope, active hope remains at the core of a winning centrist approach to political communications.

32

THE CENTRIST ORGANISATION OF THE FUTURE

Josef Lentsch

'The future is already here – it's just
not very evenly distributed.'

William Gibson

We all know why political parties must change. We also know a lot about what needs to change. What we know least about is *how*. Fortunately, there are models and examples we can learn from.

Compared to campaigning and policy, organisation is the least-understood domain of politics. In this essay I want to provide you with some insights from my work with parties around the world.

Utilise the innovation transmission belt

The future of a centrist party often lies within itself. But just as often, party leaders are unaware of this. The critical junctures, then, are: first, are party leaders made aware that there is a case for change? And second, once they are aware, what decisions do they make?

The Dutch VVD and the Canadian Liberals are two parties that have been highly successful for a long time. I have spoken to people close to Dutch Prime Minister Mark Rutte of the VVD and Canadian Prime Minister Justin Trudeau of the Liberal Party of Canada. Both have successfully transformed their parties – the former to stay in office for thirteen years, the latter to become prime minister.

What I have found are similar patterns.

The leader is not necessarily the first to recognise the need for change. In many cases, signals first emerge in the periphery, where there are fewer constraints. These signals are then picked up and amplified by what I call 'political intrapreneurs'. These are people who try to transform the party from within. They are often found in the second and third rows – close to the centre of power, but not necessarily in it. But it is the transmission of the signal to the leader and how they deal with it that is critical to success. And the connection between the periphery and the centre of power, which allows ideas to be transmitted to the leadership, is what I call the 'innovation transmission belt'. It demands a solid party foundation with a grassroots that is both sufficiently loyal and sufficiently confident to send the signals to the centre of power.

Nurture good leadership

A critical component to the future of centrist parties is good leadership. According to those close to Rutte and Trudeau, the underlying qualities of both leaders that were crucial to a successful party transformation were a self-reflective ego, a willingness to continuously learn and improve, curiosity, and analytical thinking.

Three dimensions of leadership in particular were identified in both cases:

Openness to advice
- Willingness to listen, and to take action
- Consideration of different perspectives
- Trust in their own people

Attention to detail
- Passion for precision

- Thoroughness
- Commitment to a deep understanding of political disciplines like campaigning, media and communication

Interest in data
- A scientific and forward-looking mindset that is attracted to technological innovation
- Fascination with the potential insights, patterns and knowledge that can be extracted from large amounts of information
- Recognising the importance of data quality, accuracy and reliability

Both Rutte and Trudeau listened to their advisors, took seriously the data-based case for change they each presented, challenged it and, having accepted the arguments, acted on them. These are essential qualities for any leader, whether in business, civil society or the public sphere.

As noted above, however, the successful transmission of signals from the party periphery depends not only on the party leader receiving signals for change, but also on political intrapreneurs conveying them. How can such changemakers be fostered?

Capacitate political intrapreneurs
In business, many boards now have chief human resource officers (CHROs). As one of the most senior roles, they sit next to the CEO. In political parties, such a function is rare. HR is an underdeveloped discipline in professional politics, and a critical one for the future of the centrist organisation.

What does this mean for political intrapreneurs?

Like all effective changemakers, political intrapreneurs do not come out of nowhere – they grow into their roles. The truth is that many grow, but never flourish. On their way through the ranks (the German *Ochsentour*, the English 'slog'), they burn out, or give up. Most leave politics before they can make a transformative impact.

The answer is not simply promoting them more quickly. This may overwhelm and overstrain them, with the same negative results. The answer is capacitating them, through structured development. Investing in the talent pipeline means taking HR and personnel development in politics seriously. Two means to this end are training and coaching.

Training is long established in politics. It is instructive and skills-oriented, and comes in many shapes and sizes, from the classic in-person media training to the pre-recorded digital masterclass. Here centrist parties can learn from one another and benefit from closer international cooperation.

Coaching, on the other hand, is reflective and process-oriented. Whereas training is more incremental, coaching can have a transformative effect – exactly what political intrapreneurs who want to transform their parties need. It can help them to recognise their inner limits and to discover new perspectives.

In the definition of Christopher Rauen, 'Coaching is the individual counselling, accompaniment and support of persons with leadership or management functions realised in the form of a counselling relationship. The formal goal is to help in the accomplishment of the tasks of the professional role.'[1]

Coaching is particularly helpful when it comes to facing complex challenges for which there is no template, like dealing with emerging role requirements for political professionals, which require new behaviour. In such uncharted situations, coaching is the right approach.

By definition, coaching with its many very personal aspects is of a confidential nature. It is hard to get accurate information, and the consequence is a lack of scientific literature. Thankfully, some people have started to investigate this.

Katja Wolter writes in a great 2019 paper on counselling in politics, which is based on a survey of the members of the German Bundestag: 'Politics gets to you. The actors in politics are often lonely.' She sees a lot of potential for coaching: 'The creation of reflection islands in coaching [. . .] can enable politicians to deal with their powerlessness, their insecurity, their dependency and to shape them positively.'

For centrist parties to have a future, a genuine culture change is required and they are best placed to implement it. It may already be on its way, as younger generations are more open towards coaching.

Cultivate an innovative periphery

In addition to the party leadership and political intrapreneurs, an innovative periphery is the third critical component of an effective innovation transmission belt.

Together with my colleague Nicolas Stühlinger at The Innovation in Politics Institute, I have developed a spherical model of party transformation. It consists of seven spheres and can be used for analysis and as a basis for strategy development. The party periphery, as a part of the whole, consists of three spheres that can and should be tapped into.

- **Farside:** These are the idealists at the front and on the streets, with lots of direct voter contact. As they do not hold high office, they are mostly uninhibited by power constraints. As 'lead users' of innovations, they are a great source of new ideas. For these ideas to translate into action, however, processes need to be in place that let the great ones among them reach the centre of the party, so they can be effectively enabled there. If they are not safeguarded, they might get lost before they reach the centre of power. To avoid unnecessary frustration, the framework, scope and willingness for adopting transformative ideas and concepts should be clear from the very beginning.
- **Bothside:** Organisations which are inhabiting the outer atmospheres of the party, on the border with the outside space. At the edge of the internal and external world, these 'boundary spanners' can look both ways and provide a stage on which to display and discuss ideas coming from the inside as well as from the outside.

They can be useful platforms for exchange with civil society and business, and offer transformative impulses. These ideas, however, need to be picked up and pursued, as bothside organisations cannot implement them on their own.

- **Outside:** Sympathetic but independent organisations, like think tanks, foundations, academic institutions, social enterprises, businesses, unions or associations. Their transformative strength is their independence towards the party, which leaves them unrestrained; and they bring more intellectual and organisational horsepower to the table than individuals. Often they are a great source of new talent and new ideas. To be effective, however, they need political intrapreneurs to carry their ideas into the centre. And as the centre's time and attention are scarce, the number of really relevant outside satellites is usually limited to two to five.

Unrestrained by old, bureaucratic party structures and outdated ways of thinking, centrist parties can ensure that their best days are ahead of them by combining the three elements of nurturing good leadership, capacitating political intrapreneurs and cultivating an innovative periphery.

33

THE CENTRIST METHOD

Polly Bronstein

The 1990s was a golden decade for the political centre in the West. The Cold War – perhaps the starkest expression of the global conflict between left and right – was over, and the stage was set for the arrival of a string of political leaders who could best be described as carving a new centrist path: Tony Blair, Bill Clinton, Jacques Chirac. These leaders and others did not lead centrist parties or necessarily define themselves as centrists themselves, but their ability to attract votes from both sides of the political map was in part a result of their ability to give voice to the priorities and values of the silent, pragmatic majority in the political centre through their personal character and their policy positions. They represented a desire for stability, economic growth, security and opportunity.

The crisis that has been engulfing Western democracy in the last decade is first and foremost a consequence of the collapse of the political centre, and with it the collapse of those values that generated growth and stability and slow, careful, positive progress. The first hints of the impending crisis could be seen in the Brexit referendum and Donald Trump's first presidential campaign partway through the last decade. From there, it grew and spread to most democratic countries around the world. This crisis, which is reflected in abnormally high levels of political and social polarisation, was above all a response to the loss of a supranational identity which served as a glue that bound democratic societies together despite the huge gaps between the different constituent groups of each state.

The disintegration of a core national ethos and the rise of narrow sectoral and isolationist tendencies in its place were a result of four huge shifts in the Western world that have been accelerated since the turn of the century:

1. **Significant demographic shifts** in Western countries have rendered them more heterogeneous than ever before. Huge waves of immigration have created accelerated cultural, economic and social shifts. This in turn has led to rising tensions between different population groups which have been most notably reflected in the meteoric rise of populist and reactionary politicians and parties, coupled with an increase in extremist voices, leaders and political platforms.

2. **Unprecedented technological breakthroughs** are having an unimaginable impact on how we consume information, weakening the influence of state institutions, exponentially increasing the number of voices and distribution channels and blurring the lines between fact and fiction, creating a crisis of trust in previously authoritative bodies and heightening extremism and polarisation in the political discourse.

3. **Vast geopolitical upheaval** – at the centre of which lies the perhaps inevitable end of a long period of unipolar US dominance, and the rise of aggressive totalitarian regimes such as Russia, China and Iran – but also the knock-on effects of the COVID-19 pandemic. These have eaten away at the entire democratic liberal Western apparatus and precipitated a rise in uncertainty and a deteriorating sense of stability in most Western countries.

4. **Huge economic shifts** that have coincided with the rise of a new generation of global tech giants, the mega-tycoon class and unprecedented inequality in distribution of wealth have created a stark divide in the global financial system that has exacerbated tensions and the struggle for resources. The rapid pace of development is offering vast economic opportunities but also

leaving too many people behind; it's sparking fear as much as it is inspiring hope.

These dramatic changes, which are impacting most countries to varying degrees, require a political system with a moderating effect, coupled with a new set of political tools that enhance stability and are able to cope with the scale and complexity of the defining challenge of the twenty-first century. This vital process can only arise within the context of a new political paradigm from the centre of the political map. We have seen some sparks of this in Macron's France, Rutte's Netherlands and the approach of the Biden administration. The (re-)rise of a moderate and pragmatic centre is the necessary response to this era-defining crisis afflicting Western states. So why must it come from the centre?

1. Because the centre is **free** – free from oppressive and blinkered ideological dogma, free to raise new ideas that are beyond the rigid set of values and positions of the right and left, conservatives and progressives. The centre is free to build long-term or targeted collaborations and coalitions to get things done.
2. Because the centre is **hybrid** – it is the best of both worlds, encompassing contradictions and enthusiastically defined by them, and holding multiple values and assigning them equal weight without subjugating one to the other as the extremes must. It is able to simultaneously strive for peace and security, progress and tradition, free markets and social safety nets.
3. Because the centre is **moderate** – it recognises that every world view has valid alternatives, and where possible seeks win-win solutions, rather than a zero-sum game.
4. Because the centre is **pragmatic** – it does not engage in a fool's errand for utopian solutions or social engineering, focusing instead on identifying viable solutions grounded in the real world that have tangible benefits for people's lives. It is practical. It does not fear

the humdrum, the dry and the seemingly trivial. It is in such things that life itself is found.

But the centre is more than a methodology, it remains a political approach with a set of clear principles. And at the core of the political centre lies national liberalism. There are those who would consider liberal nationalism to be an oxymoron: nationalism is seen to be the preserve of the right, liberalism identified more closely with the left; nationalism is about the collective, liberalism about the rights of the individual; nationalism draws its inspiration from the past, liberalism looks to the future. But in practice it is only a combination of the two, nationalism and liberalism, that meets both basic components of citizens' identities in the modern nation-state: as part of the local and global spheres.

The harsh consequences of ceding the collectivist national ground in favour of globalisation and universalism, as many liberal governments have done, are being felt today. The identity crisis plaguing Europe and the USA, for example, should be a warning sign against the loss of national identity. The rise of the far right throughout the democratic world is indicative of an aggressive pushback against the loss of a collective national identity and the alienation it has brought with it.

Globalisation and democracy are vital and wonderful tools in human development when introduced alongside community and national belonging, and not in their stead. The last decade has proved as much. Throughout the world, people have begun to rebel against globalisation, against the loss of borders and national identity, against the loss of local culture, identity and production, and against changes to the communal and human tapestry.

The ideology that is underpinned by national liberal values can be converted into practical policy by employing a number of principles of centrist philosophy. These principles are the lens through which the centre reads the world, the filter through which it examines it. Here are a few of those guiding principles of the centre:

1. **Elliptical thinking** – in the same way as a circle is defined by having one centre, a focal point which is equidistant from all points in the circumference, so the ellipse has two such focal points. Elliptical thinking is the politics of both/and rather than either/or. Instead of one centre, there are two. Instead of prioritising one value at the expense of another, there are two values between which a balance must be struck, even if they seem contradictory. Sometimes one of these values offers the chosen path, in which case solutions and mechanisms are found to avoid the other being subjugated to it.

   Some call this a concession, failing to recognise that we go through this exact process on a regular basis in our daily lives. Every individual, every family and every community has its own inherent contradictions. For example, parenting and the pursuit of a career: these are two focal points in life that come into conflict with each other, yet many of us choose to hold on to both and navigate between them – on some occasions prioritising the career and on others parenting, depending on the circumstances.

   The day-to-day life of a country is no different. Indeed, it rings truer still in the life of a heterogeneous country with disparate groups who hold different perspectives and values on a range of subjects. The centre does not pass judgement between conflicting values, where these both hold value for broad swathes of the public. It is therefore able to identify solutions or frameworks that provide space to navigate between them: for example, the conflict between 'life' and 'choice' in the abortion debate that is tearing the USA apart. The centre recognises that these are two sacred and deeply held values and will therefore seek to find a solution that does not subjugate one to the other. How might that work? We'll demonstrate using the following philosophical principle:

2. **Continuum reasoning** – when the centre approaches matters of ideology or practice, it seeks to avoid binary thinking that creates a zero-sum yes/no outcome. The centre resolves problems using continuum reasoning: instead of examining questions of policy through the lens of 'this or that?' the centre asks, 'to what extent?'. For example, instead of asking 'Should abortions be legal?' we would ask 'How far along in a pregnancy should abortion be legalised?' Or 'Under which circumstances should abortions be legalised?' The answer may range from 'not at all' all the way to 'fully', but the mere act of framing the question using continuum reasoning changes the tone of the debate. If we can reach agreement that abortions are possible up to a certain stage and/or in certain circumstances, the chance of reaching an outcome that is acceptable to the majority of the public is higher than if we continue to fight zero-sum battles.

Only through the perspective of a quantitative continuum can we identify creative solutions that take into account any existing tensions. Additional examples? We wouldn't ask 'Should we allow immigrants into the country?' Rather, we would ask 'How many immigrants would we agree to let into the country? Under what circumstances? For what length of time?' Instead of asking 'Should the judiciary have the authority to exert judicial oversight over parliamentary decisions?' we would ask 'On which matters, under which circumstances and through which process would the judiciary be able to apply judicial oversight over parliamentary decisions?'

This should not be taken to mean that every question is acceptable. There are red lines; not all values carry equal weight and not every virtue is admissible. That misconception is one of the more unserious attacks on centrism. Some ideas are clearly beyond the pale. We would not ask 'To what extent and under which circumstances would it be justified to prevent women from being appointed to senior positions?' Or 'For what length of time can the children of illegal immigrants be detained?'

3. **Shrinking problems** – we often mistakenly take the view that we should seek to end deep-rooted and intractable problems in a decisive and complete manner – or else not address them at all. The political centre understands the intrinsic value of shrinking problems, even if this does not end them, and often shrinking problems is a far more achievable outcome, and one that bears significant benefits for all sides. Partial and temporary solutions often provide positive outcomes because they can galvanise public support: even if there is no consensus on a comprehensive solution, agreements can be reached on specific, tangible measures to shrink areas of conflict or challenge, without the sense of an unacceptable ideological compromise.

   We borrowed the concept of the idea of 'shrinking the conflict' from Micah Goodman's book on the Israeli-Palestinian conflict, *Catch 67*. Goodman's claim is that, while it is not possible to fully resolve the conflict at this moment in time, that does not preclude the potential for a string of measures that would shrink the conflict and the resulting impact on people. Paradoxically, both sides may oppose interim measures to shrink the conflict out of a belief that such measures risk 'normalising' the situation and preventing the desired future outcome. Yet the importance of the centre is informed by the belief that shrinking the conflict can reduce human suffering in the immediate term, lower tensions and polarisation, and thereby act to build trust between the sides and enable them to practise collaboration and achieve a more complete solution when the opportunity arises. Shrinking problems is not avoiding them, it is creating short-term benefit and long-term opportunity for comprehensive solutions.

4. **Cross-sector synergy** – cross-sector synergy is a tool that puts elliptical thinking into practice in terms of who sits around the table when we come to address local or national challenges. The centre

understands that connections between the private, public and third sectors are a key to more creative and detailed thought processes with the potential to bring far more effective results.

The combination of the obligation, the experience and the deep pockets of the state; the effectiveness, professionalism and dynamism of the private sector; and the values, expertise and connection to the needs on the ground of civil society organisations is the X factor when it comes to resolving complex and undesirable challenges.

This is usually the right tactic when setting experts and professionals from one field to creating thought processes designed to resolve problems in another field. Bringing together experts from security, health care, education, welfare, law, economics, tech, social work, urban planning, engineering and so on to work on public processes of every kind will bring surprising and innovative results.

The value of cross-sector synergy lies not only in the quality of the outputs but also in emphasising the need for diversity and an increased recognition of a sense of national duty among all the different sectors of the country, and the private sector in particular. Setting a public standard according to which representatives from the different professional sectors are invited to every problem-solving table creates a situation wherein government ministries, local authorities and civil society organisations benefit from increased engagement by the private sector, tech and academia in tackling complex issues.

5. **Trust and empathy** – without ascribing positive intentions and an ability to empathise to the other, there is no route to agreement on the rules of the national game, the division of resources and the decision-making process. The centre approaches every challenge understanding that the first stage must be listening to and learning the voices and arguments on all sides and being ready to understand their perspectives, identities and interests. Ultimately,

it is about recognising that political rivals are not enemies to be defeated. The centre does not shy away from disagreements, rather it solves problems without trampling on its interlocutors, out of a genuine effort to build trust and collaborations that seek to improve the outcome for as many citizens as possible and create improved dynamics for the future. A short-term total victory is likely to lead to a counter-reaction when the power balance shifts, as it inevitably does in democratic systems.

There is another, no less important outcome to high levels of trust and empathy that are conducive to listening and learning: our understanding of the situation improves, and our horizons are broadened. Our field of vision is naturally limited. Developing empathy as a habit enables us to listen without resorting to instinctive dismissal. The centre does not settle for its own narrow perspective. It casts its net as far and wide as possible to take in new angles, in order to get to the truth and to familiarise itself with the facts, the statistics and the different arguments. In so doing, it bolsters its ability to confront situations accurately and to develop more effective solutions as a result.

6. **50/30/20** – democratic nation-states are, to differing degrees, in the throes of a period of great upheaval. Different groups are pulling hard in different directions to ensure that the state is first and foremost in their own image, and in many cases they are rising up against the established order. This process among groups who have grown impatient with the existing reality – one in which they feel they have no say – and who are rising up and making their voices heard in response could have been natural and positive had those countries had a powerful and dynamic political centre. In practice, as noted above, the centre cracked and exposed the weaknesses in Western democracy, and its inability to address systemic contradictions in its character and among its competing groups.

50/30/20, a concept defined by former Israeli education minister Rabbi Shai Piron, is a new operating system that boosts the national liberal centre while protecting the interests, unique aspects and diversity of each group and sector. 50/30/20 takes the lessons we have learned over the last decade: a democratic nation-state requires a shared upper layer (the 50 per cent) that is robust and nationwide. Below this are those levels that provide a measure of freedom and autonomy to the different population groups – 30 per cent a localised or group-based middle layer and the lower 20 per cent a community layer.

Let's take this model and apply it to the education system. A democratic country must guarantee not only equality of opportunity to all its children, and not only an education that enables them to find gainful employment, but also to forge a shared national narrative with their peers, a set of national values and civic education that ensures that every citizen in the country is familiar with the rules of the game of democracy, their rights and responsibilities. At the same time, most Western democracies have communities who have a distinct culture, religion, language or ethnic background of their own. These groups naturally seek to hold on to their unique character and pass it on to future generations.

When applied to education, the 50/30/20 model ensures that 50 per cent of the curriculum is identical for all students across the country, including core subjects such as English, mathematics, history, sciences etc., as well as the specific civic studies that the state decides to prioritise to forge a shared ethos. Alongside this, the state permits, or even funds, 30 per cent of the curriculum that is determined by population group, in which students receive an education that is unique to their identity or geographical area. And the 20 per cent? They are entrusted to the parents or school principals, to determine the priorities for their children within the education process.

This model gives citizens greater control over their own lives and empowers them with greater responsibility, yet at the same time insists on their participation in and loyalty to the state.

These approaches reflect the ways in which the centre thinks, solves problems and develops tools to tackle the highly charged and complex reality of the twenty-first century.

34

CENTRISM AND BUILDING
A BETTER POLITICAL SYSTEM

Charles Wheelan

On 25 May 2020, George Floyd, an unarmed Black man, was murdered in Minneapolis. A white police officer kneeled on Floyd's neck until he died. Floyd's horrific death made clear the need for racial reconciliation and criminal justice reform in the USA – both difficult but important social tasks.

What the country got instead was 'defund the police', a movement that mostly served to foment a backlash. Over the next year, the percentage of Americans who wanted to cut funding for the police *fell* nearly ten percentage points: the proportion who wanted more spending climbed from 31 per cent to 47 per cent.[1] Perceptions of race relations fell to a new low,[2] and the door was shut on more thoughtful, bipartisan reforms.

George Floyd's death is emblematic of larger political challenges, in the USA and beyond. The USA confronted a hard issue – and grew more divided. The same dynamic plays out across the world around issues like immigration and LGBT rights. What might have been a unifying moment became instead more fuel for the blaze of polarisation. It is little wonder that the public is losing faith in our system. According to Pew Research, only 2 per cent of Americans trust government to do what is right 'just about always', and only one in five think government does the right thing 'most of the time'.

Complaints about government have a common theme: *it's not working*. The loudest, shrillest voices get too much attention. The political middle – the two-thirds of voters who make up the 'exhausted majority'

– are frustrated and disheartened. The politicians who are supposed to forge common ground are instead beholden to the most extreme members of their respective parties. These complaints are echoed across the democratic world.

Politicians are unable to find consensus on hard issues: climate change, immigration, personal security, public spending. In the years after my book *The Centrist Manifesto* was published, I often described this gridlock as 'political trench warfare'. I have stopped using that metaphor because our situation is worse than that. Trench warfare at least implies a stalemate. The challenges we face today grow steadily worse in the face of inaction. The appropriate metaphor is rising floodwaters. To do nothing is to invite disaster.

In fact, it is worth pausing to look more deeply at the USA's fiscal situation as a case study. Rising debt may not be the sexiest or most serious unaddressed challenge, but it is the most quantifiable. In the absence of some plan to change the trajectory of spending and borrowing, the USA's debt-to-GDP ratio will reach 185 per cent of GDP by mid-century – a clear threat to the global financial system. (As a frame of reference, EU law requires countries to keep their debt-to-GDP ratio below 60 per cent.) America now spends more on interest payments than on national defence. There are legitimate philosophical differences around the size and scope of government, but borrowing steadily more from the future is not a viable option. The numbers – a tangible measure of democratic dysfunction – don't lie.

The world's most consequential democracy is losing its capacity to govern. One prominent political journalist told me recently, 'Congress is getting dumber.' When I asked why, he replied, 'Would you want to run?' A system that rewards performers and extremists is attracting more performers and extremists. The public is growing steadily more cynical and less trusting of democracy. Talented people are choosing other professions. We face a democratic death loop as the dysfunction feeds on itself.

The remedy follows naturally from the disease: if our systems are floundering because small, non-representative groups have too much influence, the prescription is to empower the centre.

Political centrism is a term I have struggled to define for two decades. (A section of this essay is devoted to the problematic nature of the word 'centrist'.) For now, centrism means two things. First, democratic politics must reward politicians who are as representative of the electorate as possible. If there is a bell curve of public views on most issues (even on something as contentious in the USA as guns), the tails ought not be able to thwart policies that would satisfy most voters. Americans sometimes use football language: most voters' views are 'between the forty-yard lines', which happens to be the centre of the field. Our governance ought to reflect that.

Second, centrism must find a way to reward – or at least protect – those politicians who serve as the 'connective tissue' in our diverse democracies. These are the leaders with the temperament and pragmatism necessary to forge consensus. In some cases, this means probing public opinion for areas of agreement (between the forty-yard lines). In others, it requires steering the debate to a new place, or making the case for an unpopular view. The different forms of centrist leadership have a crucial commonality: *find a path forward*.

Nothing about this process, or centrism more generally, requires abandoning principle. History offers many examples of politicians with strong ideological views who were willing to work 'across the aisle' when circumstances demanded it. Every seminal peace agreement, from the Oslo Accords to the Good Friday Agreement, has been negotiated by principled leaders who made painful sacrifices for the sake of a more peaceful and durable society. The alternative is to bask in the adulation of one's own faction while beggaring the future.

The electorate are less partisan than our politicians – but they don't like the word centrist

When I wrote *The Centrist Manifesto* in 2013, there were two intended ironies in the title. The first, obviously, is the play on Marx's *Communist Manifesto*. The second is the tension between 'centrist' and 'manifesto'. Centrists are not usually the ones launching revolutions. (I even printed T-shirts with the logo 'Insurrection of the Rational'.) President Macron tried to reclaim the mantle of 'radical centrist' for much the same reason.

I have learned in the decade since *The Centrist Manifesto* was published that 'centrist' – and its linguistic cousin 'moderate' – suggest to some a lack of passion on issues that demand 100 per cent commitment, such as social justice and climate change. I strenuously disagree with this characterisation: centrists share a passion for pragmatic action rather than posturing and virtue signalling, neither of which accomplish anything. Still, one challenge for the movement is to associate centrism in the public's mind with action, positive change, and yes, passion. (Centrists of the world unite!)

Whatever the language, the evidence is strong that people yearn for a centrist path forward (as I defined it earlier in the essay). To believe otherwise is to accept implicitly that we will be unable to confront our most significant social challenges, or even that some kind of cold civil war lies ahead.

For now, the public is more pragmatic and centrist than our political institutions. The civic group More in Common used polling, focus groups and interviews to identify seven political tribes in the USA, ranging from 'progressive activists' to 'devoted conservatives'. Their Hidden Tribes report characterised 67 per cent of Americans as the 'exhausted majority'. Specifically, these citizens are ideologically flexible; supportive of finding political compromise; fatigued by politics; and feeling forgotten in political debate.[3] Readers of this book would describe them as the political centre. The Hidden Tribes report notes, 'In talking to everyday Americans, we have found a large segment of the population whose voices are rarely heard above the shouts of the partisan tribes. These are people who believe that Americans have more in common than that which divides them. While they differ on important issues, they feel exhausted by the division in the USA. They believe that compromise is necessary in politics, as in other parts of life, and want to see the country come together and solve its problems.'[4]

But the country is not coming together and solving its problems. Why is the democratic process producing outcomes at odds with what most voters say they want? And why are other democracies around the world struggling as well?

How we got here

The most significant US legislative accomplishments in the twentieth century were bipartisan, from Medicare (health insurance for all Americans over age sixty-five) to the Highway Act (funding for the interstate highway system). Bipartisanship has two advantages. First, the legislation is more likely to be durable when both parties lend support. Social security and Medicare are now considered the 'third rail' of US politics – so popular that they are too dangerous to touch. Policies that are implemented with broad support, both public and political, are far less likely to be rolled back.

Second, bipartisan legislation, in theory, should be substantively stronger. Plans presumably improve when they have input from all the room, rather than half of it. A defining feature of centrism is an openness to different political points of view and an eagerness to take the best of what is on offer as we govern diverse and complex countries.

Unfortunately, nearly every major social change has given more voice to political extremists. Cable news has blurred the line between news and entertainment and built a business model out of booking loud voices, not sensible ones. Social media creates echo chambers that feed partisan views back to those who hold them. Meanwhile, US political campaigns have become shockingly expensive, leaving politicians beholden to the interest groups who pay for them. Less obviously, the onerous fundraising keeps many pragmatic people from running for office. I ran unsuccessfully for Congress in Chicago in 2009; raising money was the only truly awful part of the experience. This may be a uniquely American problem, but other countries should be wary of replicating it.

Gerrymandering – the practice by which the party in power at the state level draws the boundaries of electoral districts in ways that advantage their own party – has always been a feature of democratic politics in systems with regional representations. Unfortunately, we are getting better at it. The combination of 'big data' and residential sorting (the tendency of individuals to live near others with similar income, education and political views) makes it easier to draw districts that are politically consistent.

Unite the USA calculated that in 2022, fewer than one in five seats were competitive between the two parties.[5] Citizens are bound to become cynical when politicians are picking their voters rather than the other way round.

Don't yell at a dog for eating off the floor

In most political systems, the major political parties select their candidates. Turnout tends to be low in these intraparty elections, and the members who participate are not necessarily reflective of all party voters, let alone the broader electorate. In the USA, for example, only 21 per cent of eligible voters cast ballots in the 2022 primary elections, compared to over 50 per cent in the general election that year.[6]

What this means for democracies across the world is that relatively small numbers of activists, or organised groups registered to particular parties, have a disproportionate impact in selecting the candidates who appear on the general election ballot. Nowhere was this clearer than the UK election in which voters were given a choice between the utterly unelectable, self-proclaimed socialist Jeremy Corbyn and the unstable Boris Johnson.

As a result of primary elections (or their party equivalent), candidates are more responsive to the views of radicals within their own party than they are to the sentiment of the broader public. Conservatives fear challengers from the right; liberals look nervously to the left.

How can we return more power to the exhausted majority? By making process changes that diminish the influence of loud but non-representative political groups. Effective governance requires pragmatism and compromise; political systems must attract, encourage and reward leaders who see this as a feature of democracy rather than a bug.

Consider a sad example from the USA that also, more happily, contains the seeds of a remarkably promising reform. Peter Meijer, a moderate Republican from Michigan, was elected to the House of Representatives in 2020. He joined the Problem Solvers Caucus, a bipartisan group of House members 'committed to finding common ground on many of the key issues facing the nation'. He sponsored more bipartisan bills than any other new member of Congress. He was one of ten Republicans in the House who voted to impeach Donald Trump.

What was his reward for not marching rigidly to the party tune? He was challenged in the Republican primary by a Trump-endorsed candidate and lost his seat after one term. This is hardly an inspiring lesson for any politician who cares about job security. And it is not unique to the USA.

Many democracies are struggling because they have an electoral system that punishes politicians who don't pander to the most committed members of their own party. One of my colleagues often remarks, 'You can't yell at a dog for eating off the floor.' His point is that anyone who doesn't like a dog eating off the floor should drop less food. There is a political lesson in the aphorism: elected officials respond to the incentives we create; better incentives will produce better outcomes.

Impactful, achievable, non-partisan

Katherine Gehl, co-author of *The Politics Industry* and founder of The Institute for Political Innovation, created the 'impactful, achievable, non-partisan' rubric for evaluating reforms. Most efforts fail one leg of the test.

For example, Unite America learned a humbling lesson in 2018 when we backed a slate of Independent candidates for state and federal offices. Our theory of change was that a handful of centrist Independents – not beholden to one party or the other – could be a catalyst for overcoming partisanship. None was elected. (Our plan, it turns out, was neither achievable or impactful.)

In 2020, the state of Alaska presented an opportunity for us to test a different theory of change: if partisan primaries are a big part of the problem, then getting rid of them could be part of the solution. Unite America was part of a coalition supporting a state-wide ballot initiative that would eliminate party primaries and replace them with a single, open primary. *All* Alaskans would vote in a primary election in which *all* candidates would appear on the ballot, irrespective of political party. (Alaska Measure 2 also required additional campaign finance disclosures, which was the more politically popular part of the initiative, albeit argu-ably less impactful. One lesson for reformers everywhere is that there can be political advantage in bundling reforms together.)

The top four finishers in the primary – again, irrespective of party – would advance to the general election with the winner to be chosen by ranked-choice voting (RCV). Under RCV, also called 'instant runoff', voters have the option of ranking their preferred candidates. If any candidate wins a majority of first-place votes, he or she is the winner. However, if no candidate wins a majority, the last-place finisher is elimi-nated, and that candidate's voters get their second choice. The process is repeated until a candidate wins a majority.

Overall, the process has four advantages. First, *all* voters can par-ticipate in *all* phases of the election. Second, the eventual winner is guaranteed to have majority support, even if he or she is not the first choice of all voters.

Third, RCV eliminates the 'spoiler problem'. In a first-past-the-post system, voters are hesitant to support Independents or minor party candidates because they fear inadvertently electing their least favoured candidate. This has made it hard for the system to gener-ate competition beyond the traditional parties. Political Independents are the largest and fastest-growing bloc of voters in the USA, yet few Independents are elected to office.

Last and least obvious, ranked-choice voting changes the way candidates behave towards one another. New York City adopted ranked-choice voting for its mayoral election in 2021. The *New York Times* reported during the campaign, 'In the fiercely competitive world of New York politics, it is hard to imagine a candidate embracing a strategy to be voters' second choice. Yet in the volatile, crowded race for mayor, such a gambit might actually pay off.'[7] A third of voters said in exit polls that the race had been more civil.[8] If we create the incentive to be civil, we will attract more candidates who are civil and begin to break the destructive loop of polarising politics.

Shocked by our success

John F. Kennedy quipped shortly after his inauguration, 'When we got into office, the thing that surprised me most was to find that things were just as bad as we'd been saying they were.' After the Alaska reform referendum passed in 2020, our reaction only one election cycle later was the opposite: we were amazed that it worked as well as we said it would.

For example, Lisa Murkowski, a centrist Republican senator who had voted to impeach Donald Trump, was re-elected. She almost certainly would have lost if she had been forced to run in a Republican primary. The big lesson here is not about Republicans, or even about impeaching Trump. The point is that the Alaska reform promoted centrism. Republican primary voters would have sent Murkowski packing; but when *all Alaska voters* were able to vote in both the primary and general election, they sent Murkowski – consistently ranked as one of the most bipartisan US senators – back to Washington.

Glenn Wright, David Lublin and Benjamin Reilly, political scientists at the University of Alaska Southeast, American University and the East-West Centre respectively, wrote after the session, 'Our research suggests that Alaska's new final-four election system – a single-vote primary for all voters to select up to four candidates, followed by a ranked-choice vote general election – has helped arrest these trends [of intransigence over compromise] in Juneau and maybe even reverse them.'[9]

Beyond the USA, there are three lessons from Alaska for those interested in promoting centrist politics. First, there is a clear public appetite for fixing our politics. Most voters – that exhausted majority – want government to work better.

Second, incentives matter. We will not get centrist politics if there are strong incentives to pander to the extremes. The most impactful reforms are those that make the system more representative. Incidentally, that is also good branding. *All voters should be able to vote in all elections.*

More broadly, politicians dance to whatever music gets them elected; if we want a different kind of dancing, we need to change the music.

Third, promoting centrist politics is not tilting at windmills, but it requires resources and unflagging commitment. The Alaska referendum passed by the slimmest of margins (50.55 per cent to 49.45 per cent). It would have failed without financial and logistical support from Unite America and a broad coalition of other reform groups.

After Alaska, however, winning has been contagious. Donors and politicians believe you can succeed after they have seen you succeed. Nevada passed a nearly identical referendum in 2022. (The state constitution requires that the referendum pass again in 2024 before becoming law.) The Oregon legislature passed a bipartisan bill in July of 2023 that puts a state-wide ranked-choice voting proposal on the ballot in 2024. That means Oregon voters will have the final say on whether the state adopts an Alaska-style system.

As difficult as promoting centrism can feel at times, the good news is that success begets success: by attracting resources; by creating models that can be replicated; by persuading sceptics that change is possible; and by showing that reforms produce more functional governance.

The alternatives are grim. Democracy is under siege. Authoritarianism is on the rise. The world's democracies face enormous challenges, many of which will grow worse in the face of inaction. Bad governance breeds more bad governance and erodes public faith in democracy.

Centrism is crucial to the future. We must act when there is broad public agreement and create consensus when there is not. Democracy depends on it.

35

CENTRISM AND BUILDING
A BETTER SOCIETY

Daniel Lubetzky

When I was nine years old, my father began talking to me about his experience living through the Holocaust and surviving the Dachau concentration camp. I can remember my mom begging him to stop. 'Roman, why are you telling him these stories?' she asked. 'He's only nine years old.' My father replied, 'He's nine years old and needs to hear this. I was nine years old when I had to live through it. He must know what took place so that it never happens again.'

At that early age, the motivation behind my life's work was instilled. When I look back at my efforts thus far, I recognise that my drive to build bridges between people has been inspired by my personal understanding of the horrors that can be unleashed upon society, including sophisticated democracies, when extremist forces divide people against one another. Through my professional endeavours, how I choose to raise my kids, and even in my daily interactions with complete strangers, I am always, on some level, trying to prevent what happened to my father from taking place again.

Since the 7 October 2023 attacks on Israel and the free world in which Hamas terrorists raped and murdered 1,200 people, including women, the elderly and children, and took 249 Israelis and internationals hostage, my understanding of the problem of hateful absolutism and violent extremism – from whatever side it originates – has deepened, and my sense of duty to awaken moderates to become Builders has taken on increased urgency. Never in my lifetime have the horrors my father, my family and over 6 million Jews endured felt so dangerously within the realm of possibility.

Today, it seems clear that the future of our world lies in the hands of Builders. But what is a Builder, and what will it take for us to stop being part of the problem so that we can start solving problems instead?

My answer to that question began to take shape in the late 1980s. Driven to combat antisemitism and help defend Israel, I had come to believe that the best way to fight hatred against Jews and to ensure a secure future for Israel was by building bridges with others, including by forging relations between Israelis and their Arab neighbours.

In 1993, shortly after law school, I started a company called PeaceWorks, which produced food products, like tapenades and spreads, using raw ingredients procured through trading across so-called enemy borders. Turks, Jordanians, Egyptians, Palestinians and Israelis all needed to work together to complete the supply chain. They would then share in the profits of their collaborative efforts, incentivising them to cooperate, and through that process to discover one another's shared humanity.

In the summer of 2000, I was back home in New York working to grow PeaceWorks when President Clinton hosted Israeli Prime Minister Ehud Barak and Palestinian Authority Chairman Yasser Arafat at Camp David for negotiations. The meetings gave many in the West hope that a final peace breakthrough was imminent. Instead, not only did the negotiations break down, but the Second Intifada, a major Palestinian uprising against Israel, broke out with gruesome events such as the lynching of Israelis in downtown Ramallah.

For months I felt saddened, paralysed and betrayed. My Arab friends had been moderates, but according to the news they wanted all Israelis dead. *Why had they become so extreme?*

When I finally gathered the strength to go back to the region, I met my Palestinian friends and business partners to challenge them. 'What happened to your people? Why did you endorse violence?' I asked.

My friends were livid. They claimed that it was not them but the Israelis who had become oppressors. I proceeded to describe the images I had seen on TV, depicting all Palestinians as terrorists and militants attacking Israeli citizens. In disbelief, my Palestinian friends switched on the broadcasts from Al-Manar, Al-Arabiya and Al-Jazeera to show me their side of the story.

What I saw was terrifying. The Arab news programmes portrayed Israelis exclusively as evil perpetrators bent on killing children and harassing women. It was the opposite of what Western and Israeli media was depicting.

As it turned out, my friends hadn't changed. The overwhelming majority of humane and thoughtful Israelis and Palestinians were both still there. But to each side, the media had made it *seem* that everyone 'on the other side' had been transformed into a cruel and unrelenting enemy.

At this moment I recognised a pattern that exists in virtually every society across the world: even though the vast majority of people are moderates who want common-sense solutions that benefit a community as a whole, a small group of the most radical members of society tend to wield disproportionate power over media, politics and life more broadly. Moderates who are more balanced and less inclined towards action unintentionally cede ground to these extreme figures by failing to speak out, step up and exercise their power – which lies not least of all in their numbers.

While we moderates tend to recognise our agency and responsibility to shape our professional and family lives, we often fail to step into our important role in influencing civic life. This abdication of responsibility leaves a vacuum that those with extreme agendas are willing to fill. While such people wake up in the morning and think, 'How can I advance my mission?', moderates, by contrast, wake up and ask themselves, 'What can I have for breakfast?' The imbalanced approach to activism can have the unfortunate outcome of allowing a small group of people with radical positions to hijack the entire political agenda.

Our challenge as moderates is to bring our drive to the civic realm – to understand that if we *don't* participate in our democracy (voting in primaries, holding representatives accountable, running for office, standing up against injustice and defending constitutional norms), we cannot expect that our government will simply work for us. If we want our political system and parties to stay relevant to our lives, we cannot allow the pillars of democracy to sway wherever the most passionate (often radicalised) activists and special interests take them. We must become a force in our own right.

For moderates to start winning, we need to take action to become Builders. Especially during periods of conflict, war and widespread disruption, such as those we are experiencing globally now, all of us are at greater risk of simplifying the world and its many problems into a reductive framework of 'us vs them'.

This false dichotomy is reinforced to us by mainstream media and social media companies whose business models operate on fear and sensationalism. Social media is particularly pernicious for three reasons: 1) its algorithms enforce binary divides by isolating groups into bubbles in which their feeds are filled with views that affirm existing beliefs rather than inform original ideas; 2) its bite-sized content, built for decreasing attention spans, spreads information at surface level, denying media consumers the opportunity to 'go deep' on issues by exploring their nuances and complexities; 3) contentious, even false information tends to drive clicks and travel furthest, awarding outsized influence to extreme positions that fuel polarisation, misinformation and hate.

Power-hungry politicians have long manipulated these divisive narratives to their advantage. Ruling through division is an effective means by which politicians can stay in control without having to serve the interests of a unified supporter base. Politicians are also incentivised to pander to the most extreme members of their party, whose political activism and higher voter participation in primaries award them more control over party agendas. The more extremely politicians behave, the more media attention rewards them, further fuelling their radical stances.

This media and political landscape is coupled with a social climate in which many people feel underserved, under-represented and left behind. But many diversity, equity and inclusion initiatives designed to combat social injustices have had the unfortunate impact of compounding 'us vs them' narratives by simplifying the world into 'victim vs oppressor' frameworks. Instead of solving problems constructively, this paradigm removes personal agency from both 'victims' and 'oppressors', casting 'victims' as unable to take action to improve their lives and 'oppressors' as evil, regardless of how they behave. Ultimately, neo-Marxist theories that fail to address the root causes of all hate towards all people end up replacing one form of bigotry with another.

The first step for moderates to become Builders is to recognise that these 'us vs them' fallacies permeating most aspects of our lives present a pathway to problem creation, not problem-solving. They lure us into powerlessness by giving us a free pass on assuming personal responsibility for society's ills. Rather than enforce accountability, these frameworks operate on the idea that everything wrong with society is the fault of another group. By dividing us against our fellow citizens, they fuel hatred, dehumanisation and mistrust.

When this paradigm infiltrates society, chaos, conflict and destruction follow. Once a community builds an extreme mindset, that hatred takes on a life of its own and metastasises beyond its original targets. While the intolerance is often initially addressed towards a perceived enemy outside our own group, as a community's fears grow, its window of acceptance becomes narrower until only the most tribal within the group are deemed part of the tribe. Even within the tribe, extremist thinking transforms cultures and the people within them, breeding intolerance, insensitivity, assumption of negative intent, lack of civility and destructive tendencies. It follows that extremist ideology not only hurts a society's enemies, but also eventually attacks from within and harms the community in which it originated. This scenario has played out in Saudi Arabia, Germany, Hungary, Poland, Israel, Brazil and countless other nations.

Even the USA, the world's most influential democracy, has not been immune to these challenges. Far-right populism and nativism claiming to be predicated on national pride have contributed to major attacks, like the 6 January 2021 insurrection at the Capitol Building, on our country's own government. At the same time, while the far left claim to promote radical acceptance, their extreme intolerance for more conservative viewpoints and adoption of the radical neo-Marxist frameworks previously described has fed the rise of 'cancel culture', limiting freedom of speech and expression and causing hate. Without drawing false equivalencies, these parallels highlight the co-dependency of extremes, which wind up unintentionally reinforcing one another. The more extreme one side becomes, the more the other side's extremists are strengthened by the backlash. Both sides become unwitting allies, bound together by their shared hatred and rigidity.

To move to a place of constructive solution-building, moderates must recognise extremism itself as the real problem. Doing so requires all of us to admit the extremism that exists inside all groups including with our own, where we have the greatest blind spots. Only then will we discover that what we thought was the problem – one another – is really the solution. Only then will moderates unlock the opportunity to start working together.

The good news is that we have the power to do this. While extremism begets more extremism, moderation begets more moderation. In 2019 I, alongside a group that has grown to 250 prominent figures like José Andrés, Dr Peter T. Coleman, will.i.am and Dr Bernice King, launched Starts With Us BUILDERS, an initiative to mobilise moderates to use their voices and actions to overcome extremism in all its forms. In addition to creating a home and community for the majority of people who reject hateful absolutism, BUILDERS is empowering moderates to use their voices and actions to build constructive solutions to the challenges dividing our world. In the USA, BUILDERS is equipping citizens with tools to supplant rigid indoctrination on the left and nativist populism on the right with a culture of curiosity, compassion and problem-solving. In the Middle East we are building a human infrastructure to empower moderate Israelis and Palestinians to dismantle the shackles of violent extremism and build towards a future in which all people can live with security, freedom, and dignity. BUILDERS Ukraine is focused on keeping Americans engaged in Ukraine's fight for freedom and safeguarding democracy from totalitarian threats.

Our work in the Middle East has evolved over the last two decades. Following the breakdown of the Camp David negotiations of 2000 and the breakout of the Second Intifada, around 2002, together with my Palestinian Israeli colleague Mohammad Darawshe, I co-founded the OneVoice Movement to amplify the voices of moderate Israelis and Palestinians and move towards a negotiated resolution of the conflict. Through grassroots work, the partnership of Palestinian and Israeli volunteers and many international supporters, the OneVoice Movement became the largest movement of moderates in the Middle East, engaging nearly 1 million Palestinians and Israelis in advocating for a negotiated resolution to the conflict. We birthed a youth leadership programme that spanned an unprecedented spectrum of politics, with young leaders from the Shas, Mafdal, Likud, UTJ, Labor, Meretz and Arab parties working together across lines of difference and eventually also meeting their Palestinian counterparts across many sectors and viewpoints. We showed the government alternative ways to strike compromise and find common ground – including through 'Citizen Negotiations' that educated hundreds of thousands of Israelis and Palestinians on the issues and the art of principled and enlightened compromise. We were even credited with helping to bring about the Annapolis negotiations in 2008. The OneVoice Movement eventually led to grassroots organisations that are not directly related to conflict resolution but are advancing moderate voices and aiming to safeguard the rule of law and democracy. Zimam, 'Our Reigns' in Arabic, is one of the largest grassroots movements across the West Bank and Gaza, while Darkenu, 'Our Road' in Hebrew, and DemocraTV are two of the most vibrant civil society enterprises in Israel.

Drawing on lessons from the OneVoice Movement, BUILDERS USA's Citizen Solutions project is giving Americans new pathways for participating in political life through their engagement in common-sense solutions to wedge issues on which there is hidden consensus. We are tapping into the power of moderates to seize back the agenda from the most hyper-partisan figures in government and media who are feeding a vicious cycle of more extremist thought. Through that process, we are advancing concrete proposals for how to resolve many of the 'intractable' issues of our time – from immigration to voting rights, from education in our schools to gun safety – thereby gaining the tools to influence the future of our nation and world. These concrete proposals are not about splitting the difference but building agreement, understanding that broader consensus creates policy that the public is able to buy into and support in the long term. A core tenet of centrism is moving from politics of total victory over the other side to politics that delivers practical and enduring solutions.

Whether in the USA or the Middle East, when moderates allow extremist hate to proliferate, it always catches up with all of us. In today's flat world, extremism and hate know no boundaries. They will impact all communities unless moderates become Builders and unite on a global scale. How do we do that?

To build, we must commit to honing skills that empower us to solve problems together constructively. The Builders toolkit is Curiosity, even for ideas you feel inclined to disagree with; Compassion, even for people whom you find it hard to forgive; and the Courage to transcend divides and work together. Just as we may work out or practise other routines, we must make it a daily habit to strengthen our muscles for

'The Three Cs'. We can model the kind of world we want to live in by re-examining and concertedly addressing how we show up in our daily lives, particularly in moments of tension and conflict.

No matter what pain befalls our own people, we cannot miss the opportunity to empathise with the suffering of 'the other'. We may feel that acknowledging the pain of the other side weakens our people's moral claim. In fact, it's the opposite. Recognising the humanity of all people can strengthen alliances among moderates. This will empower us to build a better future for all our peoples, stand against all forms of violent absolutism and hateful extremism, and solve problems together for the sake of future generations. On the flip side, we undermine our causes when we align ourselves with radical extremists whose only real cause is hate. By acting with hate ourselves, we unwittingly play into the agendas of violent extremists.

It follows that absolutist solutions that deny the humanity or rights of the other side will never fulfil the aspirations of our own people. For peace to prevail, both sides must be willing to search for consensus and ask themselves what concessions they are willing to make so that both sides can live with security, freedom and dignity. When, instead, we take an 'all-or-nothing' position, we condemn people on both sides to never-ending conflict. There are a great many Palestinians who have not come to terms with the recognition of Israel as the homeland of the Jewish people, and the recognition that, for them to have a better future, they must accept Israel as their neighbour in peace, just as there are also Israeli Jewish extremists with absolutist visions. The task is monumental, but if we are serious about forging a future in which people live in harmony, we must reach out to those from outside our group and team up behind the shared objectives of freedom and peace.

The overwhelming majority of people don't cause problems, but we aren't the ones getting them solved either. To build a future in which all people can live together in dignity, we must join as Builders to overcome the forces that divide, destroy and diminish. In their place we must unite, build and bring light to the world. If moderates do not step up, extremists will step in – and history's worst atrocities, like the kind my father lived through, will repeat themselves. But if we realise our responsibility and power to shape our future, we will break the cycle. Like so many other contributors in this book, I'm optimistic that Builders will join forces to do this.

36

CENTRISM IN A WORLD OF EXTREMES

Kathryn Murdoch

A historian looking back on this moment in time would assume that many countries around the world were highly internally divided. With strongmen seemingly ascendant, democracy under threat and wild swings in policy from election to election, we struggle to make lasting or meaningful progress on important issues like technology regulation, women's rights and the future of our planet.

Meanwhile, to read the headlines of our major newspapers or scroll through the channels of our social media, there is divisiveness and an inflammation of extreme views everywhere. It is becoming clear that democracy alone is not enough to unify a people or a country's political leadership.

Take, for example, the world's leading superpower: despite technological, military and economic dominance, trust in government is low and our politics seem more divided than ever. But talk to the American people in their homes or look at the polls on even the most contentious issues and something different appears. Over 90 per cent of Americans want to see universal background checks on guns; 80 per cent agree that DREAMers (minors who entered the country illegally but grew up in the USA) should be able to remain in the USA and find a path to citizenship; 77 per cent want to see the government reduce its debt. Two-thirds (67 per cent) agree that government is doing too little to address climate change.

On one thing the country definitely agrees: 96 per cent believe that Congress is not working for them. This cynicism and the apathy it produces gives ever more power to those who do actively participate.

When asked which of the two parties they align with, most Americans pick neither. A full 50 per cent consider themselves Independents, with only 25 per cent each going to Democrats and Republicans.

Like much of the democratic world, the USA is not a divided nation as much as a poorly represented one. The real tragedy is not that the country is being torn apart by insurmountable ideological disagreements on major issues. It's the opposite: that the two political parties, and the media systems that feed them, are snatching divisiveness from the jaws of public consensus. Too often, citizens end up voting not for the party that best represents them but rather against the party (or person) they hate the most.

In the same way that we are stuck with an education system whose rhythms conform to an erstwhile agrarian economy, our political systems, and many of the old political approaches, are not fit to serve the modern electorate. It's time for a change and centrists should be the ones to lead it.

Our representatives are not delivering adequately in terms of legislation and action because they are not incentivised to do so. While the reasons vary from country to country, in too many cases the ideological extremes are vastly overrepresented. In the USA, that's because of a primary system by which, in 84 per cent of districts, the primary determines the winner of any election and these primary voters average about 6 per cent of the actual electorate. Greater voter turnout in primary elections would certainly help, although once a state or district is dominated by one party that becomes less likely, due to those in power being disincentivised to open up the primary process.

By aligning incentives for better representation and compromise, structural reforms to our electoral systems offer a high-leverage way to increase competition, participation and accountability in our politics. In a growing movement across the USA, engaged citizens are tackling gerrymandered districts, closed primaries and first-past-the-post voting through state legislatures and ballot initiatives.

Non-partisan primaries – in place in California, Washington, Louisiana and Alaska – ensure that candidates, from day one, are running to represent all of their voters, not just the base of their own party. Ranked-choice voting – adopted state-wide in Maine and Alaska, as well as in cities across the country – allows voters to rank their candidates in order of preference, rather than just picking one.

These sorts of initiatives, fitted to each country's specific context, incentivise candidates to run more positive campaigns, while guaranteeing a majority winner and eliminating any third-party 'spoiler effect'. Vote at home election systems can boost voter participation by mailing ballots to all voters, especially in otherwise low-turnout primary elections where the fringes tend to dominate.

Voting reform efforts in other parts of the world offer up ideas to imitate. As Malcolm Turnbull outlines in his essay, in Australia everyone is required to vote. The system, initially put forth by conservatives in 1924, has been in place, successfully, for almost 100 years. Ninety-two per cent of Australians voted in their last election, compared with the 60 per cent of Americans who voted in the 2016 presidential election. In their book *100% Democracy*, E. J. Dionne Jr and Miles Rapoport argue persuasively that an Australian-style universal voting system would make our democracy more inclusive and more legitimate, more representative. It's not as radical an idea as it sounds. Compulsory voting systems already exist in more than twenty countries, including Uruguay, Belgium and Greece. Few ideas have as ample a proof of concept as does universal voting.

Not only does Australia have the highest participation rate of any democracy, it also uses ranked-choice voting (RCV). Although Australia has many different political parties, its two major parties have largely dominated the political scene. Thanks to RCV, the 'Teal Independents' – a new party of conservatives who supported climate action – were able to gain a large number of seats in legislative bodies comprised of increasingly complacent liberals and conservatives.

In Northern Ireland – a place with a notoriously bloody history in politics as recently as 2019 – voters cast ballots using proportional ranked-choice voting. That system has been credited with curtailing tribalism and giving voters more to choose from than the narrow, tightly focused options of unionism versus nationalism. If these reforms can work in a country as fractured as Northern Ireland, other countries can create voting systems that bridge sectarian differences as well.

There are additional ways to strengthen our social fabric and bring attention to the moderate, centrist majority. Citizens' assemblies – a process whereby a demographically representative slice of the population comes together to solve problems – can have profound effects on participants' levels of polarisation, civic engagement and attitudes towards democracy and each other. New tech tools and platforms around community listening can support this deliberative process and hold the promise of bringing underheard voices to the centre of a stronger public dialogue. This has the crucial added benefit of strengthening societies and a sense of common purpose.

Reforms are crucial, but they are not in themselves enough (nor can they be passed quickly enough) to meet the urgency of the moment. Indeed, there are other systemic factors at play. Traditional media is slowly dying, like its ageing audience, and as it goes it grasps at anything that feels like a return to the 'good old days'. Cable news has long shown us how fear and rage drive audience numbers; meanwhile social media and advanced data analysis allow targeted hits of adrenaline and cortisol to juice the brains of the media consumer even more.

Moderates and consensus builders struggle for coverage because they don't trigger these rage responses. A recent Starts With Us study shows that top media covers hyper-partisan politicians up to ten times as much as it does problem solvers; the fringes get more coverage than the centrists. Both political parties use the extreme wing of their opponents to brand the other side as enemies. Extremists and their antics are front-page news while major bipartisan wins are under-reported and their significance is poorly understood. A business model that uses 'clicks' as metrics amplifies this tendency. Fear and rage are drivers of engagement, and so the spiral continues.

It's not enough for centrists to complain about this problem. We must find ways to either overcome it or circumvent it. There are media initiatives that provide interesting models – sharing positive news stories, insisting on in-depth analysis, promoting centrist voices and rejecting hyperbole. The cycle can be broken by a combination of politicians who refuse to play the game, journalists who shift the focus of their coverage and a public which begins to reward that approach with eyeballs and clicks. Centrists have an alternative approach at their fingertips; the counter to a politics of fear is a politics of hope. That plays to the strengths of centrism without giving ground to the extremists in the battle for emotional connection. It is possible to create a media narrative of positive, heart-warming stories that reinforce a sense of community and build people's belief that society rewards those who invest in our common good.

Recent initiatives in venture philanthropy are helping to revitalise local and non-profit newsrooms that involve and reflect the public they serve. We need to invest in local media, because journalists who cover city hall or state capitals are an important bulwark against cynicism and corruption. They are far more likely to help us build the strong and positive local identity which can then filter upwards to the national scene.

Philanthropy can only be a part of the solution at scale. We must also explore new business models that encourage community rather than clicks. We need to reinvent the ad model, perhaps around trust levels rather than ratings. And news-gathering needs to focus more on explanation to the public and less on speed. Breaking a story should be less important than getting it right. Indeed, anyone involved in media has a special responsibility to focus on business models that serve the people, not just shareholders.

What can each of us do to improve the centrist democratic project? A lot. Citizens can support candidates who are committed to putting country over party and working together to advance policy solutions, whichever party they come from. We can support reforms in our city or state that will amplify voters' voices and improve their choices and oppose those who try to take this away from us. We can raise up the voices we want to hear more of, rather than amplifying those we actually want less of. We can consume media more thoughtfully, pausing to check the sourcing of outrageous claims before passing along to others and supporting the journalism we appreciate.

We can think about the 'other side' as complex people like us, and we can listen to each other in an effort to bridge understanding and find common ground. We can participate in our democracy and teach our children about the rewards and responsibilities that come with it. We can believe that we can make it better. Only then can we do so.

CONCLUSION:
A CENTRIST ROADMAP

Yair Zivan

This book is a call to arms – centrists of the world, unite. By now, I hope, a compelling case has been made across its pages. An approach to politics that offers the antidote to extremism and polarisation, and a set of policies that provide genuine answers to the challenges of the modern world. Centrism is both a philosophical and a practical framework for politics and society – a theoretical approach based on core principles combined with the pragmatism needed to put those principles into practice. It can be a winning strategy electorally and a successful strategy for governing. What, then, is the next step in making that happen?

First, centrists will need to avoid two temptations in their attempts to win over voters: giving ground to the extremes on either side and mimicking their tactics, resorting to conspiracy, fear or immoral campaign tactics. Both are bound to fail. Voters will never buy a cheap imitation when they can vote for the real thing and no moderate voter will reward the behaviour they abhor in others.

The radicalism of centrism will be a rejection of the direction which politics has taken in recent years: not a half-hearted and apologetic edging away from the extremes, but a principled and proud counter-approach. Where extremists use fear, centrists need to inspire with hope. Where they seek to divide, we need to advocate for, and sometimes create, bonds that unite us. Where they try to use the freedoms that democracy affords them against it, we need to protect the institutions that hold it together. Where they use simplistic slogans, we need to offer honest answers. And where the extremists fail to deliver on their promises (as they inevitably will), centrists will need to show the public that our way produces tangible results.

Centrists need to be brave and articulate a clear agenda. Some of that agenda exists within the pages of this book, some will be dependent on the specific challenges of each country. Centrist movements will need to adapt to their own political contexts and ensure they are offering a coherent approach that meets the needs of their country and society. They will have to enlist an ecosystem of support that is reflected by the authors in this book. Centrism can benefit from the help of the business community that is attracted to its plans for progress, a think tank community with innovative and well-developed ideas, media personalities looking to push back against sensationalism and experienced former leaders who can provide guidance and direction.

The principles and approach of centrism are constant, but not every political system is the same. There are differences which emerge in this book between developing and developed countries, as well as between the political traditions of Asia, Europe or Latin America. Crucially, there is a substantial structural difference between two predominant systems – multi-party systems, and those dominated by two major parties – which requires centrists to approach the political arena differently.

In multi-party systems, where possible, centrists must unite into a coherent political force and take on the politics of polarisation – there is nothing to be feared from creating a new political force and driving it into the heart of the political arena. There are successful models of this across the world, for example in France with Macron's *En Marche!*, in Israel with Yesh Atid, and Austria with NEOS. It requires the creation of a genuine political operation with solid political foundations and a process that builds a broad base of support. It also requires charismatic and media-savvy leadership able to take the message to the public in a way that is compelling. One is not sufficient without the other. Without charismatic leadership it is hard to break into the public consciousness, but without a genuine political movement it is impossible to remain there.

When creating something new, centrists must offer a more detailed policy plan than others in order to counter the perception of a light-weight middle and show that something new is on offer. Centrists must be unafraid of complexity, honest about challenges and imperfections, create ambitious but attainable goals and show the public what a better future looks like. That successful model was repeated by the three parties mentioned above, all of which created detailed manifestos after going through a public-facing process. New centrist parties will need to distinguish themselves from the left with their patriotism, respect for tradition and embrace of the free market, but also from the right with their tolerance, commitment to equality of opportunity and openness to the rest of the world.

The challenge in multi-party systems is to grow from the centre outwards rather than from the left or right inwards. Centrist political movements will need to co-opt existing centrist figures in the system rather than push them away, dictate an agenda by forcing the old parties to respond to them and build momentum that the media can't overlook. None of this is simple, it might not succeed every time, but it is attainable, and the rewards are worth the effort.

In systems dominated by two parties, the success or significant impact for a new party is nigh on impossible. Here, centrists need to find the most effective way to dominate the big parties and take on the extremes of their own party. The role of centrists is to drag their parties into the political centre, ideally from a leadership position, and if not then as a necessary counterweight to the extremes. The leader of a major political party, if not a centrist themself, should know that their centrist faction is as passionate, as committed and as demanding to be heard as their most extreme members.

Centrist politicians in these systems often find they have more in common with moderates from an opposing party than radicals in their own. The temperament, the principles, the approach to government are all shared by centrists. In the USA, centrist Democrats and centrist

Republicans have more in common with one another than with the far left or radical right. In the UK, the moderates in the Labour and Conservative parties share more common ground with each other than with the old Marxist wing of the Labour Party or the nationalist wing of the Tory Party. The same is true in Australia, where centrist Liberal and Labor politicians have more in common with one another than with the fringes of their own parties. But the goal isn't to create one party made up of former Labour and Conservative, Democratic and Republican, or Labor and Liberal politicians. Political disagreement and competition between parties is a positive. It drives better policy through debate, and it gives the public genuine choice without resorting to the extremes.

The goal is to have two parties competing for the centre ground, forcing each other to improve and to reject the influence of the extremes. Those two parties will disagree and will have to work to convince the public of the justification of their approach, but they'll do it around a set of shared principles and, crucially, a shared understanding of the rules of the game. Both major parties will be committed to the basics of liberal democracy – a strong and independent judiciary, a free press, parliamentary oversight, equality before the law, a non-politicised police force, peaceful transfer of power, and free and fair elections. Both will also be committed to considering the minority opinion when they govern and understanding that, whatever their disagreements, they need to stand firm against extremism. Politically, an environment that can showcase effective governance benefits centrists and undermines the extremes.

Nothing will do more for the major political parties in these systems than delivering for the public when they are given the opportunity. Centrists want results, and whichever party they are from, achieving results will benefit the entire centrist camp. They want to deal with the real issues facing their countries rather than imagined threats from within or outside. And, critically, they don't want to beat the other side out of a sense of political tribalism. They want to win the argument and take the best of what others have to offer along the way.

That approach, and those principles, are at the heart of centrism, and they come through in every contribution in this book. It's why centrists feel repelled by the radicals in their own camp (and I'd guess the feeling is mutual). The radicals choose purity of ideology over pragmatism; they'll reject and attack anything that is less than 100 per cent in line with their beliefs. Centrists must forcefully reject that approach and offer their own path forward.

A final word

My first political memory, and in some ways still the defining political moment of my life, was the assassination of Israeli Prime Minister Yitzhak Rabin in November 1995. I was ten years old and living thousands of miles away from Israel, but I can still recall the shock of that night. As I grew older, I came to understand why that was so instinctively significant: it was my first interaction with genuine extremism, with a violent rejection of democracy, of pragmatic leadership and of the search for peace and progress and a better future.

Political violence is the near-inevitable endpoint of unchecked extremist politics: a total belief in the righteousness of an ideology and a complete demonisation of those who dare to think differently.

From there the question has always been, how do we defeat extremism and offer something better? Over the years it became clear: the answer was centrism.

Centrism can win. It can overcome the politics of polarisation. It can counter extremism. It can present and implement a way forward for democracies in the modern world. If extremism offers total solutions and a utopian end state, centrism offers a never-ending effort to make life better, more prosperous, more secure.

Centrism will benefit and grow from being an open political movement that evolves and improves over time, that can adapt to a changing

THE CENTRE MUST HOLD

world and build on the core principles outlined in this book to keep creating political movements which deliver for the public locally, nationally and internationally.

We can't ignore the challenges – liberal democracy is under sustained assault, democracies have failed to adapt to rapid technological advances, our politics is coming apart at the seams and we face a series of global events more complex than anything we have seen before. But disaster is far from inevitable.

Humanity has repeatedly shown a capacity to overcome obstacles that seemed unsurmountable when inspired by well-governed societies infused with hope. Centrism offers the framework with which to do so once again. The struggle between the politics of fear and of hope, between the extremes and the moderates, will define the future of democracy and it is a struggle that can only be won from the political centre.

And there is one thing that shines through on every page of this book – centrists are hopeful. We are hopeful about the future and optimistic about human nature. We are not naive, nor are we searching for utopia, but we believe that with the right approach we can make progress, move society forward, improve quality of life for people, solve problems and create opportunities without losing our sense of identity, community and purpose.

At a time when politics can feel bleak and when politicians trade in fear and anger, that sense of hope is among the greatest contributions centrism brings to public life. Maybe, more than ever, that's exactly what we all need.

ACKNOWLEDGEMENTS

It's hard to know where to start in thanking all those who helped bring this book together.

The idea had been floating around in my mind for a few years but it took Lorne and the team at Elliott and Thompson to turn it into something real. Without his willingness to take a chance, it would have stayed stored away on my computer alongside other ideas that will never see the light of the day. Lorne believed in the concept and in my ability to make it happen and for that I'm incredibly grateful. The guidance provided by my two editors, first Robin and then Pippa, and their patience for my never-ending questions and requests gave me confidence throughout the process. Pippa's painstaking edits and insightful comments have had a tremendous effect on the final text. I'm incredibly grateful to the whole team at Elliott and Thompson who have been a pleasure to work with.

This book is a collaborative effort with over forty writers who so generously gave of their wisdom, experience and time. Each of them suggested ideas for the book beyond their individual essay, connected me with someone else, opened another door and enriched my thinking. They all share a commitment to the ideas in the book and if these are the people who share my political thinking, then I'm confident in the future of centrism, knowing that I'm in such esteemed company. I'm grateful to them all for their contributions and I hope this book is only the start of our cooperation in the future. I'm particularly grateful to Tony Blair and William Galston who agreed to write essays before the book had even started to take shape. There are also countless others who couldn't contribute to the book for a variety of reasons but pointed me in the direction of someone who could or simply encouraged me along the way.

A decade ago, I finished working for President Shimon Peres as he ended his term as president of Israel. It had been an incredible privilege to work for one of the greatest leaders in Israel's history at what was then a relatively young age. It had also been intense, and I planned to take some well-deserved time off before deciding what comes next. Instead, my boss at the time asked me to join her in working for Yair Lapid, the leader of a new centrist party called Yesh Atid, who was serving as finance minister.

Saying yes was the most consequential decision of my working life. I found in Yesh Atid a political home and a second family. The team around Yair Lapid is as close-knit as I've seen in politics, bound together by a shared vision, sense of patriotism and determination to make a difference. Working at the front line of politics as part of this brilliant and supportive team for over a decade has sharpened my thinking and given me a chance to see how the theories I believe in work (or don't) in the cauldron of political life. Their feedback on the book helped shape much of the content but hours of discussions with them shaped the ideas long before I put pen to paper. They have been a constant support throughout this process and I'm grateful to them all, especially to Gili, who has listened to me talk about this project endlessly.

At the head of the team stands Yair Lapid. There is perhaps no one I am more closely aligned with in terms of political thinking, no one who has given me more to think about, challenged me more or given me more reading assignments over the years. He shares a passion for centrism and after a decade of working with him it is sometimes hard to know where his beliefs end and mine begin. I hope the contents of this book do justice to the ideas he has helped shaped not just in Israel but among centrists worldwide. He gave me the opportunity to work at the front line of politics and to meet many of the contributors to this book; it simply wouldn't have been possible without him.

There is a long list of people who also deserve my gratitude and only when sitting to write this do I realise quite how long that list is. I can't possibly mention them all without offending others, but you know who you are. I'm particularly grateful to my parents and family who are not only ever supportive of my endeavours but also created an atmosphere growing up where discussing politics was encouraged, and debates welcomed. The Friday night dinner table in a Jewish family might just be the best place to test political ideas and learn how to build a convincing argument. I'm also especially grateful to my younger brother, Sahar, whose translation of a number of the essays in this book and editorial advice made a huge contribution.

And finally, to Becca. Unlike everyone else above she didn't only contribute to the content of the book but to the sanity of the writer. Her endless patience, honesty, advice and support didn't only make this book better but make me better. She always knew when to challenge me, push me, offer support or just put a glass of whisky in my hand. The majority of the work on this book was done throughout 2023 and early 2024, a challenging time for us for a host of reasons. Despite that, she found the strength to support me and the patience to put up with me. Without her this book would never have come together.

Finally (really) to my two boys Eitan and Matan, this book is for you. There is nothing that drives me more than trying to do my small part to make the world you grow up in a better one.

Thank you.

LIST OF CONTRIBUTORS

Baroness Ruth Anderson is a former MP who now serves in the House of Lords and as the CEO of Index on Censorship.

John Avlon is an award-winning journalist and author. He was a CNN anchor and senior political analyst and his books include *Independent Nation*, *Wingnuts*, *Washington's Farewell* and *Lincoln and the Fight for Peace*, which was named one of the best books of 2022 by *Vanity Fair* and *Foreign Affairs*. Previously, he was the editor-in-chief and managing director of *The Daily Beast* and served as chief speechwriter for the mayor of New York during the attacks of 9/11. He lives with his wife Margaret Hoover and their two children in New York where he is now a candidate for congress in the first district, running a decidedly centrist campaign.

Matt Bennett is senior vice-president for public affairs and a co-founder of Third Way. He previously served as a deputy assistant to the president for intergovernmental affairs for President Clinton.

Ann Bernstein is a South African analyst and commentator who serves as executive director of The Centre for Development and Enterprise.

Tony Blair is the former prime minister of the UK and founder and executive chairman of the Tony Blair Institute.

Michael R. Bloomberg, founder of Bloomberg and Bloomberg Philanthropies, served as mayor of New York from 2002 to 2013. He is the UN secretary-general's special envoy on climate ambition and solutions and co-author of *Climate of Hope: How Cities, Businesses, and Citizens Can Save the Planet*.

Børge Brende is the president of the World Economic Forum and former minister of foreign affairs, minister of the environment and minister of trade and industry of Norway.

Dr Daniel Brieba is a Fellow in Political Science and Public Policy at the London School of Economics and Political Science (LSE). He is also an assistant professor at the School of Government in Universidad Adolfo Ibáñez, Chile. He holds a DPhil in Politics from the University of Oxford. He was awarded the Sir Walter Bagehot Prize for best dissertation in the field of Government and Public Administration by the Political Studies Association.

Polly Bronstein is the CEO of The One Hundred Initiative and author of *How I Became a Moderate: A Journey from Left to Center*.

Dr Marco Buschmann is the German federal minister of justice and senior member of the centrist Free Democratic Party.

Professor Mauricio Cárdenas is a Colombian economist and politician who was minister of finance and public credit, minister of mines and energy, minister of transport and minister of economic development. He served on the Independent Panel for Pandemic Preparedness and Response examining the response to the COVID-19 pandemic. He is currently Professor of Practice at Columbia University's School of International and Public Affairs (SIPA).

Philip Collins is a columnist at *The Times* and the *Evening Standard*. He is a visiting fellow at the Blavatnik School of Government, Oxford University and the London School of Economics. He is the founder and writer-in-chief of The Draft.

Aurelian Craiutu is Professor of Political Science at Indiana University, Bloomington and senior fellow at the Niskanen Center, Washington DC. His previous books include *A Virtue for Courageous Minds: Moderation in French Political Thought, 1748–1830* and *Faces of Moderation: The Art of Balance in an Age of Extremes*. His new book is *Why Not Moderation? Letters to Young Radicals*.

Simon Davies, a partner at Number 10 Strategies, is an international political consultant and pollster who has devised and executed winning strategies for numerous presidents, prime ministers and business leaders on four continents over two decades.

Arne Duncan served as CEO of the Chicago Public Schools from 2001 to 2008 and as US secretary of education from 2009 to 2015. He is a managing partner with Emerson Collective.

Lanae Erickson is senior vice-president for social policy, education and politics at Third Way. She served as a member of President Obama's advisory council on faith-based and neighbourhood partnerships and as legislative counsel at Alliance for Justice.

Jonathan Evans, Lord Evans of Weardale, was a member of the British Security Service MI5 for thirty-three years, specialising in countering terrorism from Irish Republican groups and subsequently from Islamist extremist groups such as Al-Qaida. From 2007 to 2013 he was director general of MI5. He now sits as a crossbench (non-affiliated) member of the House of Lords.

Michèle Flournoy is the co-founder and managing partner of WestExec Advisors, chair of the board of directors of the Center for a New American Security (CNAS) and former under-secretary of defense for policy.

Richard Fontaine is the CEO of the Center for a New American Security. Prior to CNAS he was foreign policy advisor to Senator John McCain, including during his 2008 presidential campaign, and worked in the State Department, National Security Council and Senate Foreign Relations Committee.

Chrystia Freeland is the deputy prime minister and finance minister of Canada. She is a Liberal Party member of parliament representing Toronto and, in the past, has served as minister of international trade, minister of foreign affairs and minister of intergovernmental affairs. Before politics she served as managing director at Thomson Reuters, deputy editor at *The Globe and Mail* and US managing editor at the *Financial Times*.

Professor William Galston is an author, political theorist and political advisor. He is a senior fellow at the Brooking Institute, writes the weekly 'Politics and Ideas' column in *The Wall Street Journal* and was executive director of the National Commission on Civic Renewal. He served from 1993 to 1995 as deputy assistant to President Clinton for domestic policy.

Dr Micah Goodman is an Israeli philosopher and best-selling author of six books exploring contemporary society.

Sandro Gozi is a former member of the Italian parliament with the centrist Democratic Party and currently a member of the European Parliament representing President Macron's Renaissance Party.

Joshua Hantman, a partner in Number 10 Strategies, is a strategic communications and political advisor who, following stints in the prime minister's Office, Ministry of Defence and Foreign Ministry, has worked on high-level communications campaigns in over twenty countries.

Yair Lapid is the former prime minister, foreign minister and finance minister of Israel. He was an award-winning author and journalist until entering politics a decade ago. He is the founder and chair of the centrist Yesh Atid Party and currently serves as the leader of the opposition in Israel's parliament.

Josef Lentsch is the founder of PartyParty, partner and chief innovation officer at the Innovation in Politics Institute and founding director of the NEOS Lab in Austria. He is the author of *Political Entrepreneurship: How to Build Successful Centrist Political Start-Ups*.

Daniel Lubetzky is best known as the founder of KIND Snacks. He also founded and built OneVoice, the largest grassroots movement of moderates in the Middle East. Seeing an intractable conflict growing in the USA, Daniel and 200 foremost leaders launched a non-partisan civic movement, Starts With Us, to empower Americans with tools to overcome extremism with curiosity, compassion, courage and common-sense solutions.

Kathryn Murdoch is the co-founder and president of the Quadrivium Foundation. She is co-chair of Unite America, co-chair of the Climate Leadership Council, a trustee of the Environmental Defense Fund and a board member of Citizen Data. She is a founding board member of SciLine, which provides scientific expertise and context for journalists.

Rachel Pritzker is the founder and president of the Pritzker Innovation Fund, chair of the Democracy Funders Network, and chair of the boards of Third Way, the Breakthrough Institute and the Energy for Growth Hub. She is a co-author of *An Ecomodernist Manifesto*.

Matteo Renzi is a former prime minister of Italy and former mayor of Florence. He is a senator and the leader of the centrist Italia Viva Party as well as serving as editor of *Il Riformista*.

Jennifer Rubin is a *Washington Post* opinion columnist covering politics and policy. She is also an MSNBC contributor and the author of *Resistance: How Women Saved Democracy from Donald Trump* and is host of her own podcast, 'Green Room'.

Stéphane Séjourné is the minister for Europe and foreign affairs of France. He previously served as leader of Renew Europe in the EU Parliament and general secretary of President Macron's Renaissance Party.

Dr Tomohito Shinoda is a professor at the International University of Japan and a former advisor to the minister of defence who has authored numerous books on Japanese politics and national security.

Representative Haley Stevens is a Democratic member of Congress from Michigan who is a member of the New Democrat Coalition and the Problem Solvers Caucus. She is the ranking member of the House Subcommittee on Research and Technology.

Jamie Susskind is a barrister and best-selling author of *The Digital Republic: On Freedom and Democracy in the 21st Century* and the award-winning *Future Politics*. He has held fellowships at Cambridge and Harvard and has written for the *New York Times*, *Financial Times*, *The Times*, *Guardian* and more.

Simone Tebet is minister of planning and budget of the Federal Government of Brazil and former centrist candidate for president.

Dr Shashi Tharoor is an Indian member of parliament and chairman of the Standing Committee on Information Technology. He served as a diplomat at the United Nations and a columnist in each of India's three-top English-language newspapers as well as writing over twenty books in English.

Malcolm Turnbull was prime minister of Australia from 2015 to 2018. Prior to that he was opposition leader from 2008 to 2009, environment minister in 2007 and communications minister from 2013 to 2015. He was leader of the Parliamentary Liberal Party from 2008 to 2009 and 2015 to 2018.

Professor Andrés Velasco is professor of public policy and dean of the School of Public Policy at the London School of Economics and Political Science. He was a presidential candidate in Chile in 2013 and minister of finance of Chile between 2006 and 2010. During his tenure he was recognised as Latin American Finance Minister of the Year by several international publications. He has also served as a professor at Columbia University, the Harvard Kennedy School and New York University. He holds a BA and MA from Yale University, a PhD in Economics from Columbia University, and was a postdoctoral fellow in Political Economy at Harvard University and the Massachusetts Institute of Technology.

Professor Charles Wheelan is a bestselling author who wrote *The Centrist Manifesto* and is the founder and co-chair of Unite America. He is a former correspondent for *The Economist* and is faculty director of the Center for Business, Government & Society at the Tuck School of Business at Dartmouth College.

Professor Eduardo Levy Yeyati is an Argentine economist and author who is dean of the School of Government at Universidad Torcuato

Di Tella, where he also directs its Center for Evidence-based Policy. He has served as chief economist at the Central Bank of Argentina and in various roles as an expert advisor for the government.

Yair Zivan is a committed centrist. He has served as foreign policy advisor to Yair Lapid, leader of Israel's largest centrist political party since 2014 throughout his tenures as finance minister, leader of the opposition, foreign minister and prime minister of Israel. Before working for Mr Lapid he was international media spokesperson for President Shimon Peres. His work has been published in media outlets across the world.

NOTES

Epigraph
1. Arthur M. Schlesinger Jr, 'Not Left, Not Right, But a Vital Center', *New York Times*, 4 April 1948

SECTION 1

4. The 'Vital Centre' as a Face of Moderation
1. Aurelian Craiutu, *Why Not Moderation? Letters to Young Radicals* (Cambridge: Cambridge University Press, 2024), pp. 118–26.

2. See the extensive discussion on this topic in Michelle Diggles and Lanae Erickson Hatalsky, 'The State of the Center' (Washington DC: Third Way, 2014).

3. Aurelian Craiutu, *A Virtue for Courageous Minds: Moderation in French Political Thought, 1748–1830* (Princeton: Princeton University Press, 2012), pp. 19–22.

4. David Hume, *Essays: Moral, Political, and Literary* (Indianapolis: Liberty Fund, 1985), p. 46.

5. Aaron Bastani, 'Centrists are Pining for a Golden Age that Never Was', *Jacobin* (8 September 2020), https://www.jacobinmag.com/2020/09/centrism-clinton-bush-party-politics?fbclid=IwAR0LZZYl4V2ubo08SokkGF-X9-wxgyH3PM0I-_Xu-5A-ltPaTxQtCtWBLzk.

6. John Patrick Leary, 'The Third Way Is a Death Trap', *Jacobin* (3 August 2018), https://jacobinmag.com/2018/08/centrism-democratic-party-lieberman-ocasio-cortez

7. David Adler, 'Centrists Are the Most Hostile to Democracy, Not Extremists', *The New York Times* (23 May 2018), https://www.nytimes.com/interactive/2018/05/23/opinion/international-world/centrists-democracy.html?mtrref=www.google.com&assetType=PAYWALL&fbclid=IwAR0m3HvKhZ4h02QwNo65XtBcehKHxxdy9PCNw6mNrY5JbPRdWA5Sr0WsT9Y.

8. Osita Nwanevu, 'Centrism is Dead', *Slate* (25 July 2018), https://slate.com/news-and-politics/2018/07/third-ways-centrism-is-dead-the-left-has-already-won-the-debate-over-the-democratic-party.html.

THE CENTRE MUST HOLD

9. Lexington, 'Manchin in the Muddle', *The Economist* (22 July 2023), p. 21.

10. Ibid.

11. Thomas E. Mann and Norman J. Ornstein, *It's Even Worse Than It Looks: How the American Constitutional System Collided with the New Politics of Extremism* (New York: Basic Books, 2012), p. xiv.

12. On liberalism as a doctrine of the centre, see Alan S. Kahan, *Freedom From Fear: An Incomplete History of Liberalism* (Princeton: Princeton University Press, 2023).

13. Arthur M. Schlesinger Jr, *The Vital Center: The Politics of Freedom* (Boston: Houghton Mifflin, 1962), pp. x–xi.

14. Karol Soltan, 'Liberal Conservative Socialism and the Politics of a Complex Center', *The Good Society*, 2002, 11(1): p. 22.

15. Craiutu, *Why Not Moderation?*, p. 125.

16. Leon Wieseltier, 'The Radical Liberal', *White Rose* (12 February 2021), https://whiterosemagazine.com/the-radical-liberal/

17. Wilhelm Röpke, *The Humane Economy: The Social Framework of the Free Market* (Wilmington, DE: Intercollegiate Studies Institute, 1998), p. 89.

18. See Daniel Bell, *The Cultural Contradictions of Capitalism* (New York: Basic Books, 1976).

19. See Craiutu, *Why Not Moderation?*, pp. 129–34.

20. Abraham Flexner, *The Usefulness of Useless Knowledge* (Princeton: Princeton University Press, 2017), p. 52. I have commented on these issues in Craiutu, 'Liberal Education as Spiritual Exercise: On the Life of the Mind in the Age of Social Media', in Justin B. Dyer and Constantine C. Vassiliou (eds.), *Liberal Education and Citizenship in a Free Society* (Columbia: University of Missouri Press, 2023), pp. 173–96.

21. For more details on these projects, see https://www.nytimes.com/interactive/2019/08/14/magazine/1619-america-slavery.html; https://trumpwhitehouse.archives.gov/wp-content/uploads/2021/01/The-Presidents-Advisory-1776-Commission-Final-Report.pdf; https://1776projectpac.com/

22. See Craiutu, *Faces of Moderation*, p. 128.

23. Elinor Ostrom, 'Beyond Markets and States: Polycentric Governance of Complex Economic Systems', Nobel Prize lecture, 8 December 2009. For a public policy agenda 'beyond market and democratic fundamentalism', also see Brink Lindsey et al., *The Center Can Hold: Public Policy for an Age of Extremes* (Washington DC: Niskanen Center, 2018), https://www.niskanencenter.org/the-center-can-hold-public-policy-for-an-age-of-extremes/

24. Greg Berman and Aubrey Fox, *The Case for Incremental Change in a Radical Age* (Oxford: Oxford University Press, 2023), p. 7.

25. Ibid., p. 159.

26. Ibid., p. 8.

5. The Evolution of Democratic Centrism

1. 'The Clinton Lectures', https://www.georgetown.edu/news/the-clinton-lectures/

SECTION 2

10. Centrism and Global Cooperation

1. https://www.imf.org/en/Blogs/Articles/2023/01/16/Confronting-fragmentation-where-it-matters-most-trade-debt-and-climate-action

2. https://press.un.org/en/2020/sgsm19934.doc.htm

3. https://www.foreignaffairs.com/israel/statecraft-age-connectivity

4. https://www.reuters.com/world/us-climate-envoy-kerry-says-china-has-invited-him-talks-2023-05-03/

5. https://www.imf.org/en/Blogs/Articles/2023/02/08/charting-globalizations-turn-to-slowbalization-after-global-financial-crisis

6. https://www.dhl.com/content/dam/dhl/global/delivered/documents/pdf/dhl-global-connectedness-index-2022-complete-report.pdf

21. Centrist Economic Policies and Identity Politics

1. R. Cummings and N. Mahoney, 'Asymmetric amplification and the consumer sentiment gap', *Briefing Book*, 13 November 2023. Available at: https://www.briefingbook.info/p/asymmetric-amplification-and-the?utm_source=profile&utm_medium=reader2

2. D. Autor, A. Beck, D. Dorn and G. H. Hanson, 'Help for the Heartland? The Employment and Electoral Effects of the Trump Tariffs in the United States', NBER Working Paper 32082, January 2024. Available at http://www.nber.org/papers/w32082

3. Assistant Secretary for Planning and Evaluation (ASPE), 'Health Coverage Under the Affordable Care Act: Current Enrollment Trends and State Estimates', Issue Brief, 23 March 2023. Available at https://aspe.hhs.gov/sites/default/files/documents/8e81cf90c721dbbf58694c98e85804d3/health-coverage-under-aca.pdf

4. R. Reis and A. Velasco, 'The London Consensus: Fiscal Policy and Public Debt', Working Paper, LSE, November 2023. Available at https://personal.lse.ac.uk/reisr/papers/23-reisvelasco-London.pdf

5. T. Pope and E. Shearer, 'The Coronavirus Job Retention Scheme: How successful has the furlough scheme been and what should happen next?', London: Institute for Government, 9 September 2021. Available at https://www.instituteforgovernment.org.uk/publication/coronavirus-job-retention-success#:~:text=The%20IfG%20paper%20finds%20that,recovered%20to%20pre%2DCovid%20levels

6. A. Mian and A. Sufi, *House of Debt* (Chicago: University of Chicago Press, 2014).

7. OECD, 'Employment Outlook: The Future of Work', Paris, OECD, 2019. Available at https://www.oecd-ilibrary.org/employment/oecd-employment-outlook-2019_9ee00155-en

8. D. Rodrik and S. Stantcheva, 'Fixing capitalism's good jobs problem', *Oxford Review of Economic Policy*, vol. 37, no. 4, 2021, pp. 824–37. Available at https://drodrik.scholar.harvard.edu/files/dani-rodrik/files/fixing_capitalisms_good_jobs_problem.pdf

9. R. Rajan, *The Third Pillar: How Markets and the State Leave the Community Behind* (New York, Penguin Press, 2019)

10. Rodríguez-Pose, A., 'The Rise of Populism and the Revenge of Places That Don't Matter', *LSE Public Policy Review*, 2020, 1(1): 4, pp. 1–9. Available at https://storage.googleapis.com/jnl-lse-j-lseppr-files/journals/1/articles/4/submission/proof/4-1-39-2-10-20201013.pdf; and Soskice, D. 'The Technological Revolution, Segregation, and Populism – A Long-Term Strategic Response', *LSE Public Policy Review*, 2020, 1(1): 6, pp. 1–8. Available at https://storage.googleapis.com/jnl-lse-j-lseppr-files/journals/1/articles/6/submission/proof/6-1-25-2-10-20201013.pdf

SECTION 4

27. The Future of Liberal Democracy in Latin America: In Search of a Centre

1. https://www.jstor.org/stable/44483088

2. In Latin American history, the term *caudillo* usually denotes a popular, typically nationalistic warlord, often with authoritarian overtones.

3. UNDP, 2021.

4. World Bank, 2021.

5. https://openknowledge.worldbank.org/server/api/core/bitstreams/0367ebcf-2954-5f4e-87bc-9e23f7c61d71/content

6. The Spanish term comes from Giuseppe Tomasi di Lampedusa's novel *The Leopard*, and is summarised by the novel's one-liner: 'Everything needs to change for everything to stay the same.'

SECTION 5

32. The Centrist Organisation of the Future

1. https://www.rauen.de/coaching-report/definition-coaching/was-ist-coaching.html (2017)

34. Centrism and Building a Better Political System

1. https://www.pewresearch.org/short-reads/2021/10/26/growing-share-of-americans-say-they-want-more-spending-on-police-in-their-area/

2. https://news.gallup.com/poll/318851/perceptions-white-black-relations-sink-new-low.aspx

3. https://hiddentribes.us/

4. https://hiddentribes.us/

5. Unite America Institute, *State of Reform*.

6. https://bipartisanpolicy.org/report/2022-primary-turnout/

7. Emma G. Fitzsimmons, 'In the N.Y.C. Mayor's Race, Being Second Might Be Good Enough to Win', *New York Times*, 10 June 2021.

8. https://docsend.com/view/wurzmdn5rrcze66w

9. https://www.adn.com/opinions/2023/05/26/opinion-budget-deal-shows-alaska-is-already-reaping-ranked-choices-rewards/

INDEX